Studies in Modernity and National Identity
Sibel Bozdoğan and Reşat Kasaba, Series Editors

Studies in Modernity and National Identity examine the relationships among modernity, the nation-state, and nationalism as these have evolved in the nineteenth and twentieth centuries. Titles in this interdisciplinary and transregional series also illuminate how the nation-state is being undermined by the forces of globalization, international migration, and electronic information flows as well as by resurgent ethnic and religious affiliations. These books highlight historical parallels and continuities while documenting the social, cultural, and spatial expressions through which modern national identities have been constructed, contested, and reinvented.

Modernism and Nation Building:
Turkish Architectural Culture in the Early Republic
by Sibel Bozdoğan

Chandigarh's Le Corbusier:
The Struggle for Modernity in Postcolonial India
by Vikramaditya Prakash

Islamist Mobilization in Turkey:
A Study in Vernacular Politics
by Jenny B. White

Islamist
Mobilization
in Turkey

A STUDY IN VERNACULAR POLITICS

JENNY B. WHITE

UNIVERSITY OF WASHINGTON PRESS

Seattle and London

Publication of *Islamist Mobilization in Turkey* is supported by a grant
from the Institute for Turkish Studies, Washington, D.C.

Library of Congress Cataloging-in-Publication Data

White, Jenny B.
    Islamist mobilization in Turkey : a study in vernacular politics /
Jenny B. White.
        p. cm. — (Studies in modernity and national identity)
    Includes bibliographical references (p.) and index.
    ISBN 0-295-98223-3 (alk. paper)
        1. Islam and politics—Turkey. 2. Turkey—Politics and
government—1980— I. Title. II. Series

BP173.7 .W45 2002
324.2561'082—dc21   2002022515

The paper used in this publication is acid-free and recycled from 10
percent post-consumer and at least 50 percent pre-consumer waste. It
meets the minimum requirements of American National Standard for
Information Sciences—Permanence of Paper for Printed Library
Materials, ANSI Z39.48-1984. ∞ ⊛

In Memory of
Oma Rosa Schneider

CONTENTS

PREFACE

I became interested in questions of political process when I returned in 1994 to the working-class neighborhood of Ümraniye in Istanbul, Turkey, after having spent considerable time there over the preceding eight years in the course of a different research project. During that time I had noticed that, while Ümraniye's residents seemed quite informed about the platforms of political parties (and on occasion organized themselves to protest an issue or demand assistance from the local government), there was little evidence of what the literature would call civil society: participation in formal civic organizations. This impression was confirmed by surveys that showed little or no participation in civic organizations in Turkey's poorer urban areas, particularly among women. Yet, at the same time, scholars of civil society were pointing to the large and rapidly increasing numbers of civic organizations in Turkey. This lack of fit between civil society and participation caused me to wonder who belonged to these many civic groups, if large parts of the population of Turkey's cities did not. It also placed into puzzling relief the civic activism and political engagement I had observed in Ümraniye. How did people organize themselves, around what issues, and why?

Spurred by curiosity, I began to investigate civic and political activism over two months in the summer of 1994 and again in 1995, with funding from the Institute of Turkish Studies and the University of Nebraska at Omaha. Initially, I studied secularist activists involved in setting up voluntary schools that taught skills and literacy to low-income women. Soon after the 1994 elections that brought the Islamists to power in Ümraniye, I turned my attention to local Islamist activists. In 1997, a Social Science Research Council grant allowed me to spend seven months in Istanbul to take a closer and more sustained look at the activities of both groups.

What I learned led me to reconsider the categories of knowledge that I had brought with me into the field and that had guided my original questions, including the much debated concept of civil society. In order to grasp the multiple levels and unexpected convergences of what otherwise would be artificially distinguished as civic, political, and cultural/religious phenomena, a new conceptualization—and a new term—was needed. The term, *vernacular politics,* makes an argument for looking at political process as a hybrid form. This makes possible a new vision of "politics" in societies, like those in the Middle East, that generally have been examined using a precut yardstick that measures the degree to which democratic institutions have been instituted and civil society developed. The hybrid political movement in Turkey raises theoretical issues of import not only for understanding mass mobilization in Islamic societies, but also in the United States where the new megachurches also cross lines between civic, political, and cultural realms. The book as a whole makes an argument for rethinking the terms we use to understand how people are mobilized to be active participants in public life.

In Turkey, I interviewed and observed activists and officials at the local and national levels, including the Islamist mayor of Istanbul, Recep Tayyip Erdoğan, and attended rallies and other organized events. The staff at the popular Islamist television station Kanal 7 kindly allowed me to sit in on internal discussions and strategy sessions and offered insights into the Islamist movement and the Welfare Party, with which the station had an ambivalent relationship.

I did not live in Ümraniye during this time, since my research necessitated moving between two ideologically opposed groups of residents. In addition to the obvious problem of a perceived division of loyalties, my visits to the secularist group sometimes called for a different style of clothing, not quite as modest, with a bit of makeup. Since these things have important resonances within the groups, it would have been exceedingly difficult to live with, say, a more devout family and explain why I was dressing in short sleeves and putting on lipstick—taboo in that environment—to visit others in the neighborhood. Consequently, I set out mornings for Ümraniye from my rented room in European Istanbul. On a good day, the trip took around forty minutes. On a bad day, it could take up to two hours. On occasion I spent the night there; some families would not allow me to take public transportation alone at night.

My introduction to the people of Ümraniye reaches back some twenty years. I came to know the area well during the two years, 1986 to 1988, that I researched informal-sector economic production in Istanbul's squatter areas (White, 1994). Although I worked in several different neighborhoods at the time, some of my closest relationships were developed with families in Ümraniye and it is here that I returned on every visit. By the mid-1990s, the young men and women in these families had grown up and most had married. Whenever they coincided with my visits, I attended engagement ceremonies and weddings, and admired the babies that followed. The addition of new in-laws and my continual exposure at family and community functions over a decade expanded my network of acquaintances tremendously. Most important, and for me immensely gratifying, was the fact that my closeness to these families transferred my network membership to the families into which they had married, and, in this manner, I was privileged to meet a whole new set of interesting, admirable, and helpful people.

To protect the privacy of the kind people who opened their homes and their lives to me, I have changed their names, along with nonessential details about their lives and places of residence. This was also made necessary by the increasingly hostile political climate toward anyone suspected of being active in the Islamist movement. Since public officials already are publicly identified as Islamists, I have not changed their names, but have taken care not to link them directly to statements that might be used against them.

Note on Turkish Pronunciation and Spelling

For readers unfamiliar with Turkish pronunciation: *ö* and *ü* are the same as in German, *c* is *j*, *ç* is *ch*, *ş* is sh, *ğ* is silent but lengthens the preceding vowel, and *ı* is pronounced like the *o* in "atom."

ACKNOWLEDGMENTS

In its earliest stages, when my research was still focused on civil society, I was gently pushed to think outside the box by other scholars at a Social Science Research Council meeting in Cairo in March 1997. Since then, I have benefitted immensely from extended conversations with Haldun Gülalp, Augustus Richard Norton, and Ayşe Önal. They and a number of other colleagues have offered insightful and unsparingly honest critiques of earlier versions of this work, some generously reading through multiple drafts. In particular, I would like to thank Thomas Barfield, Benjamin Campbell, Dale Eickelman, Akile Gürsoy, Reşat Kasaba, Nancy Lindisfarne, Gwenn Okruhlik, Kevin Reinhart, and Ariel Salzmann. The ideas contained herein, however, remain fully my responsibility. Stephen Kimmel and Belkis Kümbetoğlu generously introduced me to their wide circles of acquaintances. Thanks are due as well to Kathy Kwasnica and Janet O'Neil at Boston University's Department of Anthropology and Gülden Güneri at the American Research Institute in Turkey for their assistance and unfailing good cheer, to Armağan Güneri for her excellent transcription work, Aslı Baykal for keeping me up to date, and Yasmine Ziesler for keeping me organized. Finally, I am deeply grateful to Michael Freeman, who commented on endless drafts and whose patience and encouragement sustained my momentum and enthusiasm throughout the writing of this book.

ISLAMIST MOBILIZATION IN TURKEY

A Study in Vernacular Politics

INTRODUCTION

In November 1997, people in living rooms and offices all over Turkey were hotly debating the seemingly inexorable progress of the Constitutional Court toward a decision to shut down Turkey's most prominent and successful Islam-based political party, the Welfare Party. This party had attracted a much greater variety of supporters than any previous Islam-inspired party: conservative townspeople and poor urban migrants, but also up-and-coming professionals, intellectuals, and wealthy industrialists. Many working-class and conservative women became political activists for the first time, going door to door to get out the vote for Welfare. Even people who were against the party, or any Islamic party, having a place in national politics spoke with awe of the extent to which the party had organized its followers, street by street.

Whatever the party was doing, it was working. In the local elections of 1994, the Welfare Party doubled its votes nationally and captured almost half the mayoral seats in provincial capitals, including six of Turkey's fifteen largest cities. To the great consternation of the country's secular elites, Istanbul, Turkey's most cosmopolitan city, elected a Welfare Party mayor, as did the capital, Ankara. In the 1995 general elections, Welfare won the largest number of seats in parliament. The political interests of its constituents ranged widely, from social and economic reform to replacing the secular state system with one founded on Islamic law.

Ataturk banner in Beyoğlu, Istanbul's shopping and entertainment district.

The Constitutional Court, arguing that the party posed a threat to the laic foundations of the state, opened a case against it. *Laicism,* one of the founding principles of the secular Turkish state, refers to the subordination of religion to the state. The laicist state aims to control all public expressions of Islamic practice, down to training the prayer leaders of mosques and vetting their sermons. Public debate revolved around whether or not an openly Islamic party should be allowed to participate in the political system. People against the party speculated darkly about what would happen if it came to power. Others were conflicted and mused that closing a legitimately elected party of any kind was undemocratic, although perhaps that was the price that had to be paid to keep the country secular. Given the political elite's hostility to the party and anxiety about the party's ultimate intentions, it seemed a foregone conclusion that the party would be closed down.

To my great surprise, Welfare Party activists seemed unconcerned. When I asked what they would do if the party was closed, they invariably answered that nothing would change. Some scoffed that closing the party was meaningless. One bearded businessman, a Welfare Party member who volunteered with an Islamic charity foundation, looked bemused at my question. "If they close the party, then a few politicians lose their jobs; that's all. It has no effect on us. We're a social movement, not a party." Others gave similar explanations. They shrugged and said that their social and political networks would not be affected by closing the party.

I found this calm unconcern striking, given the decibel level of national debate and the assumption behind the court action—that closing the Welfare Party would eliminate the threat of Islam in politics. It gave me to wonder, if not party politics, then what kind of politics was I witnessing? If the party was dispensable, how then were people organizing themselves politically? In such a tightly run party, how did activists remain independent? Perhaps, I speculated, they formed civic organizations that worked together with the party while remaining autonomous. But the number of civic organizations involved with Welfare, and their range of activities and membership, did not account for anywhere near the level of organized activism mobilizing behind the party. And what was mobilizing them? How important was Islam in all this, given the wide variety of supporters?

The global spread of Islam-based politics gave these questions broader importance. They concerned the nature of political processes that were developing in major urban centers worldwide, attracting hybrid populations and frequently taking inspiration from Islam. The questions also seemed applicable to political mobilization that did not revolve around an Islamic interpretation.

In February 1998, the Welfare Party was closed and its leader temporarily exiled from politics. Another Islam-inspired party, the Virtue Party, was formed within days and continued to attract a strong and equally diverse following. Before long, a case was opened against Virtue, but its activists remained, as always, confident, committed to a movement that Virtue shared but clearly did not control.

This is a book about that political process. It challenges the premise that political Islam and Islamist political ideology can fully be understood as national political phenomena apart from the cultural beliefs, local practices, and often contradictory motivations of their adherents. Likewise, the book questions the usefulness of analytically separating "modern" civil society and party politics from "traditional" communalistic practices, institutional from individual relations, or political ideology from cultural beliefs. A fresh look at political process is suggested with the introduction of vernacular politics, a concept that reconnects political ideology and culture, organization and process.

This requires us to think outside the categories we have inherited for understanding political life. We tend to conceive of society and politics in terms of familiar solidarities, based on the communion of family, clan, tribe, religion, and ethnicity, or on the liberated individualism of modern urbanism, civil society, bureaucracy, liberal, secular democracy, and the market. In studying political movements, analysts look for shared motivations, whether these be ethnic affiliation, religious ideology, class interests, or national identity. The logistics of solidarity also come under scrutiny, acted out in local networks or as civil society, interest groups, political parties, and ethnic and religious organizations.

"Vernacular politics"[1] helps us refocus on the political process in a new way that makes no assumptions about motivation or form, allowing us to grasp the hybrid nature of modern urban-based political processes. The Islamist movement in Turkey in the 1990s and at the beginning of the twenty-first century is a community- and value-centered political process that, despite its local roots, is able to draw large numbers of people of diverse backgrounds into national politics. I use the term *Islamist movement* to mean a general mobilization of people around cultural, political, and social issues that are presented and interpreted through an Islamic idiom. What I will refer to as an Islamist movement is by no means coherent in organization, ideological interpretation, goal, or method. Like any loosely drawn movement, it aims to unify people around a shared ideology and social and political goals. Islam is the central idiom to which all participants appeal.

However, from a different angle, the Islamist movement in Turkey encompasses a variety of people with contradictory motivations and goals and sometimes radically differing interpretations of fundamental religious principles and political platforms. "Islam" itself takes a variety of forms. What binds people together in the Islamist movement is neither ideology (be it political or religious) nor any particular type of organization (whether civil society or "tribe"). Rather, the movement is rooted in local culture and interpersonal relations, while also drawing on a variety of civic and political organizations and ideologies.

While the cultural values underlying this political process are not new, their power to mobilize large numbers of diverse people is new.

This can be directly linked to conditions of urban life as new populations have entered the cities and over the span of two generations developed communities made up of people from a variety of backgrounds and facing distinctly urban problems. New types of solidarity, resting on familiar cultural values, recreated a sense of community and simultaneously allowed the community to become a political force.

In Turkey, the Islam-inspired Welfare Party found in this participatory local politics a powerful tool for mobilizing the population. Welfare and its successor, the Virtue Party, owed much of their success to their ability to incorporate hybrid populations and to build on local community networks. To gain access to these community networks, the party itself had to become "intimate." It did so by interacting with constituents on an individual level through known, trusted neighbors, building on sustained, face-to-face relationships, and by situating its political message within the community's cultural codes and norms. The Islamist activists also worked through a variety of institutions, from the political party and its municipal institutions to civic groups. Seemingly unrelated types of acts, from neighborly visits and marriage counseling to volunteering for a charity foundation or demonstrating in front of a mosque for religious freedom, were braided together and brought up to the national level within the political and ideological frame of party politics.

In other words, to comprehend the nature of Islamism in Turkey and its place in a political democracy, it is necessary to take a closer look at how Islam and politics are lived, not only at how they are theorized and proselytized. Gudrun Kramer has warned that "it is not possible to talk about Islam and democracy in general, but only about Muslims living and theorizing under specific historical circumstances" (Kramer, 1993, 4). It is only by looking at how people (local activists, supporters, and dissenters, as well as intellectuals and politicians) think and act politically that we can hope to understand the interconnection of religion and politics, politics and culture, and civil society and democracy. It also behooves us to remember, as Robert Darnton (1984, 4) famously put it, that ordinary people think with things. This entails, for us, investigating practices that have been labeled "Islam," "politics," and "civil society" as they are interwoven with the material conditions governing the lives of ordinary people under very concrete circumstances in Istanbul, Turkey. In order to do so, we must look at process, not static institutional models, at organizing, not organizations.

Islamist practice does not take place in isolation, but is set off against *Kemalist* secularist activism. Kemalism, the term used by secularist supporters of the status quo, is a highly charged worldview. It derives from the governing principles set in place early in the twentieth century by Mustafa Kemal Ataturk, the founder of the Turkish Republic, who initiated a great social and political experiment designed to modernize and Westernize Turkey. Like *Islamism,* the term *Kemalism* cannot be taken at face value as an analytical category. In practice, it refers to a varied and changing complex of behaviors and beliefs. However, *Islamist* and *Kemalist* are widely used as self-referential categories and it is in this spirit that I use the terms here.

While these appear as competing dyads in Turkish public life, in the factualness of everyday life they form a continuum. The meanings and parameters of Islamism and Kemalism overlap; they rely on similar institutions and share constituencies. What, then, gave Islamist political practice its edge? To answer this question, this book follows the activities of two sets of local activists, one Islamist, the other secularist, in the working-class Istanbul neighborhood of Ümraniye.

The analysis will work outward from the manner in which religion, politics, and economic status are embedded in daily practice, to the manner in which these are expressed institutionally at the national level and in party politics. The premise for this onion-like exfoliation is that the latter cannot be understood without the former. A focus on institutions, ideology, and the utterances of elites inevitably suggests certain conventional interpretations; a focus on the local or cultural suggests other interpretations that have been discussed above. The interplay of both, it is hoped, will suggest a new formula for interrelating elements that generally have been considered discretely.

An Initial Conversation

When embarking on this project, I explained to my acquaintances and friends in the working-class Istanbul neighborhood of Ümraniye, where I had done research a decade before, that I was interested in how local people participated in political and civic life. This led to discussions of demonstrations and community involvement. When, during my stay in 1995, I expressed an interest in the inner workings of the Islam-inspired Welfare Party that had recently won the municipal elections away from the secularist Republican People's Party, my friend Sevgi confided that her new husband's younger brother, Halil, worked for the Welfare Party municipality. I visited Sevgi and her husband Hasan in their rented apartment in an outlying district of Ümraniye.

Ümraniye is a large, bustling neighborhood on the Asian side of Istanbul, with a population of over two hundred thousand. It is primarily working-class, with some quite poor areas. It began, as did many Istanbul neighborhoods, as a squatter area that over the years was gradually absorbed into the city proper. Despite this bureaucratic and infrastructural incorporation, Ümraniye's residents hold a tentative position as urbanites that must be continually negotiated. This insecurity extends from the precariousness of their livelihoods to their unacceptability as "urban types" to other city dwellers who see themselves as being more modern and Westernized.

Sevgi and Hasan lived in a newly developed area with broad, multistory apartment buildings set along wide, chalky streets, still barren of gardens or trees. There were a few small shops (mostly groceries) on the ground floor of some of the buildings, but none of the hustle and bustle of life in downtown Ümraniye. In fact, Sevgi complained, there was nothing to do—no place even to stroll and look in the shop windows. She spent most of her days at home.

Their apartment was a third-floor walk-up, with two other apartments on the same floor. It was a new building, with a wide staircase, but the apartments were small. To the left of the entryway, where we traded our shoes for slippers, was a long kitchen leading onto a narrow balcony that ran the entire side of the apartment. There were cabinets in the kitchen, and on that day a large flowered cloth lay on the floor, piled high with hazelnuts drying in their green husks. Her sister-in-law, Nefise, perched on the bed-couch in the small, unadorned sitting room. Nefise's face was framed by a light, cotton, indoor head scarf, fringed with complex crochet-work that matched the color of her clothing. Nefise was slim, with a delicate, intelligent face and a sweet smile. While she spoke, her hands were busy crocheting.

I shed my coat and took a seat on a chair. I had just returned from a pre-wedding, all-women henna party[2] with Sevgi and thus wore a long, narrow, linen skirt and a loose but short-sleeved, festive gold silk blouse. My hair, as usual, was uncovered. Sevgi settled down in the armchair beside me. She had removed her coat and silk outdoor over-scarf, but retained her cotton indoor scarf, now loosened. Sevgi introduced me to Nefise and we chatted aimlessly about the events of the day. We were joined by Sevgi's unmarried younger sister, Bahire, who was visiting from her village. They asked me about my project and I explained that I was interested in understanding whether or not people in Ümraniye joined civic organizations, and, if not, how they organized themselves to participate in politics and civic activities.

They grasped right away what I wanted to know and began to tell me about their own experiences or things they had heard. Nefise, upon hearing our spirited discussion, soon lost her initial diffidence and warmed to the topic. She told me that she used to work at the Ümraniye municipality. Sevgi noted proudly that her sister-in-law had done all kinds of work there, from typing to organizing and producing reports. Nefise began to tell me about the many things her job had entailed, including advanced computer skills, when Hasan entered the room and summarized, "A secretary, that is."

Hasan was a handsome, affable man, even-tempered, with an easy smile and a welcoming manner. He was a driver for a private company and, like many men in the neighborhood, also drove a taxi during his off hours. I was pleased for Sevgi that she had married well. I repeated the description of my project and he assured me that his brother Halil would be happy to help me in my research. Then he began to describe the Welfare Party's activities in Ümraniye, the young women occasionally chiming in enthusiastically.

"The [Ümraniye] Welfare mayor is around all the time. I never saw the Republican People's Party mayor. But as soon as the Welfare mayor was elected, I saw him down the block getting a haircut. Then I saw him a few blocks away eating in a restaurant. Then a few months later I met a friend of mine in the street and he said he was going to meet the mayor at a local community place where he was holding a meeting. The Welfare folks really care about people. They go door to door and see if anyone needs anything. They eat in people's homes and, if they see that there is very little food, only a few olives and bread, they help them."

I asked, with some surprise, "They eat the poor people's food?"

"Yes, but they also bring a big basket of supplies with them. Neighbors tell them if they think a family needs help and then they go there."

"Do they know the people they go to?"

"They may not know them but they GET to know them," Nefise answered.

Hasan continued, "The [Welfare Party] mayor of Istanbul, Tayyip Erdoğan, lives in a rental apartment in Üsküdar. They offered him the official residence but he refused. He lives just like us.... During Ramazan [the month of fasting] they set up tents with donated food, rice, meatballs, so that people can eat if they can't get home right away [when the day's fasting ends at sunset] or if people are poor. They can eat for free. There are also tents for cheap school materials when school opens in the fall. And tents with inexpensive used and donated clothing. They started it; it was their idea, although the other parties do it now too."

Bahire asked, "What did the Republican People's Party ever do for us?"

"A course in sewing," Nefise offered, disparagingly.

"Yes, at the municipality," Sevgi replied. "I went to that. And they had one in cloth painting"—turning to me—"and things like that."

Halil came into the room, looked startled (perhaps at my attire), and sat down on the couch next to Nefise, his wife, who said not a word after this. He was a slim, lean man with a sharp face and a thin moustache. He wore black slacks and a white shirt, adding to his austere appearance. He listened to our discussion and reiterated the story about the tents, adding emphatically that, while Turkey was not a democracy, the Welfare Party did act democratically. He cited as an example of this the fact that, every Wednesday, Welfare held an open meeting (*Açık Oturum*) where the mayor sat in his office and anyone could come and make requests of or complain to him. The mayor then dealt with each concern. Halil's voice was quarrelsome and strident. The theme of Turkey not being a democracy came up again and again. I tried not to argue, but found myself defending Turkey.

"But Turkey is a democracy," I suggested mildly.

"Being a democracy means the army is under civilian rule," he pointed out. Halil was referring to the military's dominant presence on the National Security Council, which advises the government. Many of the government's anti-Islamist policies originate in the National Security Council and the military is outspoken about its opposition to any ideology that it suspects endangers the laic basis of the state.

"That isn't the only criterion," I replied. "There are elections here, unlike many other places in the Middle East."

He elaborated on the unfairness and undemocratic nature of not being able to dress as one wished. He gave the example of a friend's daughter who was unable to continue her medical studies because she wouldn't be allowed to wear her head scarf in school. Some teachers at universities, he insisted, discriminate against students with head scarves. I agreed that people should be able to wear whatever clothing they wish.

"There are no laws against this in your country," he insisted heatedly.

"True, but there are informal dress codes and infractions are punished by loss of one's job or public ridicule. And private businesses are allowed to make whatever rules they want about dress." This was not exactly correct, I realized. There are always cases where people feel their religious rights are infringed upon, but these are solved in court, according to principles that respect religious rights. I emphasized that in the United States great attention is paid to the separation of church and state, so, for instance, there is no prayer in schools.

He brought up the Turkish government's recent moves to rein in Islamist influence by cracking down on Islamist schools.

"Don't you have schools of nuns?"

"Yes," I admitted. "I went to one, but it has a similar curriculum to that of public schools."

"So do the *imam-hatip* [Islamic] schools. The only difference is a couple of additional courses in Arabic and on the Quran."

Somehow the discussion of democracy segued into a discussion of Islamic (*sharia*) law. Perhaps I was the first to bring it up, when I tried to explain why Welfare scared many secularist Turks, that people thought that Welfare wanted *sharia* law, not democracy. Much to my surprise, instead of taking the opportunity to demur, Halil fired into a heated defense of *sharia*.

"We have to follow Allah's design."

Referring to our previous conversation, I asked him whether Allah's design was democracy.

He was momentarily flustered but soon caught up again in sloganlike exclamations about the requirement to follow Allah's will. His voice was hard and almost spitting, his eyes steely, his back arched as if daring me to disagree. Beside him, Nefise squirmed, looking pained and uncomfortable. Hasan broke in occasionally to restate what Halil was saying in less radical and clearer terms, fishing out of his flood of rhetoric points of actual fact or contention (the tents, the *imam-hatip* schools, head scarves, the fact that Turkey does have some democracy). Hasan also seemed embarrassed by his brother's outbreak and sloganizing fervor. I attempted not to argue or disagree, merely to mark his points and make relevant comments, but my simple presence seemed to inflame him.

Halil's arguments matched almost word for word those of Mehmet Metiner, an advisor to Mayor Erdoğan, with whom I had had a conversation two years earlier. When I asked him what would happen to secular Muslims who did not wish to live under *sharia* law, Halil answered, as Metiner had, that Christians and Jews could live [in a kind of confessional federalism] under whatever system they wanted. When I pointed out that I was not talking about non-Muslims, but about Muslims, Halil repeated his explanation about Christians and Jews (as had Metiner). Finally, after my third reiteration of the same question, Halil muttered something about Muslims having to follow holy law, but that there was no compulsion in religion—that is, no one could be forced into doing anything against their will. Then he fell uncomfortably silent. Metiner, in exasperation, had spit out that secularist Muslims "aren't Muslims!"

I pressed the advantage of my relationship to Halil's sister-in-law, married to his elder brother, who, in this age-hierarchical society, he was expected to respect (and obey). Supported by Hasan, I told Halil that I would like to observe Welfare's activities myself and document them. Grudgingly, he invited me to come to the *Açık Oturum* and other Welfare events. I thanked him and said I would call to arrange it. He and Nefise got up to take their leave. I reached out my hand and registered a moment's hesitation before he took it to shake, fleetingly. Nefise trailed out after him. I felt very sorry for her and couldn't help but imagine that he treated her with the same unbending will that he had demonstrated here, and submitted her to merciless ideological scrutiny.

After they left, the four of us sat contemplatively for a moment, the room seeming to silently vibrate in the wake of Halil's verbal violence. Bahire broke the silence, uttering quietly and simply, "He speaks so harshly."

Another silence followed. Hasan agreed, but added that he had become like this since joining the Welfare Party. "I don't understand it."

This is the story of a journey that began here—with a large, close-knit family, a discussion of issues, and a demonstration of ideological force, framed as an appeal to both democracy and religious law. The conversation revealed generational and gender contradictions, although these were acknowledged only as personal characteristics. Not unfittingly, given my project, the conversation ended with an invitation to participate in civic and political events. My own journey of understanding traversed this ideological terrain again and again in the lives of different families, different people on both sides of the issues. The growth of mutual respect between Halil and me, perhaps even of liking, is one thread of this complex narrative. So is my warm relationship with the secularist activists of the Ümraniye Women's Center, as intolerant in some respects as Halil and his colleagues in others. It was no easy task to settle myself squarely into such highly charged opposing camps, to winnow out what I could agree with, and to keep myself from rejecting outright what I found objectionable. I took great care never to give either group to believe that I stood with them against the other, but only addressed individual issues, about which, when asked, I gave my honest opinion. Above all, I came to appreciate the sincere desire for a better society that motivated both groups, although each would probably disagree about that with regard to the other.

It feels odd to order my experiences, which are infused with the warmth, generosity, unfailing hospitality, and friendship of the people I knew, into an impersonal narrative with quite a different goal. Yet I feel that the journey down the road of understanding is worthwhile and that the people of Ümraniye would support my attempt to grasp their ordering of the political and social world.

The Negotiated Landscape

The Istanbul cityscape is like a raised Braille script that the traveler can read as a code for the different forces and interests, and the negotiations among them, that characterize the city. The cityscape is dominated by vistas of unimproved cement. It is a modern landscape, but because of the often substandard building materials and frequent disregard for building codes, ultimately insubstantial. Entire swaths of the city were tragically flattened in 1999 by a 7.4 magnitude earthquake that killed 12,000 people. Yet the vigor of the city continues to push its way inexorably out of the earth in the form of high-rise urban architecture. Even the hand-built squatter homes on the outskirts of the city optimistically sprout antennae of steel rods, ready to stabilize the next floor when the resident can afford bricks and mortar. Squatter neighborhoods I knew in the mid-1980s now are cityscapes themselves, with rows of three- and four-story buildings, the ground floors colorful with shops. With the rapid swelling of the city, its population now estimated at nearly nine million, some of these neighborhoods have been invaded by even taller luxury apartment dwellings and by gated communities, eliding geographic boundaries between migrants from the countryside and middle-class city dwellers, although differences are seemingly maintained (even heightened) by language, dress, and norms of behavior, especially those regarding women.

But even here the operative word is change, as dress and behavioral norms metamorphose in different directions among all sectors of the population. This metamorphosis can lead to (perhaps rather unexpected) convergences, as when a veiled young woman in jeans kisses her boyfriend in the park, or a secularist university student takes on the veil. It leads as well to hardened oppositions, as when a veiled woman is refused a job because of her clothing and what this is believed to imply about her social and political views. The cityscape, in other words, may be ephemeral, but the population's drive toward an urbanity of its own making is powerfully pushing up new buildings and generating new styles and relations among residents. This is demonstrated in the political arena as residents of poorer neighborhoods unite with merchants, industrialists, and the intellectual elite in new, hybrid, social movements.

The city is bisected by the Bosphorus strait. One side of the city is in Europe, the other lies on the continent of Asia. The European side of the strait is global Istanbul, teeming with young professionals, internationally connected artists, writers, and musicians, transvestites, a gay community, foreign expatriates and businesspeople, as well as artisans and shopkeepers. In summer, European Istanbul is clotted with tourists. Residents relax in the many restaurants, bars, nightclubs, and cafes, and stroll or shop in world-class shopping malls and well-stocked supermarkets. When residents of the city's Asian shore are crossing over, they say they are going "to Istanbul," or simply "to the city."

To get to Ümraniye, I took a boat to the Asian side. I passed up the ponderous, but charming, wood-paneled municipal ferries that lumber from shore to shore at scheduled intervals, preferring one of the small private taxi boats that leap from the shore as soon as they have taken on a full load of passengers. As the boat bumped along in the wake of a passing tanker, through the spray I could make out the approaching Asian shoreline. We landed at Üsküdar, site of ancient Chrysopolis and starting point for the great Roman roads that stretched eastward from Byzantium. The central square directly behind the ferry landing is surrounded by stately mosque complexes from Ottoman times, many endowed by women of the royal family. Now a conservative neighborhood of lower-middle-class and working-class people, it is still the portal to Asian Istanbul's hinterland.

Both sides of the Bosphorus are lined with hills. The highest hill, Çamlıca, is on the Asian side and is crowned by a park from which on a rare clear day one can see the entire confluence of the Bosphorus, from its mouth in the Black Sea to its intersection with the Golden Horn and the Sea of Marmara to the south. If one then turns around toward the Asian continent, there is the sudden, disorienting view of a vast sea of houses as far as the eye can see in all directions. In the center of this, like an enormous mottled and tattered carpet of indefinite colors and perimeter, lies Ümraniye.

The ship's passengers began to leap ashore across the narrowing stretch of shuddering green water as soon as the rubber tires hanging from the side bumped up against the pier. A line of blue minibus *dolmuşlar* stretched along the square in front of the mosque. These shared taxis, found all over the city, ply regular routes and charge set fees for each length of the route. The *dolmuşlar,* now ubiquitous, began service as family businesses, informal means of linking outlying and inaccessible squatter areas with the city. Eventually, *dolmuş* drivers formed politically powerful, self-organized drivers' associations that regulated appearance, routes, and fares.

Yet, until the recent government imposition of uniform standards, these vehicles remained wheeled monuments to personal creativity, from jury-rigged motors using handcrafted spare parts to car interiors as canvases for personal expression. Up through the 1980s, *dolmuşlar* were old United States automobiles, 1950s Fords and Chevrolets that had been stretched in length to add a middle bench. They could seat eight or more slightly hunched passengers. Rounded fenders gleaming, fins rampant, the brightly colored and well-tended cars paraded the streets and avenues along predetermined routes. Ignoring designated stops, they took on anyone waving them down. Standardization made itself felt slowly, first by the disappearance of interior whimsy: glass vases attached to the dashboard by suction cups, carpeted dashboards arrayed with framed photos, dolls, and soccer paraphernalia, the drivers' goat shag or colorful woven seat throws. Slowly, the elegant antique cars themselves disappeared from the road, replaced by rumbling, fume-spewing minivans. In the late 1990s, seemingly overnight, all the minivans became either bright canary yellow or a dusty blue, depending on the route. Under the dour and unimaginative bureaucratic eye of government regulation, taxis underwent the same homogenization, with the result that the streets of Istanbul now channel rivers of jockeying yellow vehicles.

Even though it is now part of the city's official transportation system, the *dolmuş* remains a hybrid creature, deeply embedded in local culture. The negotiated quality of local life, the imperative of norms and personal relationships, the triumph of ingenuity stamp the *dolmuş* system as quintessentially local. On the Ümraniye *dolmuş*, unrelated men and women tried to avoid sitting next to one another; if they had to, their body language demonstrated overt constraint. The driver made a detour to take a friend or relative closer to home. He circumvented traffic by driving over the sidewalk and through a small wooded area to emerge on the street farther along, or simply steered the minibus the wrong way down a one-way street, gingerly swerving through oncoming traffic.

The packed *dolmuş* veered along the built-up boulevards, twisting down ever smaller, dustier streets to emerge on Ümraniye's main road, which bisected the bustle of shops spilling from the bases of three- and four-story brown cement houses. The streets teemed with people, the men in dark, ill-fitting suits or patterned knit sweaters and slacks, most women in colorful head scarves and loose, enveloping clothing: skirts and sweaters or the fashionable tailored, loose coat that was part of the new Islamic *tesettür* style. In seeming contradiction, some unmarried young women wore tight jeans and form-fitting T-shirts. As modest married women, however, they would often "close" *(kapat)* themselves, that is, cover their heads and bodily curves in public. Not all women wore head scarves. There was a broad continuum of degree and style of covering, from the formless black body veil, *çarşaf,* to the colorful pastel stylishness of *tesettür,* to simple slacks and sweater, uncovered hair dyed or streaked blond.

The overall impression was of an insouciant industriousness, with earnest shopkeepers keeping vigil at their shop doors, chatting with neighbors. Women, clutching children's hands and plastic shopping bags, meandered along the rows of shops. Chains of young

Outskirts of Ümraniye.

veiled women, arms linked, joyously bounced along the sidewalk, not unobserved by the lean young men lounging on street corners. People were watching, chatting, resting, flirting, all the while plying their trades, running errands, waiting for a bus or a *dolmuş,* proceeding toward their destinations.

One end of Ümraniye's main street was anchored by a large, gray, concrete municipal building that housed, after 1995, the Islamist mayor and his staff. Next door was the municipality's clinic, run by an Islamic foundation. Apartment buildings nearby were honeycombed with rooms and suites that served public functions, hosted public lectures, and served as offices for an Islamic charity foundation and as Welfare Party regional headquarters. Municipal representatives fanned out and distributed full-color brochures and magazines to the shopkeepers of Ümraniye, praising municipal projects and showing off the civic deeds of Welfare Party officials. On a landing in a nearby building, people waited to be taken by Islamic foundation staff to the depot where they could select used winter clothing and furniture for their families. The foundation kept a neat bookcase of binders documenting the neighborhood's poor families and their needs. Volunteers worked with corporate donors to distribute food and coal. They helped people find housing, jobs, and even spouses, and to pay for weddings and circumcision ceremonies. Party activists referred to the foundation those neighbors they believed were in need.

The Women's Branch of the Ümraniye Welfare Party occupied an office down a side street. The head of the Women's Branch was a heavyset woman in a navy-blue coat and matching scarf. Two mobile telephones in her capacious handbag demanded her attention at frequent intervals. Nearly half of the more than fifty thousand registered Welfare Party members in Ümraniye were women, she told me. Although in the mid-1990s women were not represented at high administrative levels in the party, they developed their own political and civic networks and organizations and took leadership positions within them. The Ümraniye Women's Branch had fifteen representatives in each of the neighborhood's twenty districts. The activists organized fundraising activities and political demonstrations, ran discussion groups in people's homes, and regularly visited neighborhood women to offer assistance or simply company. They set up courses and conferences to educate other activists about the party's principles and activist techniques. "We can do more than the men. They're not as active." As the head of Ümraniye's Women's Branch bustled out to attend a meeting with regional representatives, one of her mobile telephones rang, a Welfare Party official summoning her to make an appearance elsewhere.

Several blocks away, in a third-story walk-up, the Ümraniye Women's Center held classes in cloth painting for neighborhood women. Several years before, these secularist, Kemalist activists had run volunteer-staffed People's Schools with assistance from the left-of-center Republican People's Party (RPP) and the then RPP-run municipality. The People's Schools were successful at bringing together a variety of participants, both conservative and liberal, and crossing age and class lines, but this success was not sustained after the activists opened the Women's Center.

The Kemalist and Islamist activists were similar in many ways. They exhibited in their activities a proselytizing fervor and strong ideological commitment. Both were grassroots groups active in Ümraniye, led by local activists, not outsiders. Both depended on face-to-face interactions, building on local networks of people sharing a history of trust. Both had ill-defined and complex links to formal party and municipal structures and civic organizations. Despite these similarities, the Islam-inspired group was much more successful in mobilizing the local population within a sustained social movement. The secularist group, in contrast, after its initial success with the People's Schools, did not seem able to mobilize a great deal of local support.

One major difference between them was the Kemalists' strong belief in "modernity," specifically a Kemalist interpretation of modernity characterized by an emphasis on the superiority of individualistic, goal-seeking behavior over deference to "traditional" forms of family and communal authority—especially when the latter converged with Islamic doctrine about the place of women in the home, in relations within the family, and vis-à-vis men. The activists clearly perceived themselves as pioneers bringing modernity to the neighborhood, and were as concerned with providing services aimed at protecting women and making them more self-reliant as with spreading the Kemalist message. Although themselves residents of Ümraniye, members of the group allied themselves, through their clothing and their message of Kemalist modernism, with the Kemalist elite, whose laicist, secularist, Western-oriented definition of modernity has been until recently the only legitimate key to social status and acceptance by the political and economic elite. As a result of this alliance with Kemalist ideology and practice, their message took on a top-down cast.

In other words, although their method of mobilization consisted of a grassroots, personalized approach, like that of the Islamists, the Ümraniye secularists did not situate their message in local cultural values and forms. Thus, while they were able to tap into local networks, they were unable to orient them toward their cause in a self-sustaining movement. Although they practiced informal, face-to-face politics, in the end they did not practice a vernacular politics that would have bridged local hierarchies and fractures and tied local to national interests in a sustainable movement like that of the Islamists.

Practicing Community

This new politics changed the face of local politics, quite literally. It crossed ethnic, class, and gender lines to an unheard of extent. It was not simply a politics of the poor, but drew people from different social classes and educational and professional backgrounds, both men and women, as well as people of different ethnic identifications and regional origins. Vernacular politics in Turkey is based on local networks of people united within a complex set of norms of mutual obligation. These widely shared norms require people to assist one another in open-ended relations of reciprocity, without calculating immediate return. A history of such relations builds up trust and mutual obligations that are powerful forms of social solidarity, integrating not just family members and people from the same region of origin, but neighbors with no other ties except those of local proximity. "Trust," Robert Putnam writes, "lubricates cooperation. . . . And cooperation breeds trust" (1993, 171). But how does trust based on personal interaction fit into the civic and political mobilization of large numbers of unrelated and diverse people?

The Islamist activists in Turkey tapped into this, in effect, by mobilizing people one by one to act within what they called "cells" (*hücreler*). A cell consists of people who share an intimate history of trust. Cells are based on preexisting networks. Linked to one another, clusters of cells easily constitute a mass movement. They are national without losing the mobilizational power of local, primary identification. These cells may be mobilized around a shared ideological focus within a social movement. Once politicized, they act as a conduit for participation in civic life and in party politics. Thus, civic and political association does not need to trade the force of primary identitification for the breadth of mass mobilization.

Islamic principles support the values of trust and mutual obligation; these are also an organic part of the organization of social and economic life. They take on greater importance in politics in neighborhoods where state and civic institutions have been unreliable mediators. Not surprisingly, interpersonal relations based on reciprocity and trust have been key to political mobilization in heavily migrant neighborhoods, but it is a mistake to assume that these are simply rural forms of association that will eventually be replaced by more "modern," individualistic, associational forms commonly associated with civil society.

Although scholars have pointed to the prevalence of collectivism and norms of reciprocity as attributes of urban middle-class as well as rural Turks,[3] these characteristics are still associated by many "modernist" Turks with rural Turkey and with rural migrants in urban squatter areas. In reality, differentiations like rural from urban and squatter areas from the "city" proper have become increasingly meaningless, as characteristic forms of clothing, lifestyle, and architecture continually change and develop hybrid forms. The differences that do affect the look and feel of a neighborhood and the style and lifestyle choices of its inhabitants often are ones of income, education, and opportunity.

It is important to remember that people involved in local network politics perceive themselves as practicing community, not just doing politics. That is the source of their movement's strength and its autonomy from political and civic institutions. Self-interest and rational choice are downplayed (although clearly never entirely absent), while kinship, religion, and communal identity act powerfully to enforce reciprocity and communal solidarity.

This political process has had two effects on the party at the national level. First, it has challenged the authoritarian, centralized, top-down paternalism of the political system, and has empowered a new generation of politicians that constituents perceive to be "just like us." The populist image of these politicians is rooted in community network politics, giving them direct access to popular support, thus potentially bypassing the party and civic institutions that generally act as liaisons between party leaders and constituents. This autonomy from institutional mediation comes at a price: party leaders must allow community politics to lead, not follow. This means pulling the sometimes unruly local groups with their contradictory positions and goals into an effective national political agenda. The autonomy of the local political process from its institutional bedfellows also means that the fate of a social movement rooted in this political process is not linked to the fate of the political party that has carried its message to the national level. In other words, closing the party has little effect on the strength or resilience of the movement, which can simply look around for another institutional vehicle.

Second, local network politics has imported into the party the contradictory evaluations and competing motivations of the communities empowered by this alternative political process. The differences and contradictions within the movement are not immediately apparent, especially when the party invokes a unifying rhetoric of religious ideology and emphasizes certain social and political issues, like freedom of religious expression. The party faithful at mass rallies and demonstrations appear in an iconic Islamic style of dress that for its part submerges status and regional differences.

The sheer variety of supporters and activists, however, means that there is a corresponding diversity of motivations, goals, interpretations, and positions on the issues. Not all elements of the Islamist movement gravitate toward the same party. Participants organize themselves within a variety of institutions, from informal networks to associations and foundations, and under different leaders. These groups may work in tandem or at cross-purposes in terms of their political and social goals. Moreover, the contradictions inherent in the different social contexts of participants (as worker or industrialist, uneducated or intellectual, old or young, poor or upwardly mobile, woman or man) resurface as quite different expectations and interpretations of the goals and platform of the political party they might support as activists.

Finally, economic and status divisions within the Islamist movement have led to the development of an Islamist elitism that potentially undercuts the movement's link with local cultural norms and the party's populist image. Islamist elites have attempted to attach a higher social status to material styles and lifestyles, like veiling and gender segregation, that represent the movement. To maintain this distinction from everyday practice, they have tried to differentiate Islamist practice as "conscious" and, therefore, superior to the presumably unconscious adherence to "tradition" imputed to local practitioners. They also have tried to legitimate the authenticity of Islamist practices by attributing to them a genealogical relation to practices of the Ottoman period. This neo-Ottomanism gives an illusion of temporal depth to Islamist practices, but also encourages Islamist elitism by identifying Islamist practices with those of the Ottoman court, not the masses. Most notably, middle-class Islamist women have begun to develop recognizably different versions of Islamic dress and lifestyle, advertised as Ottoman-derived, that allow them to retain their class distinction while remaining within the movement.

The Islamist Phenomenon

Islamists are Muslims who, rather than accept an inherited Muslim tradition, have developed their own self-conscious vision of Islam, which is then brought to bear on social and political events within a particular national context. This has occurred in a twentieth-century context of transnational discourse and debate about Muslim practices, fueled by mass education, mass communication, and the spread of global capitalism and media. Mass education played an important role, allowing ordinary people access to key theological texts like the Quran, rather than only trained specialists, the *ulema*. These new interpretations have wide distribution in other Muslim societies through publications on the world market and by means of cassette, Internet, and other media. Some attribute the Islamist phenomenon to dissatisfaction with a perceived lack of values and community accompanying the spread of globalization.

Interpretations vary with the interpreter, with liberal, modernist readings competing with restrictive positions on the characteristics of a proper Muslim life. Central components of an ideal Muslim society that appear prominently in Islamist rhetoric—obligation to authority, communal solidarity, and social justice—are contested among Muslims as to what they entail in practice. Modernization, social mobility, the influence of the media, and the role played by religion in political mobilization increasingly allow tradition to be apprehended as a set of resources and choices. Therefore, different conditions and contexts fragment the religious and political imaginations of Islamist activists and movements.[4]

Turkey's experience is exceptional in that education does not grant direct access to the theological literature, which is still memorized and recited in Arabic, since the Quran was dictated to the Prophet Muhammed in that language. Translated, the Quran would no longer be "the word of God." Most Turks have no knowledge of the Arabic language and rely for Quranic interpretation on the sermons, lessons, or published Turkish-language works of their religious teachers. There are lively debates among Islamist intellectuals who either are able to read and understand the Quran or have access to internationally circulated interpretations. Turkish Islamist intellectuals also have brought into their debates wide-ranging literatures from Western social and political sciences. Perhaps it is this disconnect between Islamist elites and the masses that, in Turkey, makes the Islamist movement more dependent on cultural, rather than ideological, forms of mobilization.

The study of the Islamist phenomenon in Turkey generally has reflected two strategies. One approach has been the analysis of the political ideology of Islamist or Islam-inspired political parties or organizations and their role in the development of Turkish political life (Gülalp, 1999a; Yavuz, 1997), and of the ideas, backgrounds, and intellectual histories of leading figures (Mardin, 1989; Meeker, 1994; Yavuz, 1993, 1999a). A second approach traces how the cultural politics of the Islamist movement has opened up a world of Islamic style and consumerism, intellectual jockeying in Islamic publications, and other manifestations of a struggle to attribute social status to Islamic symbols and lifestyle (Göle, 1996; Navaro-Yashin, 2002).

Scholars and pundits alike are interested in the much debated issues of whether Islam and democracy are compatible and the relation of Islam to modernity. Turkey is perceived to be an important test case for the intersection of Islam and political practice because it has a laicist government with a history of electoral politics, along with viable Islamic parties and organizations that have become politicized and, to some extent, influenced by transnational trends. Violent attacks on the state and on Muslim and non-Muslim minorities by radical militant Islamists (Muslims who use Islam-based connections and Islamic rhetoric politically, with the aim of overthrowing the system) in places like Iran, Algeria, Egypt, and elsewhere lend weight to the suspicion that Islam-inspired political practice is fundamentally incompatible with democracy. No less important is the position of the laicist Turkish state. According to the Chief Prosecutor of the Constitutional Court, Vural Savaş, speaking in reference to the banning of the Welfare Party, "Islam and democracy cannot coexist and indeed one is against the other" (Mercan and Belge, 1997, A6). Typically, analysis and debate of these issues rely on Islamist rhetoric, publications, and the activities of organizations. This has the unintended impact of defining politics only from above, from its literate and vocal purveyors, rather than from below, from the perspectives of practitioners. In fact, important solidarities that emerge in local discourse will be missed when parsing the ideological rhetoric of Islamist groups. For instance, Islamist officials and activists in Ümraniye consistently emphasized neighborliness (see chapter 5). To neighborliness they attached values (like norms of reciprocity and mutual assistance) that commonly defined relations among kin and fellow villagers. Neighborliness and its associated values—and ultimately, neighborliness as a basis for political action— were given further legitimacy by reference to religious doctrine. In fact, doctrine and organization were intertwined with cultural values and practice.

Because a top-down analysis relies on a formal "party" approach, it cannot account for activists' belief that the Welfare Party's demise did not matter. Since opponents of the Islamists see the Islamist movement as a derivation of the party or a creation of outside agitators, or simply as *irtica,* a reactionary political response, they imagine that, once the party is eliminated, a malleable society would be reinstated. However, they fail to appreciate that institutions are products of the underlying society. Then the political party, in a sense, is peripheral to the movement, although each may advance the other's interests. Without an appreciation of vernacular politics that pays attention to the demands and motivations of those segments of society supporting an Islamist movement, as well as to the political ideology and structure of the party, the Islamist movement's independence of formal structures, and, thus, its broad mobilizing potential, cannot be appreciated. In the following chapters, I will examine such claims of autonomy and show how vernacular politics allows for a more complete understanding of the political process.

These concerns influence the layout of the book. I will explore vernacular politics from both local and national perspectives. In order to give centrality to the everyday, readers will not find a discussion of Islamist political parties until chapter 3. Chapter 1 offers a historical perspective on the characteristics, economic status, and lifestyles of the people involved in the Islamist movement—and its political counterpart, Kemalism. Urbanization and economic and political developments over the past two decades are seen to have played a decisive role in the development of new, horizontal, urban networks. Chapter 2 is an ethnographic limning of life in Ümraniye, introducing the families of Islamist activists and revealing how Islam, migration, economic status, gender, and politics are inextricably interwoven in everyday life and, by extension, in the Islamist movement.

Chapter 3 describes the diversity of religious belief and expression in Turkey at the national level and explores the complicated relationship of Islamists and Kemalists to Islam. Chapter 4 analyzes the divisions within Welfare and its successor, the Virtue Party. Differences in religious beliefs, ideological interpretations, and styles of relating to institutions and supporters are given a further twist by generational differences that threaten to tear the party apart. Chapter 5 takes us to the offices of the Welfare municipality in Ümraniye to examine the nature of its populist appeal. At party-sponsored events, politics is personalized and the party's ideological message situated firmly within local cultural norms. Chapter 6 continues to examine the vernacular politics of the Islamist movement from the point of view of the activists and describes the latitude of their autonomy. Chapter 7 pushes the discussion of hybridity and internal contradiction further by considering the contradictions between the expectations, goals and interpretations of male and female activists, and the development of an Islamist elitism which undermines the movement's populist appeal. Such strengths and weaknesses emerge with greater contrast in the final chapter, in which Islamist mobilization in Ümraniye is compared with the efforts of a local secularist, Kemalist group.

Vernacular Politics

To sum up, vernacular politics incorporates what one might expect to be discrete and even contradictory forms of organization and bases for solidarity. Thus, individualism may not be a necessary component of civil society, and interpersonal bonds of trust and mutual obligation, conceived on a foundation of local cultural and religious solidarities, seem to serve quite well as building blocks for "modern" civic and political life. Against expectations, civil society cannot be assumed to guarantee liberalism, but rather may be cast in the service of ideological political institutions, while still maintaining its autonomy. Religious ideology, dissolved in the acid of local interpretation, flows to fill the glasses of competing interests. Finally, informal grassroots politics of the kind so richly described by Singerman (1995) for Cairo and Bayat (1997) for Tehran may become the engine of a national movement or political party without losing either its informality or its local autonomy.

Indeed, it is in the transgressions of vernacular politics against conventional scholarly differentiations—religious and political ideologies embedded in local culture, civil society and political party organization based on local solidarities and interpersonal relations—that one finds the basis for Islamist success in mobilizing a varied population. It explains how the movement sustains political momentum despite the internal differences supporters bring with them, and despite attempts at suppression by the Turkish state and military. At its heart, vernacular politics is a value-centered political process rooted in local culture, interpersonal relations, and community networks, yet connected through civic organizations to national party politics.

But it is also true that the facade of homogeneity—expressed in ideological rhetoric and as shared symbolic forms, and apparent in the sight of masses in lockstep at demonstrations and rallies, or coordinating their efforts in organizational meetings and activities (like charity work and political organizing)—is itself undermined by the differing interests, motivations, and goals of participants. Working-class, merchant, and elite supporters, and men and women activists, each conceive of religious ideology within the context of their everyday needs, motivations, and desires.

What, then, mobilizes and sustains such a movement? In Turkey, as elsewhere, religion does play a role. But it is religion as local cultural idiom played out through social and political structures, and rarely religion as a philosophically thought-out and coherent ideology or political agenda. Islamic ideology embedded in a vernacular politics draws on more than religiosity. This is the key to the movement's strength and resilience, since it allows people to be mobilized across a spectrum of personal religiosity and beliefs.

In other words, vernacular politics is not simply Islamic populism, but rather a political process available to other parties and purveyors of other ideologies as well. This would require, however, that these parties acknowledge the role of cultural norms in political mobilizing, rather than simply conducting business as usual, engaging in top-down campaigning and bidding for local loyalties by establishing themselves as patrons, or allying themselves with local patrons who are then expected to "deliver" the votes of their clients. It requires instead that political behavior be seen as embedded in culture, including religious values as practiced in local contexts, rather than as a separable behavior modified by an ideological prefix—as in Muslim politics or Islamic populism—which refers to, but does not incorporate within political behavior, the lived variety of Islamic practice.

1

THE POLITICAL ECONOMY
OF CULTURE

A distinctive aspect of the Islamist movement in Turkey is the variety of characteristics and motivations of its followers. Social class, profession, educational level, age, and gender all condition what people want to get out of their participation in the movement, and how they go about getting it. These differentiations often remain unremarked in conventional analyses that situate a political or cultural Islam opposite an equally undifferentiated secular Kemalism, or that focus on the structure and ideology of the organizations and institutions that represent them.

Kemalist and *Islamist* are self-ascriptive terms referring to groups of people reactively polarized around certain issues. Kemalism and Islamism each provide the other with an oppositional social model that, while it does not need to actually exist in fact, legitimates the idealized characteristics of one by demonizing the perceived opposite characteristics of the other. The iconic Kemalist position combines a kind of authoritarian democracy with a Westernized secular lifestyle. Kemalists are concerned to safeguard laicism and its guarantees of free choice of lifestyle, particularly for women, but limited choice in the realms of religion and ethnicity. Elite Kemalists have tried to control the direction of Turkish society through authoritarian state institutions: the government, judiciary, and the educational system.

Woman in conventional rural dress.

The lifestyle, behavioral practices, and ideological positions that generally are associated with Kemalism and Islamism, however, have a broad distribution in society and overlap these categorical boundaries. A clear Kemalist-Islamist divide is also challenged by the continual emergence of hybrid forms under the influence of globalization and the market in goods and ideas: university students wearing both jeans and head scarves, commercialized Islamist fashion, leftists writing for Islamist magazines, Islamists supporting the introduction of Valentine's Day into Turkish society,[1] and neo-Ottoman nostalgia infecting Islamist and secularist alike. While Ataturk attempted to isolate the Republic from its Ottoman past, the 1980s and 1990s saw a widespread nostalgia for things Ottoman. Ottoman objects and references to Ottoman history served as markers of elite status among the old secular elite and the *nouveaux riches*. But the most pervasive neo-Ottomanism, the engagement of Ottoman objects, practices, and history in the legitimation of new social forms, was practiced by the Islamists. Cultural practices and references act as dividing lines in Turkish society, although the boundaries are by no means clear. Attributions of cultural difference obscure other, more categorical differences, like those of social class.

One thing Kemalists and Islamists have in common is a reluctance to recognize the role of socioeconomic class in what they perceive to be the division of society into Kemalist and Islamist camps. Instead, each side focuses on the cultural practices believed to characterize the other. For instance, self-defined Kemalists imagine themselves to be "modern," liberal, secular, and individualistic. They imagine Islamists to be "traditional," authoritarian, patriarchal, religiously fanatic, and collectivist. These characteristics also are attributed, in an equally undifferentiated manner, to rural populations and residents of the squatter areas that have grown up around Turkey's major cities—for instance in what some secular Istanbul urbanites have called the "Other Istanbul" (*Öteki Istanbul*). Each side imagines itself to be free of the characteristics of the other.

These same differentiations are made between lower-class and middle-class lifestyles. However, this link with social class remains unacknowledged, as does the overlap of these characteristics in practice. One consequence of this reluctance to admit to certain cultural practices that are associated with the "Other Istanbul" is that political practices based on social networks, and, thus, the power of vernacular politics, become unavailable to Kemalist-inspired parties determined to be "modern." They are available to the Islamist movement because it situates its organization and message within local cultural practices. Islam can be used to buttress and channel these practices.

The source and content of the Kemalist and Islamist categories and their transformation, internal differentiations, and overlap must be sought in the economic and political history of the Turkish Republic. Early Republican reforms and the leadership of Mustafa Kemal Ataturk laid the ground for Kemalism, as both ideology and lifestyle. Meanwhile, Islam has played a political role in opposition movements and support for political parties. It has also remained a powerful part of people's lives. Kemalists and Islamists have a complicated relationship to Islam; this complexity is reflected in the varieties of political expression of Islam.

I begin below with an exegesis of the Kemalist/Islamist categories, their history and expression in cultural and political practice. (The political expression of Islam will be treated in greater detail in chapter 3.) I describe the economic developments that created the urban populations of today, and the startling economic transformations beginning in the 1980s that recast those populations along new cultural and economic lines. The new economy created hybrid, even grotesque, social forms, while whetting the edge that divided rich and poor. This was accompanied by the transformation of cultural norms in working-class areas like Ümraniye, in particular norms of mutual obligation that, through vernacular politics, began to play a decisive role in mobilizing political support. Finally, I discuss the continued resistance on the part of Kemalists to acknowledging the political value of such norms, since these are attributed to the Kemalists' cultural Other.

Kemalists and Their Others

Over dinner at a Chinese restaurant in Istanbul several years ago, a middle-aged professional woman raised her glass of scotch to her foreign and Turkish acquaintances around the table and announced with some passion, in English, "*Rakı* is barbaric. Whiskey is civilized." *Rakı* is the national anise-flavored alcohol produced under state license and popularly consumed over drawn-out meals of meze, fish, lamb kebabs, and other traditional Turkish food. Much can be read from this simple statement: that the woman was a secularist Kemalist; that she disapproved of what she perceived to be the customs of the lower classes; that such reviled customs would include practices from *rakı* sipping to veiling and, even worse, not drinking at all for religious reasons; that she was passionately opposed to Islamist politics and Islamists in any form. It was also clear that she situated herself in an elite class. This was apparent not only in her profession—she was a lawyer—but also in the fact that she lived alone in her own apartment and could afford to eat at an expensive restaurant. Kemalism and elite status could be read in her taste in Western clothing, appreciation of Chinese food, and choice of libation.

Even hair color plays a role in maintaining a distinction between Kemalists and their civilizational Others. Seated at the back of a hall of middle-class women at a 1998 meeting of the Association for the Promotion of Modern Living, I was startled by the sea of beautifully coifed blond hair in a nation of generally dark-haired inhabitants.

Media advertisements use blue-eyed, blond models to sell Turkish products. In the poorer quarters, those women whose heads are uncovered participate in the "modern look" by streaking their dark hair blond, something middle-class women sneer at as a kind of white-trash copy of their own style.

In other words, there is an identifiable type of radical Kemalist that exhibits a predictable constellation of attitudes and characteristics. This is changing as a new generation of pragmatists and opportunists builds bridges between elite and popular culture; as people from the countryside and the lower classes strike it rich in the 1980s economy and bring their *rakı*-drinking habits into new milieus; and as some of the old elite lose their wealth and enter into partnership with the *nouveaux riches*. The unreconstructed radical Kemalist may be maladaptive in the economic and political environment of the new century, but in the present polarized climate still has a strong foothold. Radical Kemalists are gatekeepers to a set of ideals rooted in the reforms and aspirations of the early Republican elites.

The acquisition of Western cultural habits and the dethroning of Islam were institutionalized after the founding of the Turkish Republic in 1923 under the leadership of Mustafa Kemal, although movement in this direction began in the previous century. Kemal (later awarded the name Ataturk, or Father of the Turks) was a charismatic leader popularly revered for rescuing the remnants of the Ottoman Empire from division and dispersal after World War I and forging of them a nation. This patchwork land of peasants and minorities was ordered, in an exacting campaign, into a republic representing what Ataturk and his party imagined to be a "modern" society. To this end, Ataturk pushed through many changes, some of which would have toppled a less beloved and entrenched leadership. Thus were put into place the elements of a Kemalist ideal that are being revisited, challenged, defended, and recast in the present.

Under Ataturk's leadership, the new government changed the language of state from Ottoman, an amalgam of Turkish, Arabic, and Persian, written in Arabic script, to Turkish, written in the Latin alphabet. The Turkish Language Association was founded with a brief to purge Ottoman Turkish of "foreign" influences in order to create a language closer to the Turkish spoken by the common people. The institute regularly issued updated dictionaries of the "new Turkish" to be used in schools, newspapers, and government business. Consequently, post-Republican generations were literally cut off from their past, since they could not read pre-Republican documents of any kind—even grandfather's papers. Boxes of unsorted documents and papers written in Ottoman, sold in bulk by relatives after the death of an elder, moldered in the corners of used bookstores. The language transformation was still evident in daily speech in the 1980s, with older people using more Arabic- and Persian-derived words, many incomprehensible to youngsters raised with new Turkish.

The break with the Ottoman past that the language reform occasioned was not unforeseen by Ataturk. The Republic and its Turkish citizens were to seek their roots instead in the civilizations of the Hittites, who inhabited the Anatolian plateau in the second millennium B.C., and Turkic tribes that had migrated to Anatolia from Central Asia in the twelfth and thirteenth centuries. This history, taught in schools and honored in monuments and museums, deemphasized the six hundred years of the Ottoman Empire, which ended on the doorstep of the Republic. Ataturk's plan for a secular, Westernized Turkey required him to distance the nation from what he perceived to be the corrupt, religion-bound traditions and institutions of the old regime. He accomplished this symbolically and literally by moving the capital from the luxurious temptress Istanbul to a chaste, windswept, barely settled site in central Anatolia, Ankara, thereby rooting it in Anatolian soil. The icon of the capital was no longer a mosque, a royal palace, or the sensual tulip, beloved of sultans, but rather the spiky outline of the iron Hittite sun symbol entangled in the jagged horns of a Hittite stag.

Ataturk's bold and all-encompassing moves to Westernize the new Turkish nation met with resistance in the population, especially, as could be expected, from religious leaders whose legal powers had been expropriated. After abolishing the sultanate, one of the most radical aspects of the structural dismantling of the old order by the new state had been to abolish the caliphate, a venerable institution that encompassed leadership of the entire Muslim world and that had been invested over several hundred years in the Ottoman sultan. Religious brotherhoods also were outlawed. After being challenged by revolts against the new republic organized by religious leaders, who were angered by the abolishment of the caliphate and unhappy about the rest of the reforms, the Republican stand on religion hardened. Thus, its mandate came to include laicism, or state control of religion, since a laissez-faire policy toward religion could not be relied upon (an attitude which still today governs the state's response to religion). Religious authority was replaced by secular law and religious affairs came under state bureaucratic control. Instead of religion, nationalism was taught as the new unifying principle, binding together the ethnically diverse remnants of the Ottoman Empire into a republic of citizens.

A comment is needed here about my use of the terms *laic* and *secular*. The term for the Turkish state's position on religion, *laiklik*, often is mistakenly translated, by Turks as well as outside observers, as secularism, that is, as the separation of religion and state. It is more accurately represented as laicism, the subordination of religion to the state. This is a crucial difference in the Turkish context. The state controls the education of religious professionals and their assignment to mosques and approves the content of their sermons. It also controls religious schools and the content of religious education and enforces laws about the wearing of religious symbols and clothing in public spaces and institutions. Islamists have demanded an end to state control of public religious expression and many have pointed, accurately or not, to the secularism of the United States as an alternative model. Thus, I will use the term *laic* (Turkish *laik*) instead of the more common but inaccurate term *secular* to describe the Turkish state's policy toward religion and the related popular ideology. I use *secular* to refer to people who present themselves as being nonreligious or who believe their religious beliefs to be a private, rather than public, affair.

Ideally, Kemalist Republicans held the religious expression of Islam to be a private affair. Thus, religion was taken out of the classroom and all state public functions. Even religious symbols, including clothing, were banned from public institutions. Insignia of formal religious orders, from sheikhly turbans to priestly collars, were made illegal and disappeared from the public thoroughfares. In a bow to custom, the veil was not outlawed, but strongly discouraged, and those covering their heads found no place in the banks, ministries, and schools of the new nation. Photographs of the period show men and women shopping and strolling the boulevards of Ankara and Istanbul in tailored suits and hats, fashions indistinguishable from those of Europe at the time. In the dense artisanal and working-class neighborhoods and in smaller cities and the countryside, most women continued to cover their heads and wear the loose, enveloping clothing called for by customary conceptions of modesty.

Kemalism as a political doctrine cohered loosely around certain principles that came to be known as the Six Arrows: republicanism, laicism, nationalism, populism, statism, and reformism. The three principles that concern us here are laicism, discussed above, statism, and populism. Under statism, the state intervened in the economy and, in principle, guarded the economic well-being of the people through development and social programs. Reference to the populist basis of the state paid lip service to an ideal of national solidarity that put the interests of the nation and "the people" before those of any group or class. Indeed, the populist principle denied social class altogether and, when these principles were formalized in the Republican People's Party[2] program in 1931, political activity based on class interests was forbidden. The denial of class differences in the face of great disparities in distribution of the benefits of economic development and a widening chasm between rich and poor has been an important spur to the development of social movements in Turkey and an alternative Islamist populism. Kemalism as a social identity also developed over time. Zürcher describes Kemalism as more a set of attitudes and opinions than a coherent, all-embracing ideology: "As a result, Kemalism remained a flexible concept and people with widely differing world views have been able to call themselves Kemalist" (1997, 189).

Despite respect for Ataturk himself, who died in 1938, his monopolistic Republican People's Party was perceived by many in the 1930s and 1940s as representing not the people (*halk,* "folk"), but the Westernized secular ruling and bureaucratic classes and their alien culture of modern dress and Western tastes, habits, and music. This turning toward the West can be read in the very configuration of Turkey's major cities.

The German urban planner Herman Jansen created the new capital, Ankara, along axes of broad boulevards and straight streets, a radical departure from the tight labyrinths of Ottoman inner cities. An inset in a 1927 map of Turkey, still labeled in Ottoman, shows the new capital, Ankara. A small, pink bull's-eye marks the central citadel, shadowed by surrounding neighborhoods. Aimed at this target is a single broad boulevard, feathered with side streets that peter out into the unmarked surrounding area. The boulevard is connected at the other end to the railway station; thus the name of the boulevard, Istasyon Avenue. As for the old, cramped town around the citadel, Jansen considered it usefully placed for "the visual consumption of the modern city," but would have preferred it to be "covered by a bell jar" (quoted in Nalbantoğlu, 1997, 195).

In contemporary Istanbul and Ankara, much in the manner of Jansen's suggested bell jar, the "old" city has been sealed off to some extent from the lifestyles of the wealthier classes. The traditional artisanal and merchant quarters have been restored and refitted for consumption by tourists. Working-class areas are segregated by location and by the attribution of a distinct social typology. But noses are still pressed against the glass, as middle-class homes encroach on squatter areas and television programs beam the lifestyle of the elite directly into people's living rooms. Working-class families, the women in simple coats and head scarves, stroll the wide corridors of luxurious shops in the Istanbul Akmerkez mall—unable to purchase even the smallest item, but taking in the silk, perfume, diamonds, and designer clothing, artfully arranged in brightly lit windows, and the sleek, self-possessed shoppers, many of them women: tall, slim, blond, perfectly coifed, and dressed in elegantly understated but expensively trademarked and sometimes revealing dresses. On national holidays, the blue glass towers of the Akmerkez mall, brainchild of a group of determinedly secularist industrialists, are sheathed in lights that spell out support for a Kemalist laicist Turkey. At year's end, the mall is wreathed in "New Year's" decorations, much like the Christmas displays adorning Harrods of London and Lord & Taylor in New York.

Economic and Political Background

Despite the apparent similarities between the economic and cultural cleavages existing in the early Republican era and in the present day, Turkey has undergone tremendous economic and political changes that have substantially rewritten the balance of power between the Kemalist elite and the masses. Large-scale migration from the countryside to the cities has changed the nature and aspirations of the masses. Political organization and activism have broadened the nature of political tools at their disposal. Government insufficiency in protecting the economic interests of the masses and state repression of social movements have changed the relation between the masses and the state. This renegotiation of power has been accompanied by a polarization of economic status and a sharpening of the perception of social differences. (This refers to ethnic as well as Islamic identities, although we are only concerned with the latter here.) This enhancement of categories of difference has occurred at a time when the meanings and practices attributed to these categories are themselves shifting and under dispute. Below, I will examine the economic and political background to these changes.

From the founding of the Republic until the 1980s, the economic policies of the Turkish state were premised on self-reliance and state control. State stewardship of the economy led to considerable improvement in social welfare and infrastructure, such as roads and electricity. In its role as guardian of economic security and facilitator of industrialization and modernization, the state subsidized and controlled major industrial and agricultural projects and set up state banks to finance them. By the 1950s, new roads were being built, linking villages to towns and cities. Villages that had been accessible only by slow, tortuous travel over mud roads suddenly found they were linked by daily bus service to provincial capitals. Along these new roads, peasants began to move en masse to cities in search of economic opportunity. Together with other families from their region, they threw up hastily constructed houses on state-owned land, brought their families, and began to search for work in industry or in the informal sector. They hired out as laborers, set up small workshops, or worked as street vendors. The informal economy is still an economic mainstay of urban migrants today.

Bad weather and agricultural shortfalls in the 1950s increased economic hardship in a climate of political unrest. The military took over the government in 1960, returning it to civilian rule under a revised constitution. The government inaugurated an economic policy of import-substitution industrialization. That is, Turkey would produce what it needed domestically, limiting imports to essentials it could obtain no other way, like crude oil and medicines. Massive state-run enterprises provided jobs, income, benefits, and affordable, if unimaginative, products. In this decade, socialist movements, ranging from revolutionary youth organizations to labor unions, organized the workers and migrants who had pooled in urban squatter areas. Confrontations between these and factory owners, the state, and other institutions led to violent demonstrations and triggered another coup in 1971.

The rapid rise in world oil prices in the mid-1970s dealt another blow to the state's ability to protect domestic consumers. From 1975 to 1978, while I was a graduate student at Hacettepe University in

Ankara, the capital, I experienced first-hand the colorless, bare suffi-
ciency of Turkey's inward-looking economy. Most shops sold only
goods produced in Turkey. In a back street, a black-market strip of
shops that everyone called the American Bazaar sold smuggled
"imported" goods, heavy on popular items like foreign perfumes and
cigarettes. The shops operated openly, the police turning a blind eye.
The middle classes wore Turkish-made clothing, used Arçelik washing machines, and drove boxy Murad automobiles. An entire sector
existed to fix, recondition, recolor, and otherwise renew Turkish
products that people could not afford to replace. The government
continued to subsidize goods by first using up its own reserves, then
borrowing internationally. By the end of the decade, Turkey was near
bankruptcy, with triple-digit inflation, increasing unemployment, and
widespread shortages of basic commodities. Items like Turkish coffee, which had to be imported, were priced out of the reach of most
people. Many medicines were no longer available, so several physi-
cian friends asked me to get prescriptions filled for them when I traveled abroad. Even staple foods like cooking oil and macaroni became
only sporadically available.

In this climate of economic deprivation, the ideological battles
between left and right took on new ferocity, with squatter areas controlled by one or another faction. Violent factions terrorized the
streets, their battles claiming an average of twenty-five victims a day,
including some unwitting bystanders. Gunfire could break out anywhere. An example from my own experience as a student gives an
idea of the extreme ideological fractures that had split Turkish society, from the village square (see Delaney, 1991, 227–28) to the urban
schoolyard. The senseless ferocity of the violence was brought home
to me one day on the school shuttle bus taking students from the
suburban Hacettepe University campus to the city. After the bus was
under way, a number of the students began to sing a right-wing song
and chant slogans associated with the Gray Wolves, the feared, violent shock troops of the far-right Nationalist Action Party. I had been
unaware that even the buses were ideologically segregated. A young
man on the seat across from me also looked concerned at having gotten on the "wrong" bus. He froze and clutched his notebooks to his
chest. Before the rolling bus had passed the gates of the campus, a
young man arose at the rear of the bus, propped a briefcase on the
back of the seat in front of him, opened it, and reached in like a stol-
id businessman getting ready for a meeting. He extracted a sledge

hammer, snapped the briefcase shut and set it on the seat, then walked calmly forward until he was right behind the frightened young man. The students in the seat behind the young man pulled him up and held his arms while the other student swung the sledgehammer and brought it down on the young man's head. It connected with a dull thud. In the blink of an eye, they had wrestled his body to the front of the bus, ordered the terrified driver to open the door, and pushed him out of the moving vehicle onto the grassy embankment. The young men sat back down and, chillingly, the singing commenced again as if nothing out of the ordinary had happened. The singing was punctuated during the twenty-minute drive to the city center by the wailing and sobbing of the hysterical young woman next to me, who had been sitting across the aisle from the student who was attacked. As I waited to get out of the bus, I noticed scattered beneath my feet sheets from a notebook lined with neat script and mathematical notations, spattered with blood. Some of the sheets bore the imprint of muddy shoes. I scanned the newspapers the following days to check for a report of a body found, but discovered nothing. Perhaps he survived, like many others in that gray, terrifying decade whose suffering did not make it into the official statistics.

After 1978, the situation became even worse. Heating oil became so scarce that people abandoned their apartments and moved in with other families that had wood-burning stoves. In the winter of 1979 a friend wrote that she kept her oranges in the refrigerator so that they wouldn't freeze. Small businesses faced bankruptcy; industrial workers and civil servants were not paid. The government was in political gridlock, with competing parties in unstable coalitions stymying one another. The decade climaxed in 1980 with another military coup, an attempt by the generals to stabilize the country politically and economically. A new, more restrictive constitution was designed to keep ideologically minded groups on a tight leash. The left, in particular, was brutally suppressed. In the ideological mopping up after the coup, thousands of people were killed and many others arrested and tortured. More than a third of all college professors were fired and their graduate students expelled.

Moreover, the economy did not improve. Real wages, which had been declining every year since the end of the 1970s, dropped forty-four percent in 1982 alone. The money people earned lost forty-six percent of its purchasing power in the first three years of the new decade, and many workers were not paid for months at a time

(Ceyhun, 1988: 339). The military Junta restricted labor unions by forbidding them to support or receive support from political parties, making strikes difficult and costly to the strikers, and giving the government the right to impose compulsory arbitration. In their post-coup zeal to root out dissent, the generals closed the radical labor union confederation, DISK, tortured its leaders and accused them of trying to overthrow the state. In 1983, elections were held for a civilian government. In a testament to the strength of democratic instincts in Turkey, the voters elected not the army's preferred candidate, a former general, but Turgut Özal, a trained engineer and architect of the economic reform program begun in 1979 that was to transform Turkey economically and politically over the next decade.

The New Economy

Under Özal, the Turkish economy was unharnessed and opened to the world market. In response to prodding by the International Monetary Fund, the state began to privatize its industries and to dismantle the entitlements and protections, however tenuous, that had been a central aspect of its relationship with the masses. Instead, the state encouraged and subsidized businesses producing for export. Products also flowed the other way. Suddenly, all kinds of consumer goods were available in every conceivable shape, size, and brand, imported from Europe, Asia, the United States. After the disbanding of the Soviet Union, cheaper imports came in through the so-called suitcase trade, to niche bazaars on back streets where ethnic Turks from Central Asia, eastern Europeans, and Russians sold cheap products smuggled in their luggage. In a kind of mass amnesia, the violence that had characterized the preceding decades was effaced from public consciousness. No one wished to discuss it, even once the danger of arrest had receded. There was a lingering pain among a lost generation of men and women who had fought as students in the 1970s for something they believed in, had lost friends to killing and torture, and had themselves often suffered in jail or gone into hiding. Despite the visible changes in the economy, the fundamental inequities that had fueled the raging battles of the previous decades had not disappeared.

Different social groups carried disproportionate shares of the burden and benefits of the new economy. The new economy created great wealth for some, while the lives of industrial and agricultural workers, retirees, public sector workers, and other people on a fixed income became more precarious. Money purchased less, but pay raises did not keep pace. In the early 1980s, the minimum wage hovered around $80 a month. Unemployment rose from 5 percent in 1970 to 18 percent in 1982[3] (Ceyhun, 1988, 343). The state abandoned its role as guarantor of economic security through a controlled economy, ceding place to a kind of "economic Darwinism" (Ahmad, 1993, 206). World Bank reports in the 1980s placed Turkey among the seven countries with the worst income disparity. Turkey "became, in the words of John Rentoul who described a similar phenomenon in Thatcher's Britain, a society of 'the haves, the have nots, and the have lots'" (208).

Amid the unprecedented economic boom and expansion of the export and service sectors, the economic decline of salaried workers and the average family continued through the 1990s. Early in 1994, as part of the government's austerity program, the Turkish lira was devalued, in effect halving the buying power of salaries. Insupportably low salaries and severe cuts in university support pushed teachers to strike. Unemployment increased as government-subsidized public-sector and industrial jobs disappeared, replaced by work in the new economy requiring skills and education that the working class and migrants did not possess. The occupational mobility and ability to participate in the consumer culture, at however basic a level, enjoyed by the first wave of migrants and squatters in previous decades did not translate into upward mobility in social or economic terms. Faced with rising inflation and ever-narrowing opportunities, their living standards plummeted. The second and third generation of migrants, born and raised in the cities, were stuck in low-income, low-prestige work that no longer required or rewarded the job mobility of the earlier industries (Şenyapılı, 1992, 184). Furthermore, in the cities, they were able to compare their own living standards with those of the winners in the new economy.

Urban living conditions in general declined under the pressure of population growth and lack of investment in infrastructure. Istanbul and Ankara were plagued by a lack of services: polluted tap water, regular water outages, or no water at all; air pollution so severe that in winter 1993 some Istanbul residents wore surgical masks when venturing outside; congested traffic; unreliable, overcrowded public transport. Servicing the public debt crowded out spending for infrastructure, social services, and education.

In Ümraniye, staples like meat, olives, and cheese were pushed out of reach of low-income people. Families coped by bringing car-loads of food from their villages. Most Ümraniye residents retained some kind of long-term relation with their place of birth (Erder, 1996, 229). These relations were an economic lifeline, as city resi-dents traded their labor at harvest time, or in food preparation, dry-ing, and pickling, for a share of the crop. When I complimented Ümraniye women on their cooking, I often was told proudly that the vegetables came from the village, from their families' gardens. In winter, Ümraniye kitchens were stocked with jars of preserved grape leaves, strings of dried okra and peppers, sacks of powdered yoghurt and spices, bags of nuts, dried fish, and cheese from the village. Those whose villages were closer made the trip more often. Some families even brought barrels of water from the village well. While it did indeed taste better than the water bought in the city, as they claimed, it also meant the families did not have to purchase water from the poorly regulated urban water stations, where the people filled barrels in their car trunks from gas station-like pumps; there were not infrequent scares, reported in the newspapers, of people falling ill from tainted water from the stations.

Inflation bobbed between double and triple digits as the Turkish lira bled value daily. Shopkeepers had a hard time keeping up with the constant need to reprice their inventory. They also found that once they sold an item, they often could not afford to replace it. To avoid this, they kept their prices artificially high. In upscale areas of the city, shop owners and landlords gave up and simply listed prices in more stable United States dollars or German marks, but the reliance on foreign currency infected even local transactions in Ümraniye. In the fall of 1998, I overheard in the next room a woman compliment a visiting neighbor on a complex fringe she was crocheting on a scarf. The woman asked her visitor, "How much would you charge to make one of those for me?" The neighbor, not missing a beat, responded, "Thirty dollars." The woman drew her breath in sharply and protest-ed, "Now we're selling for dollars here, too?" Her neighbor answered, "These days are like that. What else can we do?"

The Economic Winners

The new economy opened channels for upward mobility through which anyone with an idea—and the skills, energy, education, resources and connections to make it a reality—could conceivably strike it rich. There was a great deal of new wealth among the provincial bourgeoisie and in the government-sheltered business sector. High inflation created instant wealth for currency speculators. Unlike people on a fixed salary, many business owners managed to avoid or minimize taxation. Citing a Finance Ministry survey, a newspaper reported in 1997 that every year about half of the country's 1,200,000 companies declared losses at tax time. Seventy percent of the total tax was paid by wage earners. A largely cash-based economy has resulted in the bizarre statistic that, based on income reported to the Turkish government, notaries, who must provide a receipt for every transaction, earn ten times the reported income of doctors and lawyers and thirty times that of dentists. The State Planning Organization estimated that the untaxed "black economy" was over $600 million annually (Sağlam, 1994, 9). The wealth was concentrated in Istanbul, Turkey's financial and cultural center. With the exception of England, the ratio of difference between the richest and poorest segments of society in Turkey was double that of any country in the European Union (Sönmez, 1997, 16).

In the two decades since the opening of the economy, Istanbul's skyline has broken out in a jagged rash of construction. Entire neighborhoods of two-story houses disappeared from view beneath spiring high-rises, the old buildings caught like debris between their flanks. Every year more and more of the old houses in the city were abandoned, finishing a process that had begun decades before. To restore an old wooden Ottoman-era house or stone villa was costly, and only one family could live in it. The shares of the other heirs would have had to be bought out, something increasingly impossible as land values skyrocketed. Since it was illegal to tear down historical buildings, the wooden structures were left to rot, their ornately painted ceilings revealed through empty window frames to craning passersby. Stone villas were helped along by mysterious fires. In their place, multistory apartment buildings rose, the apartments shared among competing heirs. Entire new high-rise city centers ballooned up throughout the city, and residential estates, luxury high-rises, and gated communities sprawled along the perimeter, in some cases displacing what had been squatter areas. World-class shopping malls, like Akmerkez, featured Turkish and foreign designer products in architecturally innovative, air-conditioned spaces. The wealthy came to buy, others to window shop and to watch the wealthy.

The newly wealthy built grand houses and were chauffeured about in conspicuously expensive cars. Often recently arrived provincial bourgeoisie, they were considered by urbanites to be country bumpkins who had to pay someone to teach them to use a knife and fork properly, and were popularly identified in the 1980s by "the three *M*'s": Marlboros, Mercedes, mistresses. Such conspicuous consumption was considered distasteful and gauche. The old urban elite, who were no longer necessarily wealthy, their properties having been subdivided too many times among too many heirs, still held a controlling interest in the cultural capital of status.

The difference between old elite and *nouveaux riches* in style and competitive display was illustrated in almost caricatured form in an experience I had with two business partners in 1991. I was invited, along with a group of visiting American schoolteachers, to the home of a wealthy businessman from an old elite family. His company had subsidized the teachers' study tour of Turkey. The luncheon was served in the garden of his Ottoman-era family villa by the side of the Bosphorus. He had invited a number of his friends who had studied or lived in the United States, he explained, in order to put at ease those of his American guests who did not speak Turkish. Waiters dressed in white served a variety of exquisite traditional dishes, prepared, according to our host, so that the teachers would have tasted the best of Turkish food. He told us that his wife herself had supervised the preparation of the food in her kitchen over a period of two days. The afternoon was pleasant and understated. The businessman, his wife, and friends moved among the teachers, chatting with them about Turkey and their own experiences in the United States. The family's English nanny was introduced when she came outside to see to the children. A side door to the villa was open to anyone who wished to use the bathroom, but it was only when several of us specifically requested it that the couple brought us into their home with its enormous antique mirrors, slightly shabby but still beautiful late-Ottoman furniture, and magnificent views of the Bosphorus.

His business partner, having learned of our visit, insisted that we also visit his home on the other side of the Bosphorus for tea. This businessman was from an eastern provincial city and had earned a fortune in the new business climate, expanding from two small clothing factories to a holding company that invested in everything from paint to fertilizer. He had a great deal of financial capital, while his partner had a great deal of social capital—the education and connections important for financial expansion, but also for social acceptance. The *nouveau riche* partner had recently built a compound of three modern luxury houses set around a common courtyard, one house for the parents, the others for their two sons and their families. From across the Bosphorus, the compound was easily visible as an enormous bald spot shaved into the crown of a wooded hill.

The man and his wife met us as we emerged from the cars that had fetched us from our lodgings. They immediately swept us into a tour of the houses. One son proudly described the full-size swimming pool he had had secreted under the wooden parquet of his house. He added slyly that, since it was illegal to build a pool on this hill, they just covered it with the floor when the inspectors came. We were led through each house in turn, the occupants standing back as the businessman or one of his sons described the house and its special features. Finally, in his own house, the businessman opened a sideboard and pulled out several pieces of a large silver tea service. He told us it had belonged to the sultan's court and directed our attention to the sultan's seal impressed on the side of each item. It proved the authenticity of the pieces, he insisted. He told us that it was a very expensive set and passed around the bill of sale.

The house was decorated in beige and white, crammed with gilded, upholstered furniture. In the midst of the shaggy, beige, wall-to-wall carpeting stood a thick pedestal of shimmering glass that opened at its top like an amorphous flower. He explained that this, too, was from the sultan's palace. It was a fountain made of glass that had been seeded with silver. He insisted that we bend our heads to get just the right angle to catch the silver cast of the glass. Other antiques were scattered about the room. A four-foot-high bronze of an elegant Roman warrior teetered on a side table. A fist-sized ball of blue plastic beads meant to ward off the evil eye dangled from the finger of his outstretched arm.

After more than an hour of this tour, the group was wilting in the heat and looking expectantly for the promised tea and pastries. We were finally settled in a flagstone courtyard. The businessman disappeared and did not reemerge. His wife served us each a glass of tea from a samovar and store-bought savouries. She sat with the teachers for a bit while we drank our tea, but did not seem inclined to conversation, perhaps since she spoke no English, although several of our group spoke Turkish. After the first glass of tea, she, too, disappeared and, finding ourselves at loose ends, we went in search of someone who could tell us how to get back to our lodgings across the Bosphorus. After some negotiation, cars were arranged and we left, never having found our hosts to thank them.

Clearly, what we had witnessed was a form of competitive display of social status, with each family legitimating its status on the basis of wealth and history. In one case, the slightly shabby but extremely valuable Ottoman-era villa and furnishings, the servants, and the special Turkish foods, with stuffed grape leaves as small as one's little finger—the Ottoman court standard— marked the family as old elite. History was their personal patrimony. Their display of mastery of the English language, a circle of educated friends who had traveled and studied in the West, and the choice of an English nanny marked the family as Republican elites possessed of social capital. The other family's legitimacy as urban elites, by contrast, rested entirely on its wealth, reinforced by the purchase and display of objects linked to the Ottoman court, rather than on any social capital.

While some beneficiaries of the new economy fit the unflattering stereotype of deracinated, status-obsessed *nouveaux riches,* others are redefining social capital and elite lifestyles. These range from successful, conservative businessmen developing a devoutly Muslim business and social style, to young secularist and Muslim professionals pushing out of categories like Kemalist and Islamist.

Secularist Strivers and Islamist Yuppies

In the late 1980s and 1990s, a new generation of ambitious, educated young men and women entered the burgeoning service sector. Many embraced Western styles—jeans, T-shirts, suits, short skirts— while some became Islamist Yuppies, riding the success of Islamic corporations, businesses, and publishers. In Istanbul, the dynamic center of the new economy, they found a different, competitive ethos and a wide array of possibilities, not only for success, but for lifestyle, relationships, and identity. Some young people, like Aslı, the daughter of a friend in Ankara, found this atmosphere alienating. On graduating from college, Aslı moved to Istanbul in order to get into the advertising business. There she found a small apartment and a job and began what she hoped was the climb up the career ladder. After about a year, she confided to her mother that she found the atmosphere in Istanbul difficult, and interpersonal relations quite different from those she was used to. Her mother's summary:

> The new generation in Istanbul has a problem. They compete with each other in jobs, so it's not easy to make friends. They are lonely, more so than similar young people would be in the United States, because they are Turks—they still expect mutual assistance, but are now afraid it will be misused [in competition]. So they say "I can do this myself" and are careful about getting too involved.

These young people can be seen all over European Istanbul, filling the pubs and restaurants, cell phones close at hand. The relationship of this generation to the state is entirely different from that under classic Kemalism. Judging from my conversations with young people like Aslı, I suggest that their secularism is less driven by Kemalist ideology and more a lifestyle choice. The introduction of choice into the construction of a secularist identity perhaps leaves more room for an acceptance of alternate lifestyles. Certainly, friendships between secularist and Islamist young people are not unknown on college campuses.

The new economy also fostered an Islamist elite that can be divided into the following general categories: 1) Successful businessmen who live modest, devout lives and contribute anonymously—or through their corporations—to charities and fund dormitories, scholarships, hospital treatments, and soup kitchens, much in the manner of the Ottoman elite, which they take as their model. 2) Arriviste "new Muslims" who vacation in the Bahamas toting special clocks that time the call to prayer and point the direction to Mecca from anywhere in the world. Their wives wear makeup and their Islamic-couture coats and silk head scarves, pinned with diamond-studded brooches, are draped so that the designer's name is visible. 3) Islamist Yuppies who waver between these two poles, tempted by the allure of success and fashion, yet determined to put their own mark on Islamic practice through political work, activism, or ideological writing. Many are or were university students, some from secular family backgrounds.

The evolution of the Islamist Yuppie, of a conservative, consciously Islamic, middle and professional class, and of a bevy of liberal intellectual Islamists, has pushed Islamist politics to the political center and has encouraged a more pragmatic, moderate leadership that will be discussed in chapter 4. These must be differentiated from the masses of devout Muslims who support the Islamist cause for various reasons, but consider the sleek, newly buffed Islamist lifestyle to be nothing more than an exaggeration of their own well-worn practices. The Islamist elite refer to them, sometimes disparagingly, as "unconscious" Muslims, reflecting one of the basic dilemmas of Islamist practice: how to distinguish oneself as an Islamic "elite" while participating in a populist movement. This issue will be taken up in more detail in chapter 7.

Finally, there are the young wannabe Yuppies, whose chances for economic mobility are severely limited, but who incorporate highly charged symbols into their own daily repertoire. Stylish veiling or a certain cut of shirt and beard give a leg up in interpersonal competition for "with-it"ness and attractiveness to the opposite sex. On the one hand, veiling implies modesty and submissiveness. On the other hand, in emphasizing exactly the sexuality of women that is to remain guarded and hidden, it is a kind of flirtatiousness. The rounded Islamist beard and distinctive Islamist collarless shirt intimate a promise of protection, support and a lack of vices, like drinking or gambling, in a man as possible marriage partner.

As with any advertised feature, of course, neither veil nor beard necessarily delivers what it promises. Bearded men may mistreat their wives as easily as clean-shaven men. Veiled women may be strong-willed and command their household or press for an education and a profession, using Islam as a lever against custom and the veil as a prow to cut through forbidden waters. And I have known educated, middle-class, secularist women who were cowed and mistreated by husbands and mothers-in-law, or expected to give up their careers after marriage or the birth of a child. Nevertheless, the political uproar and sense of siege occasioned by the government's attacks on Islamist clothing styles and institutions increase the cachet, importance, and local status of Islamist symbols. Participation in demonstrations or simply watching Islamist demonstrations on television, and wearing oneself what has become a political symbol, heighten a sense of collectivism and solidarity.

Islamist women wear a distinctive form of Islamic dress called *tesettür*. A long, feminine, loosely tailored coat, generally pastel-colored, is paired with a large, matching, silk head scarf decorated with abstract motifs that vary with each fashion season. The scarf entire-

Women in tesettür *at a wedding.*

ly hides the hair, forehead, and neck and usually, though not always, covers the shoulders and bosom. This is a relatively recent fashion, a reinterpretation of colorful, stylish, late-Ottoman elite clothing, another manifestation of the nostalgia for Ottoman respectability that permeates Turkish Islamism. Islamist magazines often feature representations of Ottoman scenes alongside discussions of contemporary Islamist fashions.

In one sense, *tesettür* is the culmination of several decades of transformation of clothing styles in response to urbanization, incorporation into the capitalist market, and commercialization. In the 1970s, village women newly moved to the city replaced their baggy country trousers with skirts worn over loose pants. Their head coverings, however, remained much the same: filmy cotton squares with elaborate, colorful, crocheted edgings. These were loosely wrapped around the head and tucked in at the side of the face or tied behind the neck. Before long, machine-made polyester scarves edged out home-embroidered scarves, much as machine-made carpets came to be (and still are, in Ümraniye) prized as home acquisitions over the hand-loomed carpets that, it was presumed, any village woman could make herself. Machine-made products required money to purchase, a rarer commodity at the time than the skill to make them, and were thus more desirable. Women who made head scarves for sale tried to adapt to this "modernizing" trend. In 1977, I was looking through some embroidery-edged scarves stacked before a woman selling them at the local weekly market. I pulled out a scarf onto which she had not crocheted the usual three-dimensional representations of flowers and other designs in colored thread or beads, but rather with a simple stitch attached a fringe of small, multicolored flowers of hard plastic. Another woman had cleverly attached colorful snippets of polyester cloth folded to resemble butterflies. These adaptations were ultimately not successful against the encroachment of the "modern" polyester square printed in colorful designs. The hand-worked, elaborately edged cotton scarf survives primarily in rural areas and as at-home attire for conservative urban women.

As a result of this diversification, it is possible on the streets of Istanbul to see an enormous variety of styles and degrees of covering and uncovering. Veiling varies from a scarf simply thrown over the head, much as I would tie one under my chin against the rain, to the elaborate and carefully composed ensembles of *tesettür*. Less common is the all-enveloping black or dark blue cloak (*çarşaf*) worn by followers of conservative religious sects. Like all fashions, *tesettür* is continually transformed. In recent years, it has become more common for women to wear the distinctive scarf not with the coat, but rather with specially designed suits or dresses that cover the body. The scarf may be draped to fall tentlike across the upper body or tied around the neck in 1950s Hollywood fashion. More recently, I have seen young women pairing the veil with slacks, jeans, and even form-fitting skirts. They stroll in the city's many parks, clutch books on their way to or from school, and move businesslike along the streets of European Istanbul. It is no longer uncommon to see them holding hands with or kissing young men on secluded park benches. An upscale version pairs a fitted dress with a turban of matching material, set high on the head over a tight wimple. An ornament, a bejeweled flower or spray of diamonds, often sets off the turban. I have seen an inexpensive version of this style, made of polyester, at Ümraniye weddings. A mixture of high couture and Ottoman chic, the effect is startlingly unlike both *tesettür* and other common forms of veiling.

Tesettür, however, is more than a style of clothing. In principle, like other forms of veiling, it is part and parcel of a lifestyle that ideally encompasses a religiocultural code of behavior prescribing the spatial segregation of men and women, appropriate spaces for the movement of male and female bodies in public places and in the home, the proper relationship between men and women, and the

Hittite monument in Ankara.

authority of fathers and husbands over daughters and wives and of men over women, as well as proscribing the interaction of unrelated men and women. In practice, however, it has paved the way for the movement of female bodies through a variety of spaces that had been closed to them in the restrictive culture of Ümraniye: shops, universities, political offices, streets, and the homes of strangers. Because of its association with the Islamist movement, in which women play a powerful role as activists, the *tesettür* style has opened the door to women's mobility. Women in *tesettür* can be seen in offices, classrooms, public meetings, and behind the counters of shops. (The political meaning of *tesettür*, its effect on social practice, and the contradictions inherent in different meanings of veiling will be discussed in chapter 7.)

The association of *tesettür* with high Ottoman style adds a sense of distinctiveness rooted in a glorious past. Neo-Ottomanist ideas and images fashion Islamism as distinctively Turkish and *tesettür* as a national Muslim style. This fashion nationalism is not in reaction to a history of foreign colonial domination, as is the case in Egypt, for instance, where in recent decades women began to veil in a distinctive manner (quite different from the Turkish) in a conscious attempt to develop an indigenous national style and thereby counter the perceived effects of cultural colonialism. Rather, Turkish *tesettür* is part of an internal national dialogue between people who choose to emphasize one aspect of Turkish history and culture over another. One is Ottoman-inspired,[4] the other Western-inspired, but both are Republican discourses. It is an intensely national conversation.

Many icons of Kemalism rooted in early Republican reforms have been undermined or transformed in this new ferment of competing and changing identifications. When the Islam-inspired Welfare Party won local elections in Ankara in 1994, the new Welfare mayor lobbied to change the official city symbol from the heathen Hittite sun to a stylized skyline centered on the outline of a large mosque. The municipality also agitated for tearing down the large statue of a Hittite stag and sun in a major square that, before the city expanded, had marked the division of the "modern" part of the city from the old quarter. There was an uproar, a debate in the media, a petition campaign against the change. In the end, the stag remained, corralled in the center of a busy traffic circle by an unending pack of blaring cars. Yet the city buses carried a new blue and white logo: a mosque cupola like a helmet, a minaret on either side, the whole bending inwards into a sickle moon with a Roman column and a large star in its pincers.

After decades of Republican purging, foreign-derived words have again entered the Turkish vocabulary. English has wide currency in the commercial and business arenas, from computer terms to product names. But where secularist Yuppies drop English words, Islamists drop Arabic and Persian. Where non-Islamist publications use new Turkish, Islamist newspapers use a form of Turkish replete with Arabic-derived words, much closer to Ottoman Turkish. I noticed an increase in Arabic-derived and overtly Islam-referenced personal names among young Islamist women in Ümraniye.[5]

The Ottoman era also has been mined for models of communal organization and administration. One idea that gained wide currency among Islamists is a religious federalism, based on a kind of laissez-faire Islamic governance loosely modeled on the Ottoman *millet* system. The idea is that, within this federation, Muslims would be governed by Islamic law, and minorities by civil laws based on their own religious precepts. The problem with this idea is that there are few religious minorities in Turkey; nor does this plan address the biggest "sectarian" difference of all, between the minority of Turks who wish to live under Islamic law and the many Turks, devout Muslims or not, who would not care to do so.

New Islamist Ankara city logo.

The Ottoman theme emerges in other ways. The Welfare-run Ümraniye municipality erected on the sidewalk in front of its offices a water dispenser, like an office cooler, to provide free drinking water to passersby. A municipal official told me that this was "just like" the public drinking fountains erected by the state and wealthy citizens during Ottoman times. Mass-produced portraits of Ottoman sultans decorated the walls of municipal offices and the offices of Islamic foundations. Islamist graduate students streamed into the Ottoman archives to satisfy their interest in Ottoman history.

The Islamists have resuscitated Ottoman imperial symbols and *mehter* music, the military music of the Janissaries, a kind of solemn

Sousa. Secularist elites, on the other hand, support Western classical and popular music. Working-class urbanites listen to Arabesk, Arabized popular music, the lyrics of which express the woes and longings of a hard life. Musical taste has been finely calibrated to politics and ideology—and social class—although these categories, too, are becoming blurred. Before elections in the mid-1980s, campaign buses crisscrossed Istanbul, the right-of-center Motherland Party buses blaring Arabesk, left-of-center Republican People's Party buses blasting songs of Zülfü Livanelli that combined Turkish pop, folk music, and leftist sentiment. More recently, however, reflecting the increasing cultural hybridity of the society, Turkish pop singers have incorporated elements of both Arabesk and Western musical styles, their MTV-like video clips and concerts appealing across class and ideological lines.

Blurring the Boundaries between Kemalism and Islamism

What impact have these changes in the social and economic makeup of the population had on the meaning of Kemalism and Islamism? Islamist successes at the polls in 1994 and 1995 caused a widespread Kemalist counterreaction. Many people wore Ataturk lapel pins and displayed portraits of Ataturk and posters with Kemalist themes or slogans in the windows of shops and private homes. A flier posted in the halls of Bilgi University in Istanbul in 1998 encouraged students to sign a petition to have portraits of Ataturk hung in the classrooms. That same year, the state directed school teachers to incorporate some aspect of Ataturk's life into subjects ranging from science to history in order to counter the perceived Islamist threat and to strengthen respect for Kemalism. Schoolbooks were rewritten to incorporate Kemalist principles. That same year a friend's son was told by his third-grade teacher not to talk to supporters of the Welfare Party and not to shake their hands because they didn't like Ataturk. The boy's mother, a middle-class professional and a leftist, protested to the school principal that this sort of ideological indoctrination was inappropriate, but told me afterwards that her message had been coolly received. Another middle-class friend and I were once hailing a cab on a busy street. An empty cab approached, but she waved it on impatiently. Puzzled, I asked her why. She explained that, since the election, she refused to patronize shops or ride in cabs if the proprietors or drivers had beards, identifying them as Islamists. Meanwhile, Islamists, as we shall see in the following chapters, hold up their own caricatures of secularists as dissolute, autocratic robber barons.

Because of the striking outward coherence of symbolic display (Ataturk's image, Muslim veil and beard) and passionate ideological projection in the public arena, the terms Kemalist and Islamist are often used uncritically as tacit explanatory elements. At a recent conference, for instance, I heard one speaker argue that "Turkey has outgrown Kemalism," while another countered that Kemalism was invaluable as the source of Turkey's security and integrity. The meaning of Kemalism, like that of Islamism, cannot be taken for granted and should be examined critically.

In practice, these groups are not distinct, nor do they clearly face one another in opposition. The lines between them are ambiguous and constantly shifting. Some Islamists have great respect for Ataturk and sympathy for his attempts to modernize Turkey, although they might wish to create more space for religious freedom and participation within the existing system. Many self-described Kemalists are uncomfortable with the lack of political liberalism in Turkey and share the Islamists' disquiet about the use of Kemalism to legitimate coercion by the state and silence opposition. At the same time, they may dig in their heels when it comes to loosening the reins on religious opposition, out of fear that their secular, Western lifestyle might ultimately be jeopardized were a religious party to come to power. Nevertheless, a sizable number of secularist voters supported Islam-inspired political parties in the 1990s, and a number of leftist intellectuals have crossed the line to join or support the Islamists. If Kemalism was being "rejected," as the conference speaker suggested, what exactly was being rejected—and what retained? Is a rejection of heavy-handed laicism in favor of a more tolerant secularist politics truly a rejection of Kemalism?

The blurred line between Kemalist and Islamist is aptly demonstrated by the results of a recent national survey of the Turkish electorate. According to this survey, the majority of Turks are practicing Muslims. A quarter of the electorate considers itself quite religious and 12.4 percent marginally or not at all religious, but most people carry out at least some of the minimal requirements of Islamic practice: pray five times a day (46 percent); attend mosque for Friday prayers (84 percent of men); fast during the holy month of Ramazan

(91 percent); give alms *(zekat)* (60 percent); would like to go on pilgrimage to Mecca (71 percent, although only 7 percent have done so) (Çarkoğlu and Toprak, 2000, 42–47). Not surprisingly, voters supporting liberal, secular parties like the Republican People's Party fell at the low end of the scale of religious practice, while supporters of religious, conservative parties like the Welfare and Virtue Parties had a high rate of compliance (Çarkoğlu and Toprak, 2000, 51). Despite this high level of religiosity, three-fifths of the electorate thought that a party operating on the basis of religion had no place in the Turkish political system (Çarkoğlu and Toprak, 2000, 58).

There is also widespread support for religious freedom, well beyond the support base of any particular party. For instance, three-quarters of the electorate believe that female civil servants and students should be able to cover their heads if they so desire. Yet most agree that even if a person does not pray (85 percent) or drinks alcohol (66 percent), or a woman does not cover her head (85 percent), he or she is still a Muslim (Çarkoğlu and Toprak, 2000, 83). Measures of tolerance for differences of belief and lifestyle were quite high, never lower than 50 percent, and a full 91 percent of the electorate agreed that tolerance and protection of differences of belief were important for social harmony (Çarkoğlu and Toprak, 2000, xi). The opposing poles with regard to these characteristics were found in members of the Virtue Party and the Republican People's Party (Çarkoğlu and Toprak, 2000, 113).

A generational change also adds to the complexity of Kemalist and Islamist practice, as younger elites with interests (and fears) different from those of their elders take control of the business and political sectors. The older generation of elites fears the physical division of Turkey, a sentiment some call the "Sèvres Syndrome," referring to the ill-fated, post–World War I treaty that would have carved up the remains of the Ottoman Empire to be consumed by the Entente powers, had the Turks not resisted. Sufferers of Sèvres Syndrome cling to a rigidly authoritarian system that uses Kemalism as the proverbial hammer that pounds flat any raised nails, be they ethnic or religious. National unity is won at the expense of liberal democracy. The new Kemalists are willing to compromise on some of these issues, to admit Islam and ethnicity into the system in the interests of stability. Groups like TÜSIAD, Turkey's main association of businessmen and industrialists, are in the forefront of this liberalization of Kemalist practice because they believe political stability is good for business. Others object to Kemalist authoritarianism because they see the hammer swinging wide and damaging freedom of speech, civil society, and the country's credibility abroad. The new generation, however, has fears of its own about the effects of liberalism. Rather than anxiety about the physical break-up of the Turkish nation, the new Kemalists worry about the danger to a secular, Western lifestyle posed by the aggressive spread of Islamist values and dress. Some believe the appropriate response is dialogue and accommodation; others support curtailment of the influence of Islam in politics. The latter position presents the dilemma of selective liberalism with which this generation must wrestle: can a liberal democracy support most freedoms, but not all? Clearly, this is not a question that can be answered here.

To think of Kemalism as the exclusive province of the urban elites, though, is to miss its strength in rural and working-class urban areas. It is true that until recently the Western lifestyle that is a Kemalist ideal has been an identifying characteristic of elite social class. Nonetheless, working-class women like those who run the Ümraniye Women's Center also are stalwart Kemalists. Although their home lives may vary little from those of women around them, they show their affiliation with Kemalism (and by extension Kemalist elites) by wearing slacks, still uncommon enough in Ümraniye to serve as a badge, wearing their hair uncovered, and moving about outside the home in pursuit of their charitable and political activities.

Despite the lack of penetration of Ataturk's ideas and reforms into the countryside in the early Republic, secular schooling, geographic mobility, and, more recently, the media have exposed even isolated villagers to secular lifestyles and different opportunities and roles for men and women. They may accept these, reject them, or remain haunted by the dissonance with their daily lives. Thus, a moderate and idiosyncratic Kemalism may be found in towns and villages across Turkey, although the particular local brand may have more room for religion and a conception of gender roles that may be unacceptable to urban feminists. Where does one draw the line as to what constitutes proper Kemalist practice?

Divergence and Convergence of Urban Cultures

Until recently, the characteristics that Kemalist modernists attributed to their traditional antipode had a named urban geographic location:

the *gecekondu* (literally, "settled at night") or squatter area. In the 1980s, over half the population of Turkey's major cities lived in such "irregular settlements"; a full 70 percent of Istanbul's population did so (Buğra, 1998, 307). In a continual process, these areas have been absorbed into the urban structure, or the city has simply ingested them in its growth. As a result, particular cultural differences can no longer be clearly attributed to specific physical locations in the city, such as the *gecekondu*. In the 1980s, a new term emerged in public discourse and the media: *varoş* (from the Hungarian for suburb). The term replaced *gecekondu* at a time when geographic location and cultural characteristics of the "traditional" masses and the "modern" citizen began to bleed into one another. *Varoş* is not a geographically or architecturally explicit term and can thus act as a container for "traditional" values and behaviors that are no longer localizable. It is necessarily a metaphoric location, since its assumed homogeneity is not, in fact, to be found anywhere within the cityscape.

Varoş locates what some have called *"Öteki Istanbul,"* the "Other Istanbul." It designates the urban location of a set of characteristics—poverty, rural origin, Muslim lifestyle, veiling, patriarchy—that function as an inverting mirror, reflecting back a Turkish modernity characterized by middle-class, urban values and lifestyle, secular clothing, and the autonomous Cartesian individual. This set of attributes characterizes what secularist elites call *kent kültürü* (city culture), in opposition to *"Öteki Istanbul."* There is a corresponding fear of cultural pollution and a sense of threat to secularist, Westernized, middle-class lifestyles. Not surprisingly, residents of neighborhoods like Ümraniye—squatter areas and former squatter areas—still use the term *gecekondu* to refer to illegal settlements or housing in their neighborhoods, rather than *varoş,* which has gained currency primarily among the middle class and elites.

What I found in Ümraniye was not the coherent, monolithic Other-*Öteki,* but rather a diversity of trajectories toward a complex, heterogenous urbanity. These days, people in what were once *gecekondu* areas dress in different ways and live substantially different lifestyles from one another. Many devout Islamists believe in the separation of religion and state (if not in the control of religion by the state) and honor and admire Ataturk. Other residents are laicist Kemalists or simply nonideological secularists, but are kept from participating fully in a Westernized, middle-class lifestyle by lack of money and opportunity for training and education. On a panel entitled *"Öteki Istanbul"* at the 1998 annual Istanbul book fair, a clearly ill-at-ease Nalan Türkeli, author of an autobiographical book called *Being a Woman in the Varoş: A Diary* (Türkeli, 1996), spoke at length about the problems caused by lack of money in her neighborhood. The other panelists, all journalists and professors, discussed the cultural attributes of the *varoş*. A lively debate with the audience ensued, focused almost entirely on the perceived cultural threat posed by the Other Istanbul; no one took up Türkeli's allusion to social class and she was asked almost no questions.

Unemployment and a lack of economic security and opportunities mean that people must negotiate their lives anew every day, but it does not mean that there is a lack of movement, change, hope, and even levity. An older couple I knew in Ümraniye moved back to the husband's village because, upon retiring after twenty-five years in Istanbul as a welder, he was unable to pay the rent on their small apartment in Ümraniye. With no sons to bring in extra income and two daughters to marry off, he was forced to sell some land in the village and buy a house there. Their two daughters went to live with them in the village, having spent their entire lives as city girls in *tesettür*, visiting girlfriends and relatives in the neighborhood, window shopping, and attending the many engagements, henna parties, weddings, and other social events where women gathered and socialized. One daughter married and moved back to Istanbul, although her wedding was postponed for two years because there was no money for an apartment into which the couple could move. Fatma, her fifteen-year-old sister, remained in the village.

Two years later, Fatma's alabaster skin had burned nut-brown from working in the fields. Her hands were rough and calloused. In her simple peasant clothes, she looked very different from the chic Fatma in lilac suit and matching lilac and brown head scarf I had seen dancing with other young women at a henna party before she left. She complained of being bored in the village, and she hated working in the fields. Still, Fatma was able to come back to Istanbul several times a year for the weddings of relatives and to visit her sister. There, by donning a fashionable *tesettür* outfit, she transformed herself back into a city girl for a short time, made the rounds of festivities, and visited her friends in the neighborhood.

At one such event, Fatma and a friend who had accompanied her from the village whispered to me that they were going to put on makeup and asked me if I wanted some. We crowded into the bathroom, where they smoothed a foundation base onto their faces and added eyeliner and lipstick. The effect was subtle, but radiant. Without their voluminous coats, slim in their tailored outfits and long golden scarves, they were very attractive. Fatma's friend pulled a photograph out of her purse to show me. It was of a pretty young woman made up with red lipstick and eyeliner, dressed in jeans, her long, black hair loose and uncovered. It was obviously a photograph of herself, although she looked quite different. She explained that she dressed like that in the village sometimes among (female) friends. (The usual at-home dress in the village consisted of the loose *şalvar* trousers or a long skirt, topped with layers of sweaters and a cotton head scarf.) Fatma hoped to marry a man who lived in Istanbul, her ticket to a permanent return. In one sense, being seen as an attractive young woman at these events was one way to advertise herself as a potential bride. But the fact that these young women, who appeared in public in (and enjoyed wearing) fashionable *tesettür*, also, in private, dressed in jeans, wore makeup, and uncovered their hair, revealed that their allegiance could not be captured by such artificial categories as "tradition" and "modernity" or Islamist and Kemalist. Rather, many new doors had opened to them, and they were, tentatively and at their own pace, looking through all of them.

The changes, the encroachment on one another of cultures and classes, the convergences and broadening of the population's symbolic repertoire, and the stagnation of economic possibility were dramatically displayed when I visited a family I knew in another neighborhood, Yenikent. When I had first met the family ten years before, the area in which they lived had been a quagmire of muddy roads and unfinished squatter homes of raw concrete blocks. The population was similar in income and origin to that of Ümraniye. At the time, in the mid-1980s, women in Yenikent tended to visit between homes along a web of narrow, crooked back alleys, while the broad main road onto which the houses fronted was dominated by a new mosque and several men's coffee houses. Benches were placed at the mosque entrance for older men to sit, chat, and watch the passing traffic. The coffee houses, too, offered vantage points for men to survey the street. Although women did use the main road for shopping and other tasks, it was mainly the domain of men. The women's social and family lives played themselves out in back of the facades of houses, either indoors or in the spaces behind and between the buildings.

The family had built their two-story house by hand, floor by floor. The front door opened onto the main road, mostly residential but dotted with a few groceries, a fruit stall, and several shops selling home appliances and clothing. In the back of the house was a large room, unconnected to the residential quarters. This was used as a workshop from which the family distributed knitting work to neighborhood women. They paid the women for each piece they finished and passed the product along to middlemen for subsequent export. That sort of business had been widespread in the working-class and squatter neighborhoods in the 1980s, but ended as government subsidies for exports declined, quotas from the European Union limited markets, and competition increased from Asian countries with an even cheaper labor force.

On every return, after several months or a year's interval, the neighborhood had become increasingly unrecognizable, so much so that I had to search each time for this family's entrance door, even though it was directly opposite a *dolmuş* stop and, thus, easily located, at least in principle. The area had become incorporated into the municipal structure, receiving bus service, paved roads, and legal electricity and water. Some of the squatter houses had been replaced by substantial three- and four-story apartment buildings of varying degrees of sturdiness. Dozens of new shops had opened.

When I returned in 1997, I flagged down a taxi to take me to Yenikent. It was an extravagance, since the area was quite distant, but I was late. I told the taxi driver my destination and he commented, "You're probably going to the *siteler*, then." *Siteler* are middle-class housing compounds; some are luxury gated communities. I felt certain he had misunderstood the name of the neighborhood. Or perhaps there were two of the same name: it wasn't beyond the realm of possibility, given the rate of expansion of the city; new neighborhoods were being added all the time. I described where it was, but he assured me that he hadn't made a mistake. In fact, he lived there. Developers, he explained, had built housing complexes in the neighborhood and middle-class people had moved in. Stunned, I prepared myself for yet another transformation.

The reality was impressive. Since the family I was visiting lived at the far end of the neighborhood, I didn't see any *siteler*, but even this end of town was radically changed. Large, affluent-looking apartment buildings set in manicured gardens surrounded the original core of haphazard housing. Lighted shops of every description twinkled in the dark of evening. Where I thought the family lived, I saw only shop fronts, no entryways to private houses. I began asking shopkeepers. In the second shop—no more than a single, brightly lit, narrow room crowded with bins containing all manner of nuts and legumes—the owner said, "Yes, of course. I rent this shop from him. He lives right above here." I looked to the right and in the darkness made out the familiar door in the now unfamiliar building.

Hatice and her husband Osman looked no different than they had ten years before. Hatice's round face and red cheeks gave her a youthful appearance. She had gained a little weight and still wore comfortable village clothing: baggy *şalvar* trousers, topped by a bright sweater and cardigan. Her hair was loosely covered by a colorful cotton-gauze scarf embroidered along the edges. It draped prettily around her face and onto her bosom. Her nut-brown hair, streaked now with white, was pulled back and only partially covered by the scarf. She had been sitting on a cloth on the sitting-room floor, peeling cucumbers into a big aluminum bowl wedged between her legs. After she greeted me and sat me on the couch, she returned to her peeling while we chatted. One of her three daughters sat next to her, helping. I remembered her as a lively and mischievous child. The young woman on the floor before me was slim and attractive, with a face of fresh, clean, angular lines. She was newly married. She wore a loose dress and a fringed gauze scarf, like her mother. Hers was brown with orange flowers and an intricate matching trim. From her trousseau, I thought. Indeed, when she later showed me her trousseau, which was piled high on a bed in her parents' house while her trousseau chest was being repaired, I was amazed at the quantities of embroidered scarves, towels and linens dripping with embroided edgings, and knitted bed shoes.

After a while, she said she needed to get back home to see to her husband's dinner. She donned the loose coat and oversized head scarf of *tesettür* and left. The girl's sister, Hatice explained, also wore *tesettür*. Their husbands had insisted on it after they married. These two sisters came by again after dinner, joined by the third, Emine, the family rebel who had run off with a local man rather than accept a marriage arranged by her parents. Emine was dressed in tight jeans and a white V-neck sweater. Her dyed blond hair was in a perky ponytail and she wore makeup. Her two-year-old daughter toddled at her side. She and her husband lived a few streets away in a small apartment below her in-laws. Her mother-in-law, she confided, was trying to get her to veil, but she had so far managed to resist. Her mother-in-law also pressured her to cover her daughter's hair, she said, eyes flashing, but she was adamant that this would never happen.

Several years before, Emine had been engaged to a young man selected by her parents. While her fiancé was away doing his military service, a friend had shown her a photograph of the young man with another woman. Instead of waiting to ask him about it, she impulsively decided to respond to the advances made by another young man in the neighborhood who had been interested in her for several years, but with whom she had had little contact. They arranged in secret to meet at the bus stop and boarded the bus together for Bursa. When they returned several weeks later, their presumed intimacy meant that they had to marry, and do so with minimal fanfare. Besides, Emine was in fact pregnant. Later, she learned that the woman in the photograph with her fiancé had been simply a friend.

Emine's apartment was furnished simply and inexpensively, with few of the substantial furnishings and decorations she and her husband would have acquired had they married through the proper negotiated channels and had all the requisite ceremonies and exchanges of gifts and bride wealth, instead of running away to marry. Her husband worked in a small carpentry shop with his father, building window frames. Every morning, Emine took her daughter up the cracked linoleum stairs to her mother-in-law, then met up with another local woman, who was divorced and lived alone, at the bus stop in front of the mosque. Together they took the bus to work. Emine answered telephones at a construction company and earned some extra money on the side selling hand cream to neighbors.

Her parents managed by combining income from Osman's occasional informal work as a plumber, rent from the shop built into the front of the house, and income from a small coffee house that had taken the place of the workshop in back. The former workshop had become a meeting room, serving tea and coffee. It was formally licensed as the Association for the Assistance of Those from ——— (the area of the Black Sea coast where Osman's village was), one of many such local associations to be found in cities, where men who have migrated from a certain region or village gathered to pass the day, exchange news, and request assistance in finding housing and jobs. Osman explained this to me as we went up the stairs to their apartment. Hatice, pausing near the top of the stairs, turned around, laughing, and called out, "It's a gambling den!"

The planned third story to their self-constructed house was still as it had been—a rough surface littered with concrete blocks and leaking bags of cement stacked against a half-built wall. Dried cement oozed from between the gray blocks. Rusting, thumb-wide, iron antennae emerged from the floor and raked the sky, ready to hold together the concrete walls and pillars of a new level. Osman and I had crawled up the stairs to what was effectively the roof. Casting his hand about, he explained that he hadn't yet saved enough money to build further, but that he was collecting supplies slowly, whenever he had enough to buy some blocks or cement. He intended the third floor for himself and Hatice; they would vacate their present apartment for their seventeen-year-old son when he married.

The layout of the rooms in their home had changed several times since I first came to know them a decade before, shifting to accommodate changes in family composition, but their standard of living had not changed appreciably. Still, they had married off three daughters, at least two of them at some expense, in itself an accomplishment and an investment. All the daughters lived in Yenikent and they and their families were frequent visitors.

While we were catching up on our news, a friend of the young women appeared, dressed in shorts and a short-sleeved T-shirt. We moved to the parlor to accommodate the crowd. There, they all sat in a row on the plush formal couch: *tesettür,* Western dress, and village dress all in the same family and neighborhood. I found it the most striking moment of all, since ten years before few women here ventured forth without a head scarf, and one young woman who worked and wore elbow-length sleeves to her (quite respectable) job had been gossiped about because of her clothing.

What can be learned from this scene? It struck me that, while working-class neighborhoods such as Yenikent or Ümraniye were considered by many urbanites to be homogenous *varoş,* they were not so, either in clothing, behavior, or attitudes. Although norms regarding gender behavior and, particularly, female chastity were still strongly enforced, women had much greater leeway in how they expressed those roles. An ambition of all those described above was to become successful participants in Istanbul's economy. They did so in time-honored fashion, by working multiple jobs, pooling resources within the family, and taking advantage of every kind of opportunity presenting itself. In the 1980s, government subsidies for textile exports made piecework distribution a popular income-generating activity in poor neighborhoods. Property ownership, sometimes as a result of squatter-area building amnesties, was exploited by renting out unused space. Even civil society provided opportunity—as in an association doubling as a coffee house and, perhaps, supplying other services as well.

Osman's daughters had chosen their own paths, from a more varied palette of options than was available before. Two daughters chose what Deniz Kandiyoti has called the patriarchal bargain (1988, 275): submissiveness and propriety, symbolized by veiling, in exchange for protection and support *(himaye)*. Their change from modest peasant dress to *tesettür* at marriage displayed their virtuous character and respect for religion. It also indicated their new status as married women, the economic solvency of their husbands, and their husbands' regard for them, since *tesettür* coats and scarves are more expensive than other types of clothing they would ordinarily wear. In the past, married women wore their wedding gold to indicate these same things. In the 1970s it was not unusual to see the janitor's wife sweeping the front walk wearing a heavy necklace of gold coins and an armful of gold bracelets. Wearing conspicuous gold has since gone out of fashion, perhaps as a result of an increase in crime. (Many homes in Yenikent had barred ground-floor windows, and I was told that car theft was a major problem.)

Emine, however, had stepped off the well-trodden path followed by her sisters. She had chosen her own husband, for which she had paid dearly in reduced economic cushioning, but which also left her without the same level of obligation to her in-laws and husband and freer to resist. This she did through her choice of clothing and refusal to cover her daughter's hair despite her mother-in-law's disapproval. Emine also worked at two jobs and, unlike her sisters, moved relatively freely through the city landscape. One day, she went downtown in a *dolmuş* because she needed to buy more face cream from her supplier, a freedom of unaccompanied movement that until recently would have raised eyebrows in Yenikent, as in Ümraniye. It could be argued that because she and her husband had not received the usual benefits at marriage—no furniture, little money and gold—Emine had no choice but to work outside the home. But years before, Emine had dreamed not of marriage, but of owning her own business. Her route, symbolized by her hair color and clothing, appears to be the Western secularist route. Blond, uncovered hair and Western clothing had been for much of the Republican era symbols of high social status, economic success, and city life. Her sisters appear to have taken the Islamist route to urban identity. Yet neither of these categorical definitions expresses the economic constraints, mixed motivations, and rich brew of possibilities that characterize the lives of Istanbul residents like Emine and her sisters, or the unexpected resources they bring to bear.

Culture as a Political Resource

What people in communities like Ümraniye and Yenikent do have in common, aside from financial struggle, is a set of values that emphasizes connectedness over individuality, social and moral responsibility over personal choice or decision making, attachment over detachment. While these values are not class-specific, they play an important role for families and individuals with few other resources. While my observations are limited to Ümraniye, Çiğdem Kağıtçıbaşı, one of Turkey's foremost psychologists, writes about Turkey as a collectivist society. In a collectivist society, what is valued in human relations is not autonomy and control—but yielding when necessary to uphold the harmony of the group, obeying your parents, sacrificing for your family, and accommodating to existing realities rather than trying to change the world. Kağıtçıbaşı argues that because psychology is a field with roots in the West, the psychologically healthy self is considered to be like the Western ideal: an autonomous, striving individual, a separated rather than an overlapping or symbiotic self. The attributes of a collectivist society have come to be associated with the deficient, the pathological: traditional, fatalistic, weak (1996, 66–67).

Characteristically, these also are attributes associated with the *varoş*. The *varoş* is a mythical conception because the characteristics associated with it are in actuality not located in any one kind of place, but rather characterize lives throughout the urban fabric, from the taxi driver, grocery store owner, and doorkeeper to the hairdresser and greengrocer down the street. I have observed collectivist attitudes, patriarchy, and veiling in middle-class and elite homes as well. Locating "traditional" attitudes and behaviors in the *varoş* keeps "modernity" pure—and Western and middle-class.

Several years ago I was interviewed by a reporter for a Turkish newspaper about my book on the informal economic sector in Istanbul (White, 1994). For over an hour, I explained how migrant families in poor neighborhoods constructed elaborate social webs of obligation. People assisted each other in myriad ways, from everyday sharing of food and labor to informal-sector activities. In essence, they were continually seeking to do things for other people, without expectation of immediate return. They had explained this to me as being like *imece,* the rural tradition in which villagers help one another at harvest, without expecting that the person a family has helped would then be obliged to help that particular family back. It was a communal obligation; everyone put in to help the community as a whole, and, in principle, the community was there for each individual member to provide whatever was needed when it was needed.

In the interview, I explained to the reporter that women's informal-sector income was not used for their own individual desires, but rather in ways that afforded support for the family. With their income from piecework, the women covered household expenses; they invested in their children's education, particularly that of sons, who were still expected to support their parents in old age; they acquired household items that would give their family status in the community, but which they had been too poor to acquire at marriage. In other words, rather than investing their money in individual goals—gold, clothing, travel—women invested in the family's welfare and status in the community, the source of their long-term support. Parents expressed a desire for schools that taught collectivist values. Women in particular relied on their children for support in old age. Thus, they were interested in schools that instilled in children a sense of responsibility to their families, rather than a wish for independence.

At the end of the interview, the reporter, a young woman in jeans and t-shirt, looked up from her notepad and asked, "Isn't it wrong for people to live like that? Shouldn't they become more like us, more modern?" Who is this "us" the reporter was referring to? Clearly, she included the foreign anthropologist with herself on one side of an opposition of "modern," middle-class lifestyle and values vis-à-vis the backward "traditionalism" of Turks in the "Other" Istanbul. Given the content of the discussion, one can infer that "us" meant "modern," individualistic, rational persons, pursuing individual goals rather than putting the needs and goals of the group (the family, the community) above his or her own. *Imece* and its analogues, however, should not be thought of as the opposite of individualism. Collectivist values, as Kağıtçıbaşı has pointed out, can also be the basis for personal striving and achievement—a socially oriented achievement, for the collectivity rather than personal gain. Individual effort raises the group. This reflects an emphasis on personhood over individuality: a person is a socially significant individual invested with personal responsibility and autonomy, but whose individualistic desires take second place to loyalty to the community.

The concept of *imece* and a related term, *himaye,* deserve closer examination because the practices to which they refer are related to political strategies in Ümraniye. *Imece,* as a norm of horizontal mutual support, is implicated in the new social networks, while *himaye* underlies vertically organized patronage relations. They are the core values of a Turkish vernacular politics that, by coordinating local networks with civic associations and political parties, boosts local interests and demands to the national level.

Imece is a community-based form of cooperation. In her ethnography of village life, Delaney (1993, 150–54) describes Turkish villagers cooperating in the spirit of *imece* to build houses for a poor, elderly couple living in a stable, for a widow and her child after their house collapsed, and for the village midwife, as well as a new mosque and a bridge over a problematic ravine which had claimed the lives of several villagers in a tractor accident. The villagers had also pooled labor and resources to lay down pipes for a sewage project and to bring water to homes. Social activities also were planned by the community as *imece,* including village-city social exchanges, intervillage sports meets, and projects to help send poor children to school. Delaney translates *imece* as "community project," generally resulting from a "consensus arrived at in fairly democratic manner, albeit one that included only men and then only household heads" (1993, 153). Each head of household had a say in the decision and could consult with members of his family and delegate someone from his household to work on the project. Men might also go into a cooperative partnership *(ortak)* with one another, pooling resources to purchase and then share heavy equipment, like tractors or combines, or a *dolmuş.* While these arrangements were expected among agnates, in practice they were often made between non-kin.

On a more informal, daily basis, much cooperative activity was carried out by women, both within and between households. Women shared food and the labor of food production, especially for large communal gatherings like weddings, holiday celebrations, and funerals. They cooperated in spinning, knitting, embroidering, and quilting, and in caring for the sick and elderly. "In an important sense the village is the nation's welfare agency," observes Delaney (1993, 151).

Imece projects in the village Delaney studied reflected a "community spirit." Projects introduced from outside the village, while requiring cooperative village labor, often were perceived by the villagers in a negative light. In one case, the state proposed a new road from the village and set out to hire villagers to build it. The villagers refused to participate. Other forces also could derail community cooperation. Delaney visited the village in 1980, just before the military coup that closed all formal cooperative associations. In the preceding years of political turmoil that had reached even the remotest corners of rural Turkey, the village had become politically polarized through the importation and establishment of two formal associations *(dernekler)* by opposing political parties of the left and the right. These associations linked local people with groups outside the village, threw cooperative action into disrepute as a "communist" activity, fractured communal ties, and even divided families, brothers against brothers or fathers against sons. As a result, when *imece* projects were proposed by one side, the other side refused to participate. It is ironic that the introduction of formal civic associations from outside the village resulted in the breakdown of the trust and cooperation that had until then driven community projects and informal organizations.

Imece cooperation in the village was based on similar principles as those governing family relations. In a family, each member contributed resources and labor, such as a paycheck or unpaid work in a family business, without thought of return payment, but could expect, for instance, to have marriage expenses paid or help in setting up a business. These would not be considered return for years of labor, but rather the obligation of family members toward one another by virtue of being a family, and an expression of loyalty and love. Similarly, in *imece,* the idea was not to do a favor and then have it returned (with the ball being in one court or the other), but rather to keep the account open (and the ball always in play), creating a durable and flexible web of mutual indebtedness and obligation.

In essence, people paid goodwill and good deeds into the community, which acted as a kind of bank for future assistance. Communal membership was affirmed through continual contribution. Withdrawals generally were not comparable to what had been paid in over the years, much as in an actual bank we do not receive back the same dollar bills we have deposited, nor do we know where or in what form our investment is at any given moment until withdrawal. In the *imece* system, interest was paid in loyalty and trust among the many people engaged. The resulting communality is more accurately called a web, rather than a network or even a community, since its boundaries are neither geographic nor demographic, nor easily traceable as single, inter-personal exchanges. Rather, *imece* describes the multiple, simultaneous relations of people interacting over time, spilling beyond communities, doubling back over networks, enfolding anyone who begins to contribute and develops trust. Crucial to the development of trust is continual face-to-face interaction.

The residents of Istanbul migrant neighborhoods used an analogue of the principle of *imece* to tie themselves to other people in the neighborhood, people to whom they were not necessarily related or with whom they even shared a common place of origin. By doing so, they constructed for themselves long-term flexible webs of support that were, in some ways, more reliable than the formal, rational institutions surrounding them. Mutual obligation wove a web of support, where everyone put into the family and community, and could rely on the resources of the family and community when they needed them.

Imece, as a principle for social organization, was brought from the countryside and adapted to city life and city needs, much as with the northern Italian mutual aid societies and other networks of horizontal civic engagement discussed by Robert Putnam in his analysis of Italian democracy (1993, 137–42). It became a pivot in the economic and political life of migrant and working-class communities. It provided economic support for community members and a basis for political and civic mobilization—without the membership lists, but with the same goal of representing and acting out community interests. In the political context, *imece* was a moral imperative to help the less fortunate, and an important tool for grassroots organizing. The Welfare Party and its successor, the Virtue Party, were the most adept at harnessing this indigenous, local basis for collective action.

Imece acted out the collectivist principles described by Kağıtçıbaşı. Thus, neighbors might be drawn into the web, regardless of whether they were kin or had migrated from the same part of the country. When asked whom they trusted, Ümraniye residents mentioned neighbors (51 percent) almost as often as kin (57 percent) (Erder, 1996, 259). Sectarian and ethnic divisions in the community, such as those between Alevi (Alawites) and Sunni Muslims or, in some instances, between Kurds and non-Kurds, may have limited daily social interaction, but Islamists claimed that their political networks crossed these boundaries as well. It is widely known that the

Welfare and Virtue Parties attracted Kurdish voters. In a national poll of the Turkish electorate, 47 percent of Kurdish speakers expressed support for the Virtue Party, compared with 40 percent of non-Kurdish speakers (Çarkoğlu and Toprak, 2000, 65).

Women also became important actors in urban *imece*-based political and civic networks, unlike in village *imece* decisions, which were the province of male heads of households. They canvassed for votes, organized and participated in demonstrations, attended rallies. Female Welfare activists, many from working-class neighborhoods and conservative families, were responsible for getting out a large part of the vote for Welfare in the 1994 and 1995 elections. In the month before the 1995 elections, in Istanbul alone, Welfare's women's commission worked with eighteen thousand women and met face to face with two hundred thousand women (Arat, 1997, 67). Welfare was successful in politically mobilizing residents of poorer urban neighborhoods like Ümraniye not only because of its message of economic justice, but also because of its method of mobilizing locally, creating cells of activists and supporters that built on already-existing webs of neighborhood networks engaged in horizontal, *imece*-like organizing.

Women who became local activists, whether Islamist or Kemalist, told me that they felt empowered, but did not perceive their goals to be personal goals. Rather, they were very clear about the fact that they were acting on the basis of a moral imperative for the good of the community. The combination of individual activism with collectivist values and motivations was reflected in the structure of their grassroots activism. The women were active not as individuals, but within what they called a *hücre*, or cell, of people who knew each other as neighbors and who had a history of interaction; that is, with people in their social web. Their relations were based on the trust that had developed on the basis of their interaction. These cells were then mobilized in tandem.

For this, the telephone has proven pivotal. The telephone has only become ubiquitous in Turkey since the 1980s. Now that most households are linked by telephone, it can be used to amplify face-to-face relations by joining together and mobilizing cells of people who know each other. If each woman and her husband called ten people in their social web, and those people called ten more, and so on, thousands of people could be mobilized very rapidly, one by one. This projection of personal relations into the political realm privatizes public space in a manner that makes it possible for women in conservative milieus to become active participants in urban civic and national political life—not as an individualist enterprise, but in the collectivist tradition.

The challenge to women's political activism came in the contradiction between their positions within horizontal neighborhood networks and within the hierarchical family. It was not unusual, as we shall see, for activist women to be expected to withdraw from their political activities at marriage or when they bore a child. Almost half of all working women in Istanbul left their jobs because of marriage. One in six of those who continued to work later left in order to raise a child (TESEV, 1997, 29). They were expected to return their energy and labor to the family pool and to submit to the support and protection, or *himaye*, of the family.

Himaye is the principle of protection by and loyalty to family, region of origin, and, by extension, political party. Wives are under the *himaye* of their husbands, children of their parents. *Himaye* embodies protection, physical and moral support, and respect, and implies an affectionate, rather than merely duty-bound, relationship.

Himaye differs from *imece* in that one party is presumed more powerful and capable of protecting and supporting the other. Thus, *imece* refers to horizontal ties among equals, while *himaye* incorporates hierarchy and patronage. *Imece* refers to the activity of pooling resources and labor, while *himaye* denotes a relationship that can be expressed in any number of ways, depending on the characteristics of the people involved and their connection to one another. A daughter under the *himaye* of her father and other male relatives is in a different situation than a young bureaucrat under the *himaye* of an older official, or a guest under the *himaye* of the household she is visiting, or a constituent under the *himaye* of the municipal administration. What is required and what is proffered substantially differ in each of these cases, but all involve protection by a higher-placed person and the loyalty of the other.

Like *imece, himaye* is an expression of the principle of mutual obligation, another aspect of the social web. However, *himaye* can take two forms. It can refer to mutually supportive relationships within family and community, but it can also be engaged to create or express unfair advantage, reflecting what one might call the dark side of the social web. These two aspects are not always easily disentangled.

The requirements of *himaye,* for instance, can lie heavily on the shoulders of women whose loving families protect them through strict seclusion and segregation. Even in the most supportive families, women may be punished for putting themselves "at risk"—for instance, by being seen speaking to an unrelated man on the street. For what is being protected in women is not only the women themselves, but the honor of the entire family. At marriage, a woman comes under the *himaye* of her husband, who may request that she cease work or end her education so that she will no longer be "at risk." It was not uncommon in Ümraniye for husbands to require their wives not to leave the home except under their supervision or with their express permission. Likewise, the new freedom and political respectability of Islamist women activists is not without its contradictions. The special *tesettür* style of veiling, in one sense, can be understood as putting women under the *himaye* protection of any Islamist man. This interpretation is borne out by the special, ostentatiously chivalrous treatment accorded by Islamist men to women in *tesettür,* from elaborate respectfulness to allowing them to step to the front of a queue. *Imece*-based customs have opened the way to a powerful vernacular politics that includes women activists. *Himaye,* with its mixture of support and control, protects women, whether as sisters of the blood or as sisters of the faith.

A clearer implementation of *himaye* for unfair advantage would be the case, for instance, when the person at fault in a car accident changes his legal status to victim by using patronage or family connections within the bureaucratic system. Mübeccel Kiray (1999, 161) has argued that *himaye* is an impediment to "modernization" in Turkey because it encourages people (indeed requires them) to solve problems personally, through connections, family, and patron-client ties, rather than submitting problems to a system based on anonymous relations and law. Indeed, until recently, the bond between state and citizen has been premised on just such a relationship: paternalistic protection and support in exchange for loyalty (Keyder, 1997, 41). Traditional party politics also relies heavily on patronage links. Political leaders of the 1960s still exert leadership in the 1990s. Powerful political hierarchies and personality cults outlive party affiliations and sometimes the parties themselves. The respect owed to elders and one's teachers and masters of the trade means that, no matter how talented and famous, a former student or apprentice will never claim leadership as long as the master is still alive. Instead, they remain under the *himaye* of the elder and receive his or her patronage in return for their loyalty.

At the community level, as used by activists, *himaye* has a broader meaning. It expresses a moral imperative to protect and share, to take under one's wing those less fortunate and weaker, in addition to those to whom one owes loyalty and obligation. It was this understanding of *himaye* as protection of the weak, combined with the *imece* model of moral obligation to one's neighbors, that inspired and coordinated local activism in Ümraniye. On one level, the underprivileged translate *himaye,* both in its patron-client sense and in its incarnation as community activism, into a negotiation of claims. *Himaye* and other political implementations of the social web are a moral assertion of popular demands in a political system where certain groups of people receive attention from the government only when it is expedient—for instance, just before elections.

However, *imece* and *himaye* are not simply tools for survival or levers for obtaining resources. At another level, this is about building and maintaining a community identity, fully engaged in urban and national life, through a vernacular politics built around these cultural norms and practices. Since vernacular politics to some extent circumvents traditional social categories and political hierarchies, it has empowered not only a new generation of activists who cross class, gender, ethnic, and perhaps sectarian lines, but also a new generation of politicians willing to make an end-run around the party elders. (The resulting divisions within the Welfare and Virtue Parties will be discussed in chapter 4.)

Imece as a principle for social organization, and *himaye* as a mobilizing bond among members of a community, are adaptations to city life and city needs. They are central principles organizing economic and political life in migrant and working-class communities. *Imece* provides economic support for community members and a structural basis for grassroots organizing. *Himaye,* as protection of the poor, provides the rationale for community mobilization. *Imece* and *himaye* also resonate with Islamic dictates about generosity, obligation, and social justice, as well as patriarchy and hierarchy, reflecting the tight weave of culture and religion in the lives of Ümraniye residents, who turn to these principles, and each other, to contend with the challenges of migration and the new economy.

This does not mean that Ümraniye and Yenikent are culturally and ideologically homogenous communities, or that these cultural attributes stop at their borders. However, self-styled Kemalists and others who perceive themselves to be part of an oppositional, "mod-

ern" Westernized city culture see in such norms and practices examples of a dangerous and polluting "traditionalism" characteristic of
varoş culture. By means of such categorization, they set themselves
off as pure of these things. Their rejection of local cultural practices
means that vernacular politics is out of their reach as well. As a
Republican People's Party representative once replied, when I asked
him why his party didn't organize on the basis of local, face-to-face
networks as the Welfare Party was doing, "We're a modern party. We
don't have time for that sort of thing." Vernacular politics represents
an investment of time and effort in developing local relationships
that has the effect of pulling together a diverse following into a political community. It is both a national politics and a politics of everyday life.

2

RELIGION AND POLITICS
IN THE EVERYDAY

What do these politicized categories and socioeconomic transformations mean to people in Ümraniye? What role do religion and cultural norms play in their political choices? People mobilize around a political or religious ideology for reasons inherent in their personal histories and in their histories as a class of people—as migrants, workers, professionals, men and women. In other words, politics, like religion, is embedded in everyday life. As such, it is colored by experiences of migration and poverty, by aspirations for self-betterment and upward mobility within the possibilities held out by urban life in the post-1980s economy.

While Ümraniye's residents varied in their political and religious affiliation and their stand, if they had one, on Kemalism or Islamism, they shared a lifestyle conditioned by a lack of money, opportunities, and choices. They also shared norms regarding mutual obligation, neighborliness, and family loyalty. Gender segregation, arranged marriages, and patriarchal lines of authority within the family were common. These were not simply rural holdovers. Rather, within the context of poverty these customs conferred resources and provided a crucial backup for those reaching for new opportunities, be it in business, education, or political activism. Education and professional skills were more widely available, yet were often insufficient in the

Ümraniye women in indoor dress.

face of a lack of economic resources that necessitated falling back on other available means of security, such as family or marriage. Islamist politics opened the door for young women to obtain an education, gain professional skills, work outside the home, and become politically active. Yet for Ümraniye's Islamist women, the door sometimes led only to a short corridor of public activity before marriage and childbearing closed it again. Without the economic basis that would give professionally trained women the ability to buy equipment, rent space, open their own businesses, and establish an income sufficient to support an alternative lifestyle, they had to rely on the sometimes restrictive support and protection of their own families or husbands. Much discussion among Islamist and intellectual circles was devoted to "the new Islamist woman," and, indeed, examples abounded in Ümraniye. But the ability of women in Ümraniye to persevere in their Islamist activism had less to do with religious ideology than with an economic reality that narrowed their choices. (The political and professional opportunities and choices specific to female Islamist activists are addressed in chapter 7.)

Rather than either/or scenarios, these sets of alternate resources often required a series of sometimes conflicting choices, supported or restricted by religious and cultural norms and practices. In this chapter, I will try to give some sense of the intersection of Islam and culture in daily life as they set the framework for people's expectations and choices, and the role of economic status in making those choices. Ultimately, political practice in Ümraniye built upon expectations and desires intimately conditioned by religious and cultural practices and economic possibilities.

Economic motivations rooted in working-class life played an important role in the 1994 and 1995 elections that brought the Islamists to power. Among Ümraniye residents who voted for the Welfare Party, not one I spoke to at the time mentioned Islam as the reason for their vote. Rather, they complained about the corruption of the government, inflation, unemployment, the lack of sufficient public buses, water shortages, and scanty garbage pickup. Many mentioned a fatal methane gas explosion at the Ümraniye garbage dump in 1993 that killed dozens of people as a defining moment in their political choices. It was only in the years after Welfare had risen to political prominence and the government had reacted sternly, by, for instance, enforcing the ban on head scarves in universities, undermining religious schools, and beginning efforts to close Welfare, that I began to hear some of these same people justify their support for Welfare in terms of Islam-related issues. One could as easily argue, though, as indeed many Islamists have, that these were issues of freedom of religion, and therefore democracy, not of religion per se. Powerful though it may seem, ideology cannot be assumed a priori to be the principal agent of political mobilization. Much as the physical world is subject to the laws of gravity, ideology must be grounded in the forces of social and economic life that govern the relations of people to one another in their world.

Middle-class housing encroaching on a squatter area.

Ümraniye's Socioeconomic History

Ümraniye is a broad administrative district on Istanbul's eastern flank, with a population of over 250,000. It began as a sleepy village of under nine hundred souls, but in the early 1950s developed into a squatter area, or *gecekondu,* as rural migrants were drawn to industries that located there. After 1965, its population almost doubled every five years. Large-scale plants situated outside the city center needed to foster nearby pools of labor, so some factories extended credit to their workers to encourage the formation of *gecekondu* neighborhoods (Tekeli, 1992, 38).

Squatters built on public treasury land and, to a smaller extent, on private land, drawing nearby villages into the maelstrom of habitations. With every election, politicians handed out deeds to prospective voters in squatter areas, or declared amnesties on unauthorized housing. Over time, residents upgraded their houses, added floors, balconies, gardens, and shop fronts. Squatter areas became a checkerboard of legal and illegal holdings, jerry-built shacks alternating with five-story concrete apartment buildings. As a result of the ambiguities surrounding urban land tenure and patronage politics, most *gecekondu* dwellers held some kind of property title, shared title deed, or a government certificate that would eventually lead to legal title to their house. Many of the neighborhoods lacked basic infrastructural elements like water or electricity, although services were often extended even before the areas were regularized and formally incorporated into the city proper.

By 1987, there were 161 industrial plants in Ümraniye and its environs (Tekeli, 1992, 89). Over half of its economically active population worked in industry, with unemployment hovering around 10 percent. By the end of the 1980s, these industries had begun to organize and modernize production in such a way that their labor needs became predictable. Thus, the spatial and economic flexibility provided by *gecekondu* housing was no longer an advantage. The laborers' new problem was to insulate themselves against the reduction of real wages after 1980 and the inexorable rise in inflation. They responded by selling their properties, renting them out, or converting them into low-quality apartment buildings that created slumlike conditions. To build upward, they used money sent from family members working abroad, loans from family members, proceeds from the sale of property in their villages, or gold jewelry. Generally, they hired nonprofessionals, local developers, themselves former construction workers, whose financing was precarious and whose equipment and workers often insufficient. The plan was drawn up by the owner or contractor, with no attention paid to environmental conditions, the need for playgrounds, green areas, parking, or earthquake resistance.

Another force in the transformation of *gecekondu* areas was the interest of large-scale developers in building middle-class residences away from the crowded inner city. Developers either bought up or confiscated by force prime areas of urban land located in *gecekondu* areas and transformed them into sites of middle-class apartments and even luxury housing estates *(siteler)*. By the 1990s, about half of *gecekondu* owners were not the original settlers of their property, but had purchased it from those who originally appropriated it. Some of the funds for these new developments came from institutions set up to subsidize construction of housing cooperatives for low-income groups (Buğra, 1998, 308–13).

The result was the breakdown of previous forms of communal cohesion based on ties among kin or families that had migrated from the same region. Şenyapılı sees the outcome of this process as the development of slums and transition areas open to crime, frustration, and alienation, and consequent radical political action and civil strife. She argues that, while the first generation of migrants benefited from the initial stages of industrialization, the second and third generations of *gecekondu* dwellers born and raised in the city were stuck at the level of their parents in low-income, low-prestige jobs in industries that had advanced beyond them (1992, 184). Thus, what had been relatively homogenous *gecekondu* areas became heterogeneous urban neighborhoods, with a struggling population stuck in low-wage work and unable to move ahead economically, face to face with the tantalizing opportunities and increasingly conspicuous wealth of the new economy, sometimes in their own backyards.

In the 1990s, Ümraniye was composed of eighteen neighborhoods *(mahalle)*, varying in age of settlement, quality of housing stock, and income level of the inhabitants. The old center was a dense concentration of back-to-back buildings set along narrow, winding streets teeming with traffic. Down side streets, an occasional house sat in a tiny pocket of dusty garden. Communal rituals often took place in the street. Several years back a family I was visiting that lived on one of these narrow side streets held a pre-wedding ceremony for their son. They set up a table in front of the house at which the young man's face was ritually shaved. Neighbors and relatives sat along the side of the street in folding chairs, chatting and nibbling from paper plates piled with rice and lamb. The groom-to-be and his father danced opposite each other to music from a boom box. Every few minutes a car, truck, and even a full-size bus drove through the middle of the ceremony, the driver honking and blaring out his congratulations.

On the fringes of Ümraniye were newly settled, unimproved slums that had not yet been upgraded by the residents. Other areas were barren expanses of newly constructed apartment buildings. Infrastructural services may have been irregular, but the resolute, entrepreneurial *dolmuş* connected residents to the city transit network. There was a great deal of movement into and between different neighborhoods. At marriage, a woman tended to move to her husband's neighborhood to set up a household near his parents. Consequently, family links crossed neighborhood lines, and visits via *dolmuş,* bus, and car blurred the boundaries.

Nevertheless, residents of upgraded housing stock took pains to differentiate themselves from those still living in *"gecekondu"* housing, regardless of the official designation or history of their own area or housing. Much like the elites who differentiated their own secularist "city culture" from the alien *varoş,* long-term Ümraniye residents saw *gecekondu*-ization as something new that was happening at the fringes of their community. To some, *gecekondu* was the location of the local Other. Erder (1996), in her study of Ümraniye, found that, when asked about the status of Ümraniye as a *gecekondu,* some residents used ethnic difference as a benchmark. "A *gecekondu,*" one woman asserted, "is a Kurdish neighborhood. And a Kurdish neighborhood is outside of Ümraniye" (187). Others attempted to distance themselves by implying that a *gecekondu* was the place where the poor lived, but recognized the ambiguities inherent in that judgment. One resident pointed out that *gecekondu* women "wear gold bracelets on their arms. I can't say that they're poor, but they and their houses look poor. But on the other hand, they have televisions and electric washing machines in their homes. . . ." (Ibid.) For those living on the fringes themselves, housing quality, rather than status of land ownership or any characteristics of the inhabitants, was the touchstone for judging what was a *gecekondu* and what was not. "A *gecekondu* was a house made of briquettes topped with sheet-metal or tarpaper." A house built of reinforced concrete, by this definition, was not a *gecekondu,* even if built on untitled land (189).

More than two-thirds of Ümraniye's population was born outside of Istanbul, three-quarters in a village. The average resident migrated at age twenty and had lived in Ümraniye for more than two decades. By 1990, half the population still lived in squatter areas; the other half had at one point in their lives done so. The most common occupations in Ümraniye were factory worker, construction worker, small tradesman, driver. Many men made a living as low-level civil servants: public bus drivers, ditch diggers, road crews, garbage collectors. Others eked out a living as street vendors, carriers and delivery men, drivers, parking space guards, all-purpose assistants and gofers. Most had more than one job. Many worked one job during the day and drove a taxi at night. Even within the same family, there might be stark differences in standard of living, since a family's economic status usually depended on the man's earnings. Thus, a woman who married a man with a successful business might live a very different life than her sister whose husband was unemployed. While family members tried to help one another cope, their resources generally were limited. It was the responsibility of the man's natal family to help him financially, while a woman's family sometimes helped out with food, child care, or links to job possibilities. More than half the adult population, consisting mainly of housewives, students, and retired people, was not economically active. Most neighborhoods had no bank or post office, and fewer than five had doctors. Despite being graced by three or four mosques, the greater number of neighborhoods boasted no more than one school. Eight of ten residents had attended some school, but two-thirds had not gone beyond primary school.[1]

The families discussed in this book lived in various parts of Ümraniye and generally reflected the statistical portrait painted above. The families ranged from very poor to lower middle class. All were Sunni Muslims, some more pious than others. Some were kin. Although scattered over several different neighborhoods, they visited one another regularly and spoke on the telephone. Others were not related, but embedded in one another's social circles. These generally lived in the same area and had ties of neighborliness that extended several years into the past. Some were not related at all and, although they lived in the same neighborhood, did not know the other people in my study.

The Religious Chiaroscuro of Social Life

What are the social and economic choices available to ordinary people in Ümraniye, the costs and rewards of their actions? What roles do religion and politics play in these choices? Füsün and Zafer, their son Ahmet, and his fiancée, Mahmure, were in many ways typical residents of Ümraniye. Füsün and Zafer migrated from a Black Sea village over twenty years ago. They were devout Muslims, prayed daily, and took an interest in the religious complexion of daily activities. Zafer was active in the local mosque. Füsün had always been veiled, indoors and out, although not in the stylish new fashion. Her future daughter-in-law, on the other hand, wore chic *tesettür* outside and sweat suits and dresses at home. Ahmet was a young man armored in an irreducible amalgam of custom and Islamic belief, seeking opportunity, but limited in his resources. He was attracted to Islamist politics, but looked at the Welfare Party with a critical eye, despite his father's support for it. Ahmet's political leanings, like those of his mother and much of the electorate, were premised on a deep belief in Islamic principles, a suspicion of Islam in politics, a dislike of politicians who they sensed placed themselves above the people, and a pragmatic evaluation of what any particular party had to offer. These criteria had, in the past, led Füsün to support the right-of-center Motherland Party and Ahmet to support the young, populist leaders of the Welfare (later Virtue) Party, but not the old-style Welfare politicians who operated a tightly controlled, centralized patronage system. (The differences between these will be examined in chapter 4.)

It is true that Islam affects how people think about space and time, about social relations between men and women and among family members and neighbors. It conditions people's expectations and range of choices, from marriage to politics. However, Islam does not always determine these choices, but rather sets up a framework within which competing motivations and opportunities are negotiated. In Ümraniye, Islam blends seamlessly into cultural and political practice.

The little park at the corner of the main street in Ümraniye had changed its name again. When we drove past it and I mentioned the change, Füsün exploded. "I don't know who this man is. Who is this person that they should name a park after him?" Her son behind the wheel snapped that he was a martyr who died in Chechnya and we should respect him. Füsün retorted, "My uncle's son died and nobody named a park after him! What makes him so special?" A row of public telephones, large, green, plastic bubbles from which depended trousered legs and long skirts, stretched along one side of the park. The street was faced with small shops, their goods—inexpensive furniture, clothing, slippers, and children's knapsacks—spilling onto the sidewalk, blurring indoors and out. Minivans and taxis jostled aggressively as pedestrians gauged their speed and threw themselves into the spaces between vehicles to run across the road.

Mother dancing at home after her son's wedding.

Several weeks later, I came to participate in the festivities leading up to Ahmet's wedding. I jumped awkwardly from the high door of the minivan to the road and wound my way along the dusty lanes to the family's home. As I fumbled at the blue iron slab of the garden gate, Ahmet strode up beside me, hand extended. I guessed he had been at the coffee house at the end of the block, where his father and other neighborhood men spent most of their time when not at work. The coffee house afforded a view of the entrance to the house, but the lower face of the house was hidden behind a high metal fence painted blue. Only the dusty tops of young trees nodding their heads above the fence revealed the presence of a small garden. The entrance was on the side, up a short flight of stairs, accessible from a narrow, adjacent street. Two cavernous rooms took up the entire ground floor and yawned onto a busy thoroughfare fronting the house. This floor was rented out as shop space. The house, like most in the working-class and squatter districts, was designed with this extra source of income in mind.

I passed under the trellis of grapevines and through the tiny garden, entered the house and climbed up the narrow, curving, concrete stairs leading to the second-floor residence. Füsün called down, instructing me not to take off my shoes at the base of the stairs, as was usual, because the house was beset with workmen preparing the third floor for the new couple; Ahmet was getting married the following weekend. Because of the construction, interior space, marked by the exchange of shoes for house slippers, now began inside the private rooms on the first landing, not right inside the house entrance as it usually did. I took off my shoes on the landing, slipped on a pair of brown plastic slippers and stepped into the small living area. The day was stiflingly hot. Füsün wasn't feeling well and was stretched out on one of the couches in the parlor, fanning herself with a newspaper. Three women, relatives come to ask about the wedding arrangements, sat on the other sofa and chair. I made tea and served it, trading slippers for shoes and shoes for slippers to get back and forth from the kitchen off the landing, crossing three feet of what was now public space. After the wedding, when Mahmure came to live in the house, it would be her place to make the tea. As Füsün's friend, I took over the role of serving the guests since she was ill.

The house had been remodeled since my last visit, walls moved, a new bathroom and balcony added, the old balcony expanded and turned into a room. I had noticed this free play with space in other homes, where walls were simply moved and moved again until a satisfactory arrangement of rooms was arrived at. There was no set arrangement, although there were set functions for the rooms: formal parlor, kitchen, bedroom, toilet and bathroom, and usually a room for everyday lounging, entertaining close friends and relatives, or for the women to withdraw if there were male guests. Füsün used the parlor more casually than was common in other families, who reserved the stiffly furnished room for entertaining strangers and important guests, or for gatherings of men. Doors were everywhere, for the easy conversion of space from one use to another.

A third-floor apartment had been added, including a fancy bathroom swathed in frothy pink chiffon curtains and coverlets, a small dining room/parlor, and a tiny bedroom just big enough for a queen-size bed and an enormous wardrobe with sliding mirrored doors (there was no space for doors that opened out). The matching brown lacquered furniture set was sleek and substantial, purchased, as was customary, by the groom's family. The bride's family furnished the kitchen and bedroom. Into the parlor was squeezed an enormous china cabinet with glass windows, a long, bulky sideboard, a couch, two matching armchairs, and a small, square dining table, half of which was taken up by an enormous black boom box.

Füsün and Zafer had migrated from their Black Sea villages when they married. Zafer was somewhat successful after having tried his hand at various ventures. He now managed an automotive parts store in the neighborhood. They were able to save enough money to build their own house on a tiny sliver of a corner lot up a dusty street of similar houses. They made the most of the lot by building rental space into the ground floor, a residence on the second, and providing for the option of another tiny apartment on the third floor for their son when he married, as he was about to do. The new couple's apartment did not have a kitchen: the bride and her mother-in-law would share the second-floor kitchen. This was not an unusual arrangement, since the bride would be expected to take over much of the housekeeping from Füsün in any case. This changing of the guard was marked by the replacement of Füsün's trousseau embroideries in the kitchen by Mahmure's. Mahmure had stitched pink carnations and matching edgings onto white cotton squares that she draped in zigzag corners from the shelves. She had sewn matching curtains and even decorated the stove lid with a cloth of carnations, thus marking the territory as her own. Füsün's apartment, on the other hand, held only Füsün's embroideries.

The family was very devout. Zafer prayed regularly at the nearby mosque and donated substantially to mosque funds. Füsün prayed at home, retreating regularly into the cool, dark bedroom to kneel on her prayer cloth, head swathed in a special long, loose scarf, and murmur her prayers. If other women were present in the house, as they often were, they might join her, or take turns. The timing of the prayer after the muezzin's call from the many local minarets is somewhat flexible. The activity of prayer laced the day with subtle rhythms and punctuations, periods of quiet reflection and community. If they needed to retrieve something from the room, the other women, hushed, tiptoed respectfully around the kneeling figures.

The bride-to-be was from a family that had migrated from eastern Turkey. The engagement had caused a bit of a stir in Füsün's family, since she had chosen a bride for her son from outside the circle of her own relations or those of her husband, who came from a village near her own. There were several suitable young women in these villages who would have jumped at the chance to marry Ahmet and move to the city. Mahmure was the daughter of Zafer's business associate, a man who owned some property on the outskirts of the city. She had struck Füsün's fancy when she was ill. Mahmure had visited with her mother and had immediately gone to the kitchen to prepare tea for everyone. Füsün confided in me, a few days before the wedding, "And that's when I thought to myself, that girl would make a very good daughter-in-law."

Arranged marriages were common, usually with at least one supervised meeting and with both parties' consent. Arranged marriages were considered better thought out and more likely to be successful than leaving such an important decision up to the hormones of two young and inexperienced individuals. It surprised me to hear this sentiment expressed by young as well as old, even by young women who had married into difficult situations, with a stingy husband or demanding mother-in-law. At engagements, weddings, and all other ceremonies that brought women together, elder women busily engaged in matching the girls on view with prospective grooms. At one pre-wedding henna celebration[2] a few blocks away, I was enlisted by a neighbor who had a son of marriageable age to find out the identity of a young woman who had caught her eye. The young woman was leaning against a pillar across the room, watching the dancers. I dutifully squeezed my way through the crowd to various acquaintances until I found someone who could identify her. Unfortunately, she was already married.

Marriage candidates were chosen carefully and their qualities and those of their families weighed. Most important in a groom was a steady job or some form of income and a good family with no scandal attached. These things were investigated thoroughly through neighbors and other connections. For a prospective bride, it was crucial that there be no hint of indiscretion. She must be a virgin at marriage, and any gossip to the contrary, even as innocent as word of having been seen chatting in the street with an unrelated man, would make it difficult for her to find a husband. Some young girls in Ümraniye might wear jeans and tight sweaters while they were unmarried, but they still comported themselves judiciously, traveled in a group, and would not speak with unrelated men in public. That did not mean they wouldn't flirt. Smiles and eye contact flashed between groups of young men and women passing each other on the street. Comments made to friends in the group but meant for other ears floated on the air.

Trousseau display.

There was a fine line between displaying one's attractiveness and gaining a bad reputation. Some young women and their families refused to take the chance, and from a young age the girls dressed in enveloping clothing and head scarves when they appeared in public. Other families restricted or firmly chaperoned their daughters' appearances in public. Mahmure's family had sheltered her in this manner. She was able to attend a girls' high school, but on a tight schedule, and was veiled in fashionably colorful head scarves with matching overcoats. She believed in the necessity—and even allure—of veiling, but chafed at the restrictions on her activities, especially when it became clear that she would not be able to finish her last year at high school because she was getting married. Her husband's family thought it improper for her to be out traveling on public conveyances and neglecting her new duties as wife and daughter-in-law. Indeed, it was not uncommon among the families I knew in Ümraniye for women to need their husbands' permission to leave the house, even to take the *dolmuş* a few stops to visit a relative. Mahmure had hoped, she confided to me, to escape the restrictions of her father's house by marrying a man who would allow her more freedom. She was dismayed to find that, while her new husband was indeed on her side, he could not and would not go against his parents' wishes. Ahmet was dependent on his parents in several ways. After marriage, the couple would not only live in his parents' house, but Ahmet worked for his father in the automotive shop as well.

Although Mahmure was veiled, she had friends and some relations who did not cover their hair. Ahmet's family, on the other hand, had almost no contact with women who were not veiled, except for a middle-aged neighbor who indoors occasionally took off her light cotton under-scarf, although she generally donned a head scarf when she stepped out into the street. Her head scarf was not of the more elaborate *tesettür* style that had become popular with the rise of Islamism after 1980, but rather a modest square of polyester. There was a broad palette of styles of behavior and clothing to choose from in Ümraniye, but the range of that palette was limited by moral conventions.

Likewise, some ceremonies and festivities were mixed gender, but many were segregated, with men and women celebrating in separate public halls or different parts of a restaurant—the women in a room with curtains that could be drawn against curious men, eager to catch a glimpse of women with coats and perhaps head scarves removed, dancing among themselves. Ahmet commented that he and his family had been invited the following week to a mixed-gender wedding, but his parents wouldn't go because alcohol would be served. "Some of the girls will be veiled; they won't dance. I once asked a girl in a miniskirt to dance, but she refused. She said her parents wouldn't let her." Ahmet was miffed. "Since she was wearing a miniskirt anyway, at least she could also dance!" Some weddings, he added, were in a mosque, with prayer and no dancing. Others were mixed. "The young like the mixed weddings." However, despite Ahmet's liberal attitude with regard to his own expectations, the differences between Ahmet's and Mahmure's family, although seemingly negligible to an outside observer, caused problems at Mahmure's own henna party the night before her wedding. The women from Ahmet's family wouldn't take off their coats and head scarves and dance in the presence of a male organ player and male photographers. Mahmure's friends, dressed modestly but with hair uncovered, had no such qualms and enjoyed themselves. Mahmure was near tears at the dour reaction and recriminations of her future family.

For a girl to be marriageable, she was also expected to be skilled and diligent. An engaged woman showed off her skill and industriousness in the display of her trousseau in her natal home, before she bundled up the many items she had intricately sewn, stitched and crocheted and brought them to the home where she would live after her marriage. Several weeks before, we had visited Mahmure's parents' home to admire her formally displayed trousseau, arrayed on the walls of the living room, on cords stretched across the room, and draped on every surface. Her family had then carried it to her new home in boxes and a carefully assembled, cloth-wrapped bundle *(bohça)*.

Mahmure had arranged the items throughout her new home. Visitors ascended to the apartment at will, like visiting a museum, to view the trousseau and comment on and evaluate each item. Ornate silver-colored plaques made by the bride were displayed in the glassed-in vitrine. Brightly colored arrangements of artificial flowers were distributed throughout the room. Some had been given by the bride's family, others by the groom's; the provenance of each object was carefully explained. A pile of ten colorful satin prayer mats *(seccade)*, ornately embroidered, was arrayed on a chest in the hall, topped by two tall stacks of cotton head scarves, overlapping to display the fine, elaborate, crocheted edgings, each scarf different. Another artfully arranged three-foot-high pile of towels, crochet-worked borders dangling, and other embroidered and stitched items concealed the top of a cabinet. Gifts to the bride-to-be from her new family were also on display. The doors to the hall shoe closet were open to allow views of three new purses and six pairs of fancy new house slippers of embroidered vinyl. In the living room, the display continued: intricate hand-crocheted doilies covered every imaginable surface, including the fuse box in the hall, upon which, at Füsün's insistence, since I was taller than the others, I reached up and draped a doily.

The bride had also artfully crafted small, artificial trees and bowers of wire, beads, and cloth, having learned this skill, along with that of engraving silver metal sheets into decorative plaques, at a course in the Girl's Art School, a common form of girls' education in Ümraniye. There, girls were taught basic academic subjects, but also learned to make objects with which to decorate their homes at marriage and perhaps sell to neighbors or at craft fairs. Mahmure told me she had also taken an English course and demonstrated with a well-pronounced, "I speak English very well." Girl's Art School was considered a genteel form of education that did not imply that a girl was being educated for the labor force, as a trade school might, and did not require her to share school space with young men, as in regular schools. One way or another, making a trousseau (or earning money, for instance through piecework, to buy trousseau items and supplies) took up a great deal of women's lives before marriage. Their hands were busy with their art in school, after school, and during the evenings, when they were not cooking, cleaning, or taking care of younger siblings.

Young men's lives played themselves out in a workplace, if they were lucky, or, if they were unemployed, while hanging about on the street and kicking a ball around a sports field or an empty lot. Fights were not uncommon; a manly temper in Ümraniye was a temper with a short fuse. A look or a word taken the wrong way, an unflattering rumor heard, or any kind of suspicion of "inappropriate" interaction with a female member of one's extended family could result in confrontation. The men were rarely at home, even in the evenings. If not driving taxis, they congregated in the ubiquitous coffee houses where, over inexpensive glasses of tea, they read the cafe's newspapers, exchanged news of possible jobs, played backgammon, and talked politics.

The world of the coffee house was an insular one of male companionship and limited friendships. A man's closest friends, men with whom he might share stories about women (although never women in his family) or problems at work (rarely problems at home), were usually relatives or men with whom he had bonded during mandatory military service. Coffee-house conversations could be general (about politics, about the neighborhood) or more specific (about job openings or a good car repair shop). But men never discussed their families or home lives; that topic was entirely off limits, regardless of how close a male friend was. Likewise, men never asked about a man's wife, certainly not by name. At the most, one might ask after someone's "family." Interest by other men in one's women was inappropriate, an invasion of privacy, and aroused suspicion of possibly salacious intent. Women also rarely referred to their husbands in conversation with one other, and then did not use a husband's given name, but rather referred to him as *beyim* (my gentleman, or, in its more archaic meaning, my lord). Men used the third person *hanım,* the lady or the woman. There was an intense, jealous guarding of the inner sanctum of the family home, in speech as well as in action. Only certain people, well-vetted, were allowed past the front door, then past the parlor into the actual living areas.

This vigilance at the portals to family life and the segregation of male and female activity have obvious implications for political mobilization. For instance, the coffee house was a central location for political mobilization and organization of neighborhood men, but male activists had little or no access to other family members. Female activists, on the other hand, could enter homes to mobilize women and young people and collect information about families that men could not. They attended women's social gatherings *(kabul günleri)* and helped organize prayer readings and other religious celebrations in the home. They attended wedding and birth celebrations, and visited families to offer condolences. They also held education and propaganda meetings in people's homes. The different forms of and venues for relationships among men and women are reflected in political activity, as are cultural norms and expectations. These are of one cloth with, although not reducible to, religious beliefs and devotion. That is, the culture of male-female interaction in Ümraniye was legitimated by reference to local interpretations of Islamic injunctions regarding modesty, propriety, and the "proper" roles of men and women. In this sense, the structure of the network of support that developed in Ümraniye for the Welfare Party in particular (and the Islamist political message in general) was tied to religious beliefs.

However, political support was not necessarily given for reasons of religion. In previous decades, Füsün and members of her family had voted for the left-of-center Republican People's Party, the party founded by Ataturk. At the time of Ahmet and Mahmure's wedding, Ümraniye had an Islamist Welfare Party mayor. Over tea with her new mother-in-law, Mahmure told me that she preferred the right-of-center parties (Motherland or True Path) to Welfare. The Welfare mayor, she said, "has been good for Ümraniye. He did a lot of things here, fixed the roads and the infrastructure, but otherwise the party didn't keep any of its promises." I asked what promises had not been kept. "Erbakan [the party leader] promised to lower inflation, and look—it's in three digits now. He promised a raise for the civil servants, but everyone is suffering."

Füsün admitted that she had voted for Welfare in the 1995 election because "a woman I knew came by and pressured me to promise to vote for them. I didn't want to, but in the end I promised
because the woman insisted. Then," Füsün continued, frowning, "I
actually had to vote for them so I wouldn't be breaking a promise.
But I didn't want to and next time I'm going to vote for [Tansu] Çiller
[of the True Path Party]." Later, when we were alone, I asked
Mahmure whom she had voted for. She admitted that she hadn't
been able to vote on her own yet. "The last time, my father took me
and he took my and my mother's vote and stamped them with the
party he wanted. After that I refused to go and told him that if I
couldn't vote myself, I wasn't going." Both the sacredness of an oath
and the patriarchal authority of the father, although resented and
resisted, could be (and often were) justified by reference to Islamic
beliefs. In other words, while political choices were made for a variety of often eminently practical reasons, political practice occurred
within a cultural frame reinforced by religion.

Poverty and Choices

While local culture informed by Islam set up the framework for people's
expectations and choices, poverty was the ultimate qualifier, underlying what choices were available to Ümraniye residents and undermining their ability to choose. Poverty also conditioned the terms of
and motivations for political choices and activism. Many residents
had been left out of the new economy, although not for lack of ideas
and effort. Some had acquired an education or accumulated small
amounts of capital, while others barely hung on at the extreme edges
of poverty. A general lack of education, capital, connections, and
knowledge, especially of foreign languages, hindered the integration
of local men into the booming Turkish export and service sectors.

Ahmet talked about importing good-quality, inexpensive shirts,
bedsheets, and automobile parts from the United States and reselling
them in Ümraniye at a profit. These were things in great demand, he
explained, but unavailable or too expensive. Many men dreamed of
owning their own businesses. Nihat, a newly married young man, quit
his job as a driver for a business and pooled resources with two of his
brothers to build a restaurant on some land owned by their father in
an outlying part of the neighborhood that had begun to be settled with
three-story apartment buildings. Nihat perceived that there would be a

need for services and decided on opening a restaurant, although neither he nor his brothers had any experience running a business or cooking. His wife and mother were aghast at the risk entailed in quitting a good job that paid $350 a month. To tide them over until the restaurant was ready, the brothers drove taxis and sold cheap children's clothing from the first room completed in the construction of the restaurant building. Nihat was busy collecting recipes. He showed me glossy pages he had clipped from magazines with recipes for exotic versions of local foods, like baked eggplant stuffed with lamb and cheese and arranged on the plate in the unlikely shape of a flower.

Not all families had the resources and options of Ahmet, who would inherit his parents' house, and Nihat, who shared in the financial and labor resources of a supportive extended family. Nurcan and Hüseyin illustrate the extremes of poverty, with almost no resources and limited family support. Nurcan was a woman in her mid-thirties. Her wide, pale, sweaty face wore a permanent, mildly harassed expression. Before her marriage ten years before, her young face had been calm and unlined, and I was surprised at the change when I saw her again several years after her marriage. She had only been allowed to see the fiancé arranged for her, the owner of a vegetable stand, briefly in formal, chaperoned settings. Whenever she saw him, she had blushed deeply and become tongue-tied. Her family had migrated twenty years before from a village to the north, so Nurcan had grown up in Ümraniye, in a sparsely furnished but sunny apartment with her parents, two brothers, and a younger sister. Her brothers shared a taxi; one drove it during the day, the other at night. She and her sister tended their parents' home, watered the profusion of flowers in recycled sunflower oil cans lining the window sills, and fed the caged songbirds her father favored. Her father was a retired bus driver and, other than the birds and the newspaper, interested himself in nothing else. He sat morosely all day in an armchair by the balcony window and spoke to no one. Her mother was a fleshy, always slightly disheveled woman who fussed around the apartment, occasionally plopping herself into a chair to wipe the sweat from her broad face with the dangling end of her cotton-gauze head cloth.

Nurcan, like Mahmure, looked forward to marriage as a release from the strictures of life in her parental home, more often than not enforced by her brothers, who kept a close eye on her movements. Nurcan was rarely allowed out of the apartment, except to go, chaperoned, to visit a nearby relative. Unlike Mahmure, whose family was comfortable and could afford to buy her fashionable and expensive *tesettür* silk scarves and matching coats and indoor clothing like dresses and jogging suits, Nurcan had a minimal wardrobe. A cheap cotton coat of indeterminate color and a large polyester scarf sufficed as her outdoor wear. Indoors, she wore *şalvar,* loose peasant trousers of inexpensive flowered cotton, a sweater, and, over that, a cardigan. Her gauze head cloths, though, were colorful and finely edged with embroidery. She prepared as many as she could for her trousseau, but money was short for materials, so her trousseau was not as extensive as Mahmure's would be. Still, the scarves showed a great deal of skill and prettily framed her innocent, pleasant face.

The produce stand owner, Hüseyin, was considered a good match because he was reputed to be a decent, hardworking man with no moral flaws. He didn't gamble or drink. He also owned his own vehicle, a small truck to haul fruits and vegetables from the *Hal,* Istanbul's distribution center for fresh produce. This was considered an injection of capital, transportation, and other potential advantages into Nurcan's family network. His family's reputation was spotless; they had migrated from the same region as Nurcan's and lived in Ümraniye. The latter was important for Nurcan because it meant that she could continue to visit her natal family.

After their marriage, Nurcan and Hüseyin moved into a tiny apartment in a square concrete housing block on a steep, narrow side street. Her apartment was directly across the street from the apartment of Hüseyin's parents. They were so close that Nurcan could almost join hands with anyone leaning from the balcony on the other side. Her days of close supervision had not ended at all. Hüseyin's mother came constantly to Nurcan's apartment, stayed for hours, expected to be served tea continually, and asked what Nurcan described as nosy questions about all aspects of her son's life.

By the mid-1990s, Nurcan had two children, an eight-year-old girl and a five-year-old boy. The family lived in three small rooms, with the children, a washing machine, and ironing board in one of the two bedrooms. The couple's marriage bed took up almost all the floor space in the other. There was just enough room between bed and door to sit on the bed and pull on one's socks. A dresser was crammed into the space at the foot of the bed and was approachable only by sidling crabwise along the bed frame, back against the wall. The third room was the sitting room/parlor. Unlike many other homes, there was no parlor (to house the display furniture acquired at marriage) and separate sitting room (for daily use and to receive friends and relatives). The living-room furniture had been chosen for serviceability, not display, and the wear from the activities of two children was sadly obvious. Still, this room was bright and cheerful. A sunny window looked out on treetops. The living room was too small for a dining table, so the family ate at a table set up in the hallway connecting the rooms. Since the bathroom had no working faucet, a barrel of water was set beside the sink with a plastic scoop for washing. The kitchen was just big enough for a small refrigerator, a sink set into a short, built-in counter with some wooden shelving above, and several plastic barrels to store drinking water and tap water in case it was cut off. Nurcan had decorated the shelves, refrigerator, and barrels with cheerful, hand made, decorated doilies.

When I joined her in the kitchen, Nurcan was crying. Her husband's family had refused to help them after an accident in which Hüseyin's truck had been irretrievably damaged. To purchase a new truck, Hüseyin had asked Nurcan to sell her wedding gold. As she told me this, Nurcan cried and stretched out her arm to show me her one remaining gold bangle bracelet. "What can I do? He's my husband." Gold bracelets, lengths of chain, and gold coins are given to a bride by the groom's family, her natal family, and wedding guests as wealth that is the bride's alone and is meant to be her insurance in case of illness, divorce, or widowhood, and, finally, to pay for her burial. Women rarely sell their gold unless out of dire necessity. Instead, they try to add to it. Gold coins are given the new mother at the birth of each child, and a woman can also buy gold with money earned from sewing or embroidering for neighbors or with piece-work income. Gold is an important hedge against adversity and important for survival in old age in a community where informal-sector work or work paid under the table does not bring access to pensions or social security for women. In another kind of investment in their future, women sometimes sell their gold to help their children establish a business, buy an apartment, or get out of a scrape.

Nurcan's family situation was so dire, however, that it seemed only her contribution would save them. But even after selling the gold, they were still in debt. They owed five hundred German marks to the company that had sold them the first truck, and, even though the truck was wrecked, the company still demanded payment. Hüseyin earned about $300 a month and the rent was $120. "How can we come up with that kind of money?" Nurcan asked, drying her eyes and busying herself in the kitchen preparing a meager dinner of bread, salted anchovies, and cheese. She could afford nothing, barely enough food for the family. Later, as she washed the dishes in the privacy of the kitchen and I stood beside her, dish towel at the ready, she said wistfully, "I wish we had enough money to open a small shop, maybe selling pizzas. Then I could help earn money." I turned to look at her and saw a raw desperation in her face that choked off the soothing but entirely inadequate words I had been preparing to say.

The next day was the first day of school and together we walked the forty-five minutes to bring her daughter to the public school. We spent a couple of hours milling in the courtyard of the unassuming concrete building with other parents, mostly women, the children corralled in the middle, herded by several strategically placed teachers. We listened to long, boring speeches from the school director and a teacher, welcoming parents and students and reaffirming the value of education and the greatness of the Turkish nation. This was followed by patriotic speeches by a male student and a female student, both of whom had obviously been instructed to declaim loudly into the microphone. The director took the microphone again and, in a rambling talk (punctuated by warnings and lectures to the fidgeting children to pay attention and show respect), told the parents that, while the school had little to work with, it had made improvements. Then he announced what many of the parents had been waiting for: the school fees. When he mentioned $35 for school lunches, Nurcan winced.

Afterwards, the children were herded in and we hovered around the registration table set up in the cement yard. Nurcan was waiting for her husband to come by in the truck with the $24 registration fee. I offered to lend it to her but she said she would rather wait. It became clear that she didn't know whether they even had the money—together with the lunch money, a total of $59. By the time the schoolyard had cleared of most parents, we were still waiting in the hot sun by the registration table. She took the forms anyway and the man at the desk told her kindly that she could register by Thursday; it didn't have to be that day. We began to amble back down the street, stopping to peruse schoolbooks in the shop windows. Just then Hüseyin drove up. We crowded into the cab of the truck. He apologized, saying he had been en route for over an hour; there had been a lot of traffic. As they drove, Nurcan whispered to Hüseyin what the fees were, asking, "Where will we find that much money?"

He answered softly, "We'll find it." On the way home, we passed a large tent set up by the Welfare-run municipality in a main square, where parents could purchase inexpensive school supplies during the first week of school.

Lives so constrained by need respond to even the smallest injection of assistance, whether through food shared among kin or schoolbooks subsidized by the municipality. Male pride did not permit acceptance of charity as long as a man was working. Islamist foundations understood this and couched their assistance in more acceptable ways. Chapter 6 will take a closer look at Islamist welfare activities. The concerns that resonated through Nurcan and Hüseyin's lives made them extremely sensitive to political groups addressing issues like subsidized school supplies and an end to the economic strangulation of state-run schools that led school administrators to charge parents for supplies and services, from cleaning staff to teacher salaries, that the school should have but was unable to supply.

Political Resources

The stark visibility of unequal wealth gave impetus to Islamist groups that preached social justice and an end to economic favoritism and corruption. "Once the Motherland Party was in power [in the 1980s], the elite spoke only of how to make money and how best to consume it," rather than of social welfare, justice, and the state's obligation to guarantee these (Ahmad, 1993, 209). The state forfeited the people's loyalty when it reneged on its promise to protect the common national interest through statist development. Government corruption scandals and the state's slow response after the devastating earthquake in the Istanbul area in 1999 dealt further blows to its legitimacy. This left the way open to an Islamist movement that seemed to have something to offer a sizable and diverse segment of society, from the urban dispossessed to provincial bourgeoisie and upwardly mobile young professionals. Islamist intellectuals and Welfare Party ideologists envisioned "an egalitarian petty-bourgeois paradise, a utopian society made up of individual entrepreneurs" that pitted the little man in the market against a capitalist monopoly of wealth and economic mobility (Gülalp, 1997, 423). When a working-class couple drove me home one night from Ümraniye over the Bosphorus bridge, we passed along the edge of the glittering, expensive neighborhood of Bebek. The man, Hasan, pointed out the window and said to his wife, who had rarely been to this side of the Bosphorus, "See that? There are people who live here who feed their dog every week what I earn in a month." I knew some of those dog owners; Hasan was not far wrong.

As we have seen, the concept of social class in Turkey is very much bound up with cultural practice, but neither classes nor cultures can be as clearly delineated in practice as Hasan's powerful comparison might imply. Hasan had what Robert Hefner calls a self-conscious-ness of class, that is, the simple consciousness of a group's situation in a hierarchy of wealth and power. This does not presuppose "a con-viction that those occupying common class situations actually share common interests" or a "consciousness of kind" (1990, 28). Indeed, Hasan was able to find common ground and even identify with Welfare politicians and popular Islamist figures who clearly had a great deal more wealth and power than he, but who, in their pub-lic lives, appeared to live "just like" him. The Welfare Party selective-ly used class differences to throw a mantle of commonality over its economically heterogeneous constituency by setting Islamists off against a "corrupt" and "dissolute" elite class of secularist politicians and industrialists. At one Islamist rally, a film clip showed centrist party politicians at a fancy dinner party in palatial rooms, eating from a richly laden buffet. This was followed by footage showing three young boys dressed in rags picking through mounds of garbage at the city dump. Nevertheless, within the lower ranks of the Islamist movement, a self-consciousness of class bubbled up as resentment against any conspicuous consumption by its own leaders.

In discussions of Islamist practices, the emphasis has been on culture and status, with little mention of social class as a motivating factor. This is not surprising, given the historical links between class and identity in Turkey. Since the founding of the Republic, the state attempted to propagate its concept of a secular, Westernized citizen through elite-led national institutions (the bureaucracy, the military, schools, universities, folkloric clubs, the media) engaged in shaping and honing identities. Conservative rural people gained sufficient political mass in the 1980s and 1990s and began to create an alterna-tive urban culture and their own institutions, and agitated for change in the nature of schools and bureaucracy. The contest, however, was perceived to be one of identity (urban/non-urban, secularist/Islamist), to which the other characteristics of the urban poor, such as their class position, were subordinated.

Yet, as Hasan's comment and the experiences of Ümraniye families described above indicate, a self-consciousness of class was an important lodestone that gave direction to political mobilization, even if it was not identified as such. Michael Kearney has suggested that contemporary society is characterized by many layers of internal differentiation and generally lacks the sharp cleavages that can be fitted into such categories as lower, middle, upper-middle class and so on. Under such ambiguous conditions, identities and values, expressed symbolically, do assist us in identifying people's social position. Nevertheless, the system of signs within which people express their identities must be seen as occurring within a system of class differences, "the fundamental, bottom-line economic issue in social life" (1996, 174). Thus, Hasan's, Nurcan's, and Ahmet's self-consciousness of their class is "not so much reflected [as] refracted in consciousness, in some cases as alienation and anomie and in others as ethnicity and the motive force of new social movements" (146). In the following chapters, I will examine some of the forms this "motive force" has taken in Turkish society.

3

THE INSTITUTIONAL
EXPRESSION OF ISLAM

Vernacular politics links neighborhood networks with local civic and national political institutions. Through these institutional links, different social groups coordinate their interests and move together seemingly in the same direction. In this chapter, I will discuss the diversity of religious belief and expression in Turkey at the institutional level. I will examine the background to the blossoming of the Islamist movement in general since 1980, and the reasons for the Welfare Party's electoral success in the 1990s in particular. It is important to note here that the discussion of institutionalized Islam in this chapter is meant as a *mise en scène* to put vernacular politics in a more systemic and historical perspective. This brief overview is not meant to be exhaustive; much has been written about the various actors on the Turkish political stage and references are provided to guide the interested reader further. Yet, however exhaustively we describe the vehicles for Islamic participation, an explanation of how this particular political process works is ultimately to be found in vernacular, not official, politics.

Despite the seeming convergence of religious interest and opposition around certain issues and symbols, Islamist institutions are extraordinarily diverse, both in organization and orientation. They are often structured hierarchically, even where they are allied with more egalitarian, horizontally organized networks. Their particular understanding of Islam and the role of Islam in national political life falls in a broad range from liberal to conservative, moderate to radical, and is linked with nationalism or pluralism as variously defined. A variety of positions on women's roles and economic practice are represented. All these positions, like the institutions that represent them, are subject to change. This diversity, in part, is simply emblematic of the heterogeneity of Islamic beliefs and practices that characterize the region, and a reflection of the characteristics and motivations of the different social groups that support these institutions. It is also the result of a complex history of state suppression, control, and deregulation of Islam that has brought about a proliferation of institutional bases for Islamic engagement in the political arena.

There is a long tradition of couching opposition to the state in Islamic terms. Before the introduction of multiparty politics in 1945, Islam was the only channel for protest, since the Republican state monopolized all legitimate political expression and left no room for the development of an independent civil society. This pattern is not unique to Turkey, but applies more broadly to the Middle East. Egypt, Syria, Iraq, and Iran all have pursued a national ideal in which the state monopolized the right to represent the interests of an organically conceived nation.

In Turkey, the means by which the masses could pursue their interests broadened with Turkey's first multiparty elections. In 1950, Ataturk's party, the Republican People's Party, was soundly defeated and, for the first time, an opposition party, the Democrat Party, came to power. In the period before and after the election, rural areas were galvanized by extensive grassroots organization and political participation. Villagers quickly took stock of the advantages of the new multiparty democratic system in which they could play parties off against one another to make them "heed our voices" (Lerner, quoted in Kasaba, 1997, 31). Unlike the Republican People's Party, the Democrat Party had a more populist approach. It appealed to the Islamic sentiments of the people and, thus, was able to gain the allegiance of rural religious leaders. These were able to influence the votes of their followers.

This was a populism rooted in patron-client relations between landlords and peasants, religious sheikhs and their followers, and politicians and their constituents. Patron-clientilistic relations of hierarchy and dependence were, and in some respects still are, a powerful feature of rural life. In many rural areas, particularly in eastern Turkey, tribal leaders and big landowners in effect "owned" the villages in their region. These powerful families served as patrons to the villagers, assisting them materially, mediating with the authorities, and administering their own form of justice. Loyalty, labor, and obedience were expected in return. Rural elites, like leaders of religious brotherhoods, could deliver blocks of votes at election time. The Democrat Party government, in return, brought electricity and other services to hitherto isolated villages and connected them to market towns and cities with new roads and bus service. Thus began the mutual transformation of country and city as villagers rode the buses to town, found work, and did not return, and as new ideas and ways of doing business transformed village life.

The decline of patron-clientilism in cities was suggested as early as 1975, after the first wave of urban-rural migrants had settled in, in a study of Turkish squatter-area politics by Kemal Karpat (1975). As urban migrant needs and demands became more complex and numerous, traditional patron-client ties based on kinship or region likely proved insufficient to cope with them. Karpat noted a new type of leadership emerging in the squatter areas, leadership not based on religious, tribal, or communal authority of the village of origin, but rather based on "organizational skills and the ability to represent and defend the interests of the settlement in political and administrative circles" (Karpat, 1975, 92). The loyalty to authority and the state that characterized village life, he observed, gave way in the squatter areas to ideas about social rights, equality, and freedom. However, communal demands pursued under this new philosophy still retained much of the old paternalism that colored patron-client relations, seated in the belief that the state's role was to be the providing "father." The citizen was under the *himaye* protection and benevolence of "Father State" *(Devlet Baba)*.

Nevertheless, political parties and their representatives had to be responsive to local demands if they wished to gain or retain power. Voters would not hesitate to replace a party they felt was not meeting their needs, regardless of ideological position. There was a high level of political awareness in the squatter areas. A 1968 study of voting behavior in an Istanbul squatter area found that 88 percent of men and 84 percent of women were fully aware of the platforms of political candidates and listened to their speeches, although only 14 percent of men and 3 percent of women actually belonged to a political party (Karpat, 1975, 105). Few viewed organizations as a viable means of communication with the state, much as the squatter residents in a more recent survey (Gökçe et al., 1993, 319–20). Rather, voting and petitioning local officials were seen as the primary means to bargain for community needs with political parties and with city and national authorities. In general, the relation between citizen and political party was not one of coercion or enforced loyalty (an unwilling clientilism), but rather one that on the whole encouraged party performance and accountability to voters. On the other hand, patron-clientilism in the political system also led to widespread cronyism and corruption when patronage ties took precedence over an equitable distribution of or fair competition for municipal contracts, permissions, and other resources.

Voting was accompanied by and was a prelude to bargaining for community needs. This bargaining was accomplished directly through confrontations with officials or indirectly through personal contacts. The latter drew on personal connections, or "pull" (*torpil*, from the French *torpille*, torpedo)—that is, on *himaye* relations. Politicians also were directly petitioned as representatives of the patron state. In May 1987, the young daughter of a local headman[1] in a poor neighborhood not far from Ümraniye threw herself before the Turkish president, Kenan Evren, as he was getting into his limousine while visiting a nearby high school, and thrust a written petition into his hands. In it, she requested that he intercede to stop the building of a mosque on the site of the neighborhood's only medical clinic (Gürsoy, 1994, 96). In this case, the community's efforts were in vain: the clinic was closed and the mosque built.

Patronage, in other words, has not died out in urban Turkey, but it has been challenged by vernacular politics. Relations with political parties have tended to be of a patron-clientilistic nature, where the party was expected to provide social and infrastructural services to a community in exchange for being voted into power. Voters, however, have developed a counterforce, as when Ümraniye residents applied community pressure by planting jars of their sewage-laced tapwater on the desks of municipal officials. On the strength of horizontal neighborhood networks, they have gone beyond bargaining and petitioning to changing the system so that it is more responsive. Perhaps the process of the decline of patron-clientilism that Karpat identified as early as the 1970s will begin to run its final course as nonhierarchical forms of community organization become the motive force in political life.

For now, however, vernacular politics is most visibly a force in the Islamist movement, through first the Welfare and then the Virtue Party. Within these parties, politics based on patronage and politics based on horizontal neighborhood networks were identified with different constituencies and different leaderships. Other groups within the Islamist movement have tended to be hierarchically organized, often around a central religious leader. Despite new ideological messages and forms of organization, they retained the patron-clientilistic elements of older religious brotherhoods. Below, I will examine the variety of institutionalized forms taken by Islam in Turkey.

Which Islam?

The Kemalist project of secularization has been remarkably effective among a segment of the population, specifically middle-class elites who inherited the Kemalist mantle from the Republican bureaucratic elites who had crafted it. My friend Selma is typical of this type of secularized citizen. Her parents and grandparents had been active supporters of the Republican project and her grandfather, father, and mother had all been committed Kemalists and held positions in the civil service bureaucracy. Selma, a professional woman, sees herself as secularist but apolitical. She lives a middle-class lifestyle. Like many of my friends from the middle and upper classes, she attends mosque only on special occasions. When her son reached grade-school age, Selma decided he should have a basic grounding in Islam. She wanted to inoculate her son against fanatic appeals, so he wouldn't find religion mysteriously alluring if he discovered it at a later age. She also felt that Islam was part of Turkish culture, and, thus, an educated Turkish citizen should have some familiarity with its customs and doctrines. Like any highly educated mother, she tackled this project by scouring the bookstores for books that explained Islam to children, but after some months of looking gave up because she couldn't find any that met her exacting moral requirements. She told me she particularly objected to the stern emphasis on obedience and the way the books either portrayed women as inferior or glorified them as mothers, but as nothing else. Thus, her son, like his mother, grew up with little formal religious training.

Selma, her family, and friends might go to the mosque on religious holidays or attend *mevlud* prayer ceremonies, much as secular American families celebrate Christmas and attend funeral services, as soothing cultural activities that reinforce community, but do not require in-depth knowledge of religious doctrine or even faith. The cultural rituals of secularist Kemalism have been augmented by imported customs. In 1999, supermarkets in middle-class Istanbul and Ankara neighborhoods stocked a wide variety of Christmas baubles, reindeer, and Santas for New Year's celebration, which secular elites had begun to celebrate, complete with Christmas trees and exchange of gifts.

In contrast, Islam has never been absent from the social and cultural lives of the Turkish masses or from the lives of many middle-class households. This is supported by a recent survey showing a high level of religious practice, with nine of ten adults fasting during the holy month of Ramazan and almost half praying five times a day (Çarkoğlu and Toprak, 2000, 45). However, since "middle-class" has come to be associated with a secularist ideal, religious practice among the middle classes is likely to be less visible, either because it is attenuated, is not displayed openly, or is life cycle–related, as when men and women become more religiously observant as they age. Not surprisingly, supporters of the Republican People's Party were least likely to rate themselves as very religious (2 percent, compared to 14 percent for Virtue Party supporters) and most likely to claim to be not at all religious (8 percent, compared to below 3 percent for all other parties). Most striking of all, though, is that between 40 and 60 percent of all respondents rated themselves as religious and 40 percent would define themselves as Muslim or Muslim Turk before Turkish citizen (43, 27).

Likewise, membership in religious institutions is not simply a matter for the masses. Religious brotherhoods *(tarikat)* and mystical religious (Sufi) orders have remained important institutions for the popular as well as middle classes. Brotherhoods and Sufi orders were banned early in the Republican era and their lodges closed. Although religious brotherhoods still are not allowed to practice openly, in reality the government turns a blind eye. After 1945, brotherhoods began to reappear in political life, once politicians realized that religious leaders were able to deliver blocks of votes. Former president Turgut Özal and other prominent people have admitted to belonging to religious brotherhoods.

Religious orders vary from the politically active fundamentalist Nakşibendi and Süleymanci to such philosophically left-of-center Sufi orders as the Bektaşi and Mevlevi, familiar outside Turkey as the

Whirling Dervishes. Sufi orders are active primarily at the cultural and associational level, although they may ally themselves with particular political positions. The socially and politically liberal Alevi, a non-Sunni religious minority estimated to make up around 20 percent of the Turkish population, were recently granted the right to reopen their lodges and practice openly. Others, like the Ticani and Nurcu, are organized like brotherhoods but appeared in Turkey only in this century. Their open participation in political life has been sporadic. The Ticani, a minor group, were known mainly for their periodic attacks on statues of Ataturk, which they condemned as idols. The Nurcu, on the other hand, have become an important part of the Islamist movement, generally allied with center-right political parties.[2]

A more mysterious group, the Hizbullah, is suspected of waging an armed battle to establish an Islamic state in Turkey. The name may be a gloss for a number of small but violent fundamentalist groups, like the "*sharia* fascists" responsible for a hotel fire in 1993 that killed thirty-seven people. On July 2, 1993, a mob emerged from a mosque in the eastern city of Sivas and set fire to a hotel hosting a conference of liberal journalists, writers, and intellectuals, many of them Alevi. The arsonists had been encouraged by an inflammatory sermon against the famous writer Aziz Nesin, who had translated portions of Salman Rushdie's *Satanic Verses* into Turkish. Nesin escaped, but many others died in the flames. Local Sivas officials, including the Welfare Party mayor, were accused of withholding police assistance and firefighting equipment, even when the severity of the situation was clear and orders had been given by superiors to intervene. Hizbullah is suspected to be behind assassinations of anti-Islamist intellectuals. A number of journalists, educators, and other elites have been assassinated in recent years. Prominent among them was Uğur Mumcu, an outspoken proponent of secularism and author of several books exposing and documenting financial connections between Saudi Arabia and Islamic groups in Turkey and Germany. More recently, Hizbullah has been accused of carrying out government-sponsored[3] acts of terror against Kurdish businessmen and others suspected of supporting, in deed or principle, Kurdish separatism. In February 2000, bodies of dozens of people who had been tortured and executed were unearthed in Hizbullah safehouses around Turkey. The case of Hizbullah is a clear, if sinister, example of the illegibility of the boundaries between religion, politics, ethnic nationalism, and culture. Given all the variables at play in Hizbullah actions and motivations, it would be simplistic to describe it as simply an example of Islamist extremism.

Most Islamic groups have not engaged in such violent behavior (although the distinction was lost on some radical Kemalists in the government and military who tarred the entire Islamist movement with the Hizbullah brush). The Nakşibendi order, for instance, has been a powerful presence in Turkish political life since the founding of the Republic, both in active opposition to the state and as a counterweight within political parties after 1950.[4] In Ümraniye, Halil's parents belonged to the Nakşibendi order. They considered themselves followers of a particular local religious teacher *(hoca)*. A bookshelf in their bedroom held a dozen religious volumes, mostly popular encyclopedias of Islamic topics. Those, Hasan and Halil's mother Müşerref pointed out, were her husband's books. Hers were a stack of flimsy paperbacks published by the sheikh *(şeyh)*, the head of the religious order. One was printed in Arabic letters, which she had learned to read as a child. Over glasses of tea in the sitting room, she explained to me the nature of the brotherhood *(tarikat)*. "What is a *tarikat?* You cut your hand and the blood flows, the blood of everyone in the brotherhood flows." The followers of different teachers are "like the fingers on a hand, but all the same hand." Hasan had come in while we were talking, and elaborated, "The teachers have great power. For instance, in Erzurum there was a demonstration outside a mosque and the police told them to disperse, but nobody did. Then Naim *hoca* came and all he did was say in a quiet voice that people should leave and everyone just quietly left. He stopped a demonstration that the police couldn't disperse." Clearly, moral power was perceived to be mightier than the state.

The women who followed Müşerref's teacher met twice a week, on Tuesdays and Fridays, for "Quran." These meetings differed from a *mevlud,* she explained, which were meetings held for specific purposes—for instance, to commemorate a death—at which certain religious poems and prayers were recited. She was also careful to differentiate a brotherhood from other types of religious community *(cemaat)*. In Turkey, she explained, there were only three or four brotherhoods, but many *cemaat*. "The communities have teachers too," Hasan chimed in. "They train teachers that go out and found new communities elsewhere." Halil, who had come into the sitting room, added, "Like we're a *cemaat* here. Four or five people can be a *cemaat*." Fethullah Gülen's organization, Müşerref offered, was the biggest, "an organization [*teşkilat*], an association [*örgüt*]." The impression I received from their description was of a pale, superficial association of "just anyone" in a *cemaat,* contrasted with the organic kinship and moral power of a *tarikat.*

The Enlightened Elites

Müşerref was referring to the Nurcu Fethullacılar,[5] a tight web of associations with chapters in every major city, many of them with names, like Turkey Volunteer Organizations Foundation, that obscure their connection to the Islamic fold. In the spacious, elegant offices of one such organization, the Journalists and Writers Foundation in Istanbul, Cemal Uşşak, the foundation's head of international relations, explained to me that the Fethullacılar had one or more foundations *(vakıflar)* in every city in Turkey, almost all established to support education. Mr. Uşşak used the terms *vakıf* (foundation) and *cemaat* (religious community) interchangeably. This was not surprising, since the foundations and other organizations were set up specifically to disseminate the religious ideas of Fethullah Gülen and, thus, constitute the visible body of the community.

Gülen has written about an Anatolian Islam that differs from Arab Islam in its tolerance and openness to dialogue with all segments of society, including other religions and sects. His attitude toward veiling and women in the professions is similarly liberal and focused on the importance of seeking knowledge and integration with the modern world, even if that includes incorporating Western technology, clothing, and, to some extent, lifestyle. Like other Islamists, the Fethullacılar use Islam and the Ottoman past to symbolically bridge contemporary ethnic and sectarian diversity. Gülen seeks to "Islamize Turkish nationalism; recreate a legitimate link between state and religion; emphasize democracy and tolerance; and encourage links with Turkic republics" (Aras, 1998, 29).

In his writings, Gülen emphasizes that religion is a private matter and its requirements should not be imposed on anyone. Instead, a web of organizations teaches Gülen's brand of Islamic philosophy. As Uşşak put it, the Fethullacılar do not indoctrinate using the language of the tongue *(lisani dil),* as he claimed the Welfare Party did, but rather communicated its message and taught by using the language of the heart *(lisani kalp)* or the language of behavior *(lisani hal),* that is, by example. To spread Gülen's message of the "heart," his followers have sponsored educational and cultural facilities, student dormitories, summer camps, and media organizations. Following from their belief in a fundamentally Turkish Islam, many of the schools founded by the Fethullacılar are in the Central Asian Turkic republics.

Gülen's movement is an offspring of the Risale-I Nur movement, based on the writings of Said Nursi (1877–1960). Said Nursi argued that there was no contradiction between religion and science. The Risale-I Nur, or Nurcu movement, spread throughout Turkey in the 1950s and held particular appeal for those who had been educated in the secular school system.[6] Fethullah Gülen aims his message at Turkish elites and his movement consists primarily of students, teachers, businessmen, journalists, and other educated professionals. Gülen has met with politicians of both right and left and has the support of a number of well-known liberal and secular intellectuals. Around the country, supporters, both male and female, attend regular meetings to listen to speakers and to discuss contemporary issues in the light of Islamic doctrine and the writings of both Said Nursi and Fethullah Gülen. A series of generously funded conferences bring in international scholars to speak on Islam, democracy, civil society, and related themes, raising the international profile of the movement. The Fethullacılar were one of the sponsors of a series of meetings in July 1999 of Turkish intellectuals representing a variety of activist stances on Islam and secularism. The group hammered out a joint statement on the relation of religion to society and the state in Turkey called the Abant Platform.

The popularity and opaque structure of the movement have raised suspicions among laicists, in particular the military, that the various organizations are a dissembling front for groups that really wish to turn Turkey into an Iranian-style Islamic state. Gülen and his followers deny any interest in political power, although videotapes of Gülen making statements to the contrary, revealed on television in 1999, have fueled the debate. Relations with other Islamists are not cordial, either. Despite their similarities, followers of the Fethullacılar and the Welfare Party have few kind words for one another. Each accuses the other of secretive fanaticism. The Fethullacılar have little recognition in rural and working-class areas. In Ümraniye, when I asked Füsün about the Fethullacılar, she shook her head in puzzlement and suggested, "One of those religious orders. They take young people and brainwash them." Müşerref and her sons put the Fethullacılar in the category of a voluntary religious organization, much like any other voluntary organization—based on "mere" membership, rather than the flesh and blood union of brotherhoods.

The Fethullacılar control an extensive publishing and media industry, including their own television station. Restrictions on Islamic publishing were eased in the 1970s, and the military's policy of re-Islamization in the 1980s let out the leash even further. The military had intended Islam to be a socially unifying force that would heal the societal rifts that precipitated the 1980 coup, and that would replace the left-wing ideas and discourse of Turkey's youth with a more cohesive religious culture. With the support of the Özal government, the military encouraged the building of mosques and expansion of religious education. In the Islamic boom years of the 1980s, about 1,500 new mosques were built every year, until by 1988 there was a mosque for every 857 people (Ahmad, 1993, 221). The internationalization of Islamist ideas and institutions fostered the development of a sophisticated Islamist elite and provided resources for the publication of their ideas. Groups like the Fethullacılar and the Welfare Party also had their own resources, such as donations from their many followers, including Turkish migrants in Europe. The views expressed in Islamist publications cover a wide range, from pro-*sharia* to feminist and modernist, some say postmodernist, Islam.

Islamist Party Politics

If the Fethullacılar are the well-manicured lawn of Turkey's grassroots Islamist movement, the Welfare Party arguably could be seen as a field, seeded with wheat as well as holding its share of weeds. (The party symbol was a white staff of wheat on a red field.) At the political level, Islam is appealed to by several parties, out of political expedience or conviction—including the Democrat Party's successor, the Justice Party, and other center-right parties, as well as more overtly Islamic parties like the Welfare and Virtue Parties.

Islamist party politics got off to a slow start in the 1970s. Party politics at the time was dominated by the Republican People's Party. In the 1970s, the social democratic Republican People's Party had become the biggest party, claiming up to 42 percent of the national vote and twice reigning as the leading party in government. The

Republican People's Party appealed to the new social groups that arose as a result of the mechanization of agriculture, industrialization, and consequent urbanization. The working class, organized into unions, agriculturalists in developed regions, and an educated middle class looked to the Republican People's Party's social democratic ideals for leadership in meeting social demands and getting a bigger share of the country's resources. In the 1970s, both left and right parties maintained an egalitarian ethos that sought to minimize differences between the elites and the masses. The left promised social security reforms, inexpensive health care, and universal primary education. Although the left had little rapport with the culture of the masses, its largesse and rhetoric about social and economic rights appealed to a large number of voters. The right couched its egalitarianism in paternalism. Süleyman Demirel, leader of first the Justice Party, then the True Path Party, and president of the republic, was called *Baba* (Father) in the press. Despite the populist rhetoric of both right and left, however, the structure and political culture of the hierarchically organized and tightly centralized Turkish party system and government made patron-clientilism inescapable.

Welfare was the offspring of a number of previous Islam-oriented parties, all led by Necmettin Erbakan. Party programs, ideology, and the nature of its popular support and, thus, political fortunes changed over the years in the party's various permutations. Erbakan founded the National Order Party in 1970 to represent small, independent businessmen, merchants, and craftsmen who felt threatened by industrialization. The National Order Party took a firm stand against pro-West big business. Shortly after the military coup in 1971, the party was closed down for violating the constitutional separation of politics and religion. Erbakan fled to Switzerland, but returned to lead the National Salvation Party he had established in 1973. The National Salvation Party was a conservative party with a marginal following (less than 10 percent of the national vote) among provincial businesspeople and followers of religious orders. Despite its small-business constituency, the party agreed that state-led heavy industry was necessary to achieve national independence. However, it proposed that state-led industry be supported by large numbers of small capitalists, each owning no more than a 5 percent share. It was reasoned that this would give small business a stake in industrialization, rather than being threatened by it (Gülalp, 1999a, 27). The National Salvation Party also became more radical than its predecessor, joining in the general high-pitched, anti-system radicalism of 1970s politics. It organized rallies that attacked the laicist system and even Ataturk himself. The National Salvation Party participated in three coalition governments in the 1970s, until the coup in 1980 that closed down all political parties.

In 1983, phoenix-like, the party rose again, this time as the Welfare Party. While the National Salvation Party had drawn its main support from towns in the underdeveloped eastern and central Anatolian provinces and did not do well in the cities, Welfare's voter base included the urban poor living at the margins of cities, particularly small shopkeepers and urban migrants, who had previously voted for the left-of-center social democrats. To this were added the expanding Islamist business community and young professionals who consciously situated their economic and political activities within a Muslim identity and Islamic principles.

The network of devout and politically engaged businessmen and industrialists that emerged from the period of economic reform and opportunity in the 1980s provided a stable economic underpinning for various aspects of the Islamist movement, whether in the form of contributions to political parties or the support of charitable organizations, funding of scholarships, or building of schools and dormitories. This strengthened the Islamist movement in general, the tide that raised Welfare's electoral boat. As the Islamist intellectual Abdurrahman Dilipak put it, "The Welfare Party is a rising boat in a rising Islamic sea. Welfare's gains flow into this sea. The river finds its own bed" (1994, 12).

The interaction of movement and party calls for two levels of explanation. First, this chapter will deal with the party as simply a political agent, with a cadre of supporters and its own agenda—neither cadre nor agenda necessarily consistent or unchanging. Whether a party thrives, and when, depends a great deal on such contextual factors as the state of competing parties, economic prosperity and the extent to which it is shared, and international events that impinge on the national mood. A second level of explanation is found in the symbiosis of party and movement on organizational, cultural, and ideological grounds. This level of explanation concerns the vernacular politics that is the subject of this book. This aspect of the Welfare Party is laid out in chapters 4 through 6.

The Welfare Party

The turning point in Islamist electoral fortunes came in the 1994 local and 1995 parliamentary elections. Compared to previous local elections in 1989, in March 1994 the Welfare Party more than doubled its votes nationally, capturing 28 of 76 mayoral seats in provincial capitals. Six of Turkey's fifteen largest cities, including Istanbul and Ankara, voted in Welfare mayors. It must be noted that, although the parties of both the religious and nationalist extremes (the Welfare Party and the Nationalist Action Party) doubled their votes, they still could not match the widespread support enjoyed by parties occupying the center-right on the political spectrum. The two parties of the center-right, taken together, earned 42 percent of the vote and won almost as many provincial capitals as Welfare, surpassing Welfare by far in the district centers. That is, the bulk of the popular vote went to mainstream, middle-of-the-road parties, but those votes were split between parties whose leaders could not agree to share power nor agree on much of anything else. The True Path Party of then prime minister Tansu Çiller emerged as the strongest party with 21 percent of the national vote. The other center-right party, the Motherland Party, also did well, with 21 percent of the national vote and a tremendous gain in district centers. Despite its significant rise in popularity, Welfare's 19 percent must be weighed against the strength of this combined centrist vote.

Still, the election results (and the sight of Islamist mayors in major cities) shocked Kemalists and sent them into a whirlwind of activity. Walking down a city street, one could identify the homes of secularist Kemalists by the small posters of Ataturk in the windows. Lapel pins with Ataturk's profile became popular accessories. Secularists organized within existing associations and started new ones to counter "the fundamentalist threat." Middle-class women's groups were particularly active, since they felt they had the most to lose in the restrictive *sharia*-based state they feared was the ultimate aim of the Welfare Party. A friend in Ankara, a professional woman in her fifties, appeared on the verge of packing her belongings to flee the country if the Islamists came to power. She worried aloud about where she would go; she was too old to begin a new career elsewhere. But, she stridently insisted, she would never, never live in a country where women were forced to cover their heads. While this may seem to the uninvolved observer an overreaction to rather ambiguous election results, it was symptomatic of the concern, bordering on hysteria, occasioned among secularist men and women by the change in Welfare's fortunes. Although the sixty-nine-year-old Erbakan had twice served in a coalition government in the 1970s and had a long record in politics, he frightened many people with his fiery pre-election stump speeches that railed against laicism and Westernization.

In a misguided initial Islamist euphoria after the 1994 municipal elections, several attacks were reported on women in Western dress in downtown Istanbul, and attempts were made to separate women from men on public transport. Dour Welfare mayors had statues of nudes removed from parks. They tried to close or restrict restaurants and nightclubs that served alcohol. On the anniversary of the founding of the Republic, Welfare mayors found reasons not to attend the festivities, which were heavy on Kemalist and secularist symbolism, or made disparaging remarks about them. Party zealots proposed building an enormous mosque in Istanbul's Taksim Square, a symbolic center of Kemalism, the focal point of which is a statue commemorating the founding of the Republic. One side of the square is dominated by the Ataturk Cultural Center, home to opera, ballet, and classical symphony, cultural traditions imported by Ataturk as part of his Westernization program. To build a mosque in Taksim Square would be a direct affront to the institutional legacy of Kemalist secularism. Arguably the most ludicrous attempt on the part of the radicals to put their mark on the city was the suggestion, reported in the press, to paint the curbstones Islamic green. These actions did not draw support from the Turkish public, including many Welfare supporters, but rather criticism, ridicule, and protest. This vocal disapproval underlined the party's diverse voter base and made it clear that the party platform could not comfortably accommodate religious intolerance.

It also spotlighted the fact that the Welfare Party contained political radicals as well as conservatives. Conservatives, like the Islamic modernists of the nineteenth and early twentieth centuries, supported modernization with all its technological and institutional imports from the West, so long as it could be done without jettisoning moral principles. The ideas of the radicals, on the other hand, had more in common with Western postmodernist critiques of modernism, rationalism, and universal models of law and government (Gülalp, 1997). Radicals experienced modernization as Westernization, the assumption of a culture and institutions essentially alien to the

Islamic world. In their place, they proposed a technologically advanced society based on Islamic political and social models—for instance, the state as a "confederation of faiths" with multiple legal orders.

Crosscutting these two ideological perceptions of the world as it should and could be were the political styles of the protagonists. One style favored moderation: compromise, pragmatism, and accommodation with the system in order to push its basic nature in the direction of Islamic principles and institutions. Another style was confrontational. Despite his campaign rhetoric, Erbakan was a conservative in much the same mold as Turkey's other center-right politicians, but he was confrontational, causing friction in the party with those who found his tactics unnecessarily off-putting, alienating of popular opinion, and ultimately counterproductive for instituting change. Ideologically radical members of the Welfare Party, like Abdullah Gül and Recep Tayyip Erdoğan, who were in favor of radical systemic reform, nevertheless advocated a more moderate approach. Thus, some radicals were willing to work within the system to achieve systemic change in society and politics, while others, such as the Islamist rabble responsible for the deaths in Sivas or judges reinterpreting secular law in their own Islamic idiom, aimed to topple the existing system by violence or illegal actions. Ironically, the impatient confrontational tactics of some political conservatives, indistinguishable from the defiant antisystemic actions of some radicals, together fueled public mistrust of the party. This blunted the party's ability to make its legitimate criticisms of the Turkish economic and political system heard across the spectrum of the population. Tensions arose within the party between those advocating confrontation and those in favor of moderation to achieve their aims—whether based on radical or conservative criticisms and solutions. Confrontational actions of some party members, in the end, were destructive to the party, as they were noted in and vilified by the press and duly added to the case against the party when it was banned in 1998 for threatening the laicist nature of the state.

The 1995 general elections sent a further chill through Kemalists when Welfare won the largest number of seats (158 of 550) in parliament with 21 percent of the vote (compared to the True Path Party's 19 percent and the Motherland Party's 20 percent). Soon after Welfare came to power, its popular support rose to around 30 percent (Gülalp, 1999a, 36). Called upon to form a government, the

Welfare Party was unable to do so because the two leading center-right parties refused to join Welfare in a coalition government and thereby concede power to the Islamists. Yet, due in large part to the personal enmity between their leaders, Tansu Çiller and Mesut Yılmaz, the two parties were unable to agree to a coalition themselves.

Ultimately, in the summer of 1996, after shadowy negotiation with each party, Erbakan found himself prime minister in a coalition with Tansu Çiller of the True Path Party. This was remarkable, since for many years the True Path Party had represented itself as pro-Western, laicist, and a bulwark against Islamism. Çiller herself was the quintessential secularist Kemalist elite. A professional woman from a wealthy family, she had attended elite, English-language schools in Turkey and abroad, and had dedicated herself to state service. Her hair was blond and she often wore elegant trousered suits. During the campaign, Çiller had accused Erbakan and his followers of "dragging the country back to the Dark Ages." Çiller's "conversion" occasioned cynical appraisals by voters and media alike, who accused her of being more concerned with staying in power and covering up her alleged corruption schemes than with maintaining her much-flaunted principles. Indeed, in exchange for her support, Erbakan had agreed to shield her from parliamentary investigation for corruption. This state of affairs, popularly know as the *hacı-bacı* (haj pilgrim–elder sister) coalition, lasted until June 1997, when the military engineered what has become known as a "soft coup," edging Erbakan out of power without actually taking over the government itself. In the meantime, Welfare's star continued to rise: in the 1996 local elections, it carried 34 percent of the vote in forty-one districts.

The reasons for Welfare's success in these elections is multifold. Many Kemalists believed that Welfare's success was a result of three things: a protest vote against the corruption and incompetence of the other parties; the attraction of its religious message for rural people and *varoş* dwellers; and buying votes. Some complained that the Islamist foundations *(vakıflar)* "bought" votes through their community services, passing out food, coal, cheap school supplies, and clothing in needy neighborhoods, and by providing subsidized university dormitories to students who agreed to veil and live according to Islamic strictures. There they were indoctrinated, it was said, into radical fundamentalist Islamic ideology. Welfare was accused of receiving shady financing from abroad: Saudi Arabia, perhaps Iran.

Certainly the party received a great deal of financial support from Turkish residents in Europe. According to my own observations, however, the party's alleged wealth was not obvious in its municipal activities, with the exception that Welfare municipal offices had sophisticated computer and other electronic equipment and produced large quantities of slick, colorful reports, magazines, and other propaganda. Nor were foundation activities as extensive as assumed by Kemalists (and claimed in Islamist propaganda). Furthermore, the convention of buying votes and political support is standard in Turkish political life, evidenced by the common preelection distribution of deeds to illegal squatter property by politicians seeking reelection. In the 1980s, it was said that Motherland Party leader Turgut Özal distributed postdated checks to constituents, cashable only if his party won. The distribution of blankets, food, even small gold coins, and political favors of all kinds before elections is standard for all parties and could not in itself explain Welfare's success.

Religious radicalism was not the primary motivator in Welfare support. Forty-one percent of voters for Welfare identified themselves as laicist (Kentel, 1995). Polls show a distinct lack of popular support for a mix of religion and politics (Çarkoğlu and Toprak, 2000, 58), and voters have proven this by the fungibility of their votes, supporting left-of-center parties, then Welfare and Virtue, and more recently the right-wing Nationalist Action Party. The question of the party's religious appeal is complicated by the laic state's draconian campaign against the public invocation of Islamic symbols and activities. Wearing head scarves and beards in public institutions, such as schools, and by civil servants was banned; religious education undermined; religiously based political parties and politicians banned. The repression of religious expression occasioned great social upheaval, public demonstrations, and renewed political activism, particularly in the conservative sector of the population aspiring to education and economic upward mobility. Islamists in Ümraniye often railed against the head-scarf ban as an attempt to keep young Islamist women from getting an education and entering the professions. Issues of poverty and social class fueled what appeared on the surface to be a purely religious issue.

What accounted for Welfare's appeal to nonreligious voters? Since the 1991 elections, Welfare campaigns were designed by a professional marketing agency. They used commercial television, billboards, and other advertisements to change Islam's "dark" image of fierce-looking beards and veils by making it "ordinary." Welfare voters were shown in television advertisements as people of all ages and different walks of life. The advertisements avoided religious language and presented Welfare as a forward-looking party with a vision that encompassed all strata of society, regardless of their views about political Islam (Öncü, 1995, 60–62). This strategy continued during the 1995 parliamentary elections. Welfare advertisements showed pensioners, unveiled women, civil servants—"ordinary people"—and referred to issues like pensions, affordable housing, health care, and the environment. Religious themes and images were, for the most part, avoided. A 1997 billboard and posters tacked around the city featured a bright, clean-shaven young businessman in a suit pointing to the (Welfare-run) Istanbul municipality's website address. By then, the party had a track record on some of these issues (following upon Welfare's success in the 1996 local elections).

Even residents not supporting Welfare acknowledged the efforts of Recep Tayyip Erdoğan's Istanbul municipality to resurrect the feeble and rapidly declining "lungs" (as he called the green areas) of Istanbul. He directed the planting of hundreds of trees and went up against a wealthy holding company that intended to cut down a swath of forest to build a college campus and housing. He did not succeed in the latter, but won a great deal of sympathy and support from the general public. The various Welfare municipalities brought some order to municipal services and seemed, on the surface at least, to be less corrupt than previous administrations. Streets seemed cleaner, buses ran more often, and the garbage was picked up in a timely banner by big trucks that, at least in Ümraniye, had stenciled on the back the Islamic hadith[7] "Cleanliness is a part of faith" *(Temizlik imandan dır)*. Welfare also attracted widespread support among women, a phenomenon that will be dealt with in a later chapter.

In other words, Welfare appealed to different groups of people with a variety of aspirations and motivations, and was able to pull these diverse interests together and obscure differences within a populist image. The party's approach—a particular framework of structure, method, and message that will be discussed in detail in the following chapters—made this broad-based populism possible. Welfare (and, later, the Virtue Party) had a face-to-face, personalized political style that mobilized "cells" of neighbors through a system of associations, foundations, and informal organizations not formally connected to the party. People of different social status and with diverse interests in the same neighborhood interacted on a horizontal basis that obscured their differences within the personal matrix of network relations. That is, the political process took shape in the relations among activists, rather than in the relation between activists and party. Unlike other top-down, highly centralized parties that brought their projects to the voters for support, Welfare built on local solidarities and wedded local projects and sensibilities to the party's project. The involvement of local grassroots organizations and the mobilization of people on the basis of local solidarities (rather than simple party loyalty) lent flexibility and endurance to the Islamist political project, even in the face of the banning of Welfare in January 1998 and jailing of its politicians. This key element of Welfare's populism will be taken up in greater detail in chapter 6.

Vernacular politics was a political process that linked the Islamist social movement with the Welfare Party in such a way that activists ultimately were independent of the party, although party and movement reinforced and strengthened one another. That is, the relation between the Welfare Party and its supporters was not as patron to clients, but rather as mutually beneficial, but ultimately autonomous, forces, a nexus of network and institutional relations. This reliance on networks and horizontal relations differed from the political culture of other parties that, underneath their populist rhetoric, still relied heavily on patron-client ties. The Welfare experience also differed from previous expressions of Islam in politics in that it was not predicated on top-down manipulation of religious sentiment. That said, however, it is important to remember that the Welfare and Virtue Parties were themselves creatures of the Turkish political environment and, thus, shared its characteristics. Vernacular politics was an important part of Welfare and Virtue Party politics, but not the only part.

Vernacular politics may be the key to Welfare's populism, endurance, and flexibility, but the weakness and venality of the other parties amplified its appeal. The Welfare Party profited from widespread disenchantment with other parties that were increasingly sinking in a slime of corruption, kleptocracy, interpersonal feuds, and ineffectualness. Prime Minister Tansu Çiller faced serious corruption charges involving tax evasion and extensive investments in the United States. Political parties (including Welfare) stood by as journalists and professors were jailed for their writings or views. Relations were uncovered between the government and shadowy criminals tied to assassinations, gunrunning, and drugs in what has come to be known as the "deep state." In a national poll, 67 percent of the electorate admitted to being often or always angered by the economic situation, and 65 percent by the political situation (Çarkoğlu and Toprak, 2000, 36). At the municipal level, politicians were accused of hiring relatives and misusing funds. Erbakan, too, came under fire for having a hoard of gold in his possession that he claimed to have purchased from his earnings as a teacher. Another Welfare official was accused of embezzling funds that had been collected for relief aid in Bosnia. Nevertheless, corruption accusations against Welfare paled compared to the thick sludge of gunrunning, assassinations, unaccounted funds, and self-enrichment that clung to several other parties in power.

The political spectrum was splintered into parties representing the right and the left, although there was little difference in their platforms. Instead of focusing on their campaign promises, parties in power engaged in virulent ad hominem power struggles. The spread of electricity and television in the 1980s into every village and almost every home brought citizens nose-to-nose with their politicians. After watching a shouting match in parliament on the afternoon news one day in Ümraniye, Füsün turned to me disgustedly and exclaimed, "These are the politicians we elected?" By comparison, the Welfare Party seemed fresh and untainted, if largely untested.

Welfare's Populism and the Decline of the Left

The party also had the advantage of a strong ideological message that appealed across class, ethnic, and gender divides. In previous decades, the Turkish left had carried the banner of ideological resistance to economic injustice. But the left had fallen victim to a double knockout punch: the postcoup military crackdown and the global decline of socialism. Both left- and right-of-center parties abandoned the terrain of economic justice for more global issues. Islamist institutions and party platforms took over the role of the left as champions of economic justice, although the Islamist conception differed quite substantially from the class-based ideas of the left. Islamists also came up with controversial new designs for dealing with Turkey's ethnic multiculturalism. Below, I will discuss the development of an Islamist position on economic issues and the relation of Islamists to the Turkish left.

Over the previous three decades, positions on the economy by Islamist parties changed along with their constituencies and transformations in the economy itself. Despite Erbakan's conservatism, the Welfare Party's platform in the 1980s differed substantially from those of its Islamist predecessors. Instead of state initiative, Welfare supported private initiative. Where the National Salvation Party wanted to protect the domestic market, Welfare sought to open it to the international market. In 1993, Erbakan set out the goals of what he called a "just economic order." This loosely worked-out vision of a utopian society included the positive and excluded the negative aspects of capitalism and communism—thus, Erbakan claimed, surpassing both. "It is against interest but not profit, against monopoly but not free competition, against central planning but not state regulation" (Gülalp, 1999a, 27). Welfare's economic model was one of competitive capitalism with minimal state intervention, but also incorporated an ethical stance. Like the National Salvation Party, Welfare was concerned to protect small businesses from unfair competition and from tax and lending structures stacked in favor of big business. Both were opposed to the self-interested materialism of capitalism (by which was meant monopolistic big business: multinational corporations and large, government-supported industrial enterprises).

The economy that was envisaged was based on "relational capital," that is, investment funds secured by mutual trust, rather than formal regulation (Buğra, 1999, 27). This model was put into practice by, among others, the large, self-consciously Islamist enterprise group Kombassan Holding. The head of Kombassan claimed, for instance, that no shareholder had invested more than $100 in the company.[8] Many Kombassan shareholders were Turkish workers in Germany. The company's holdings were almost entirely in cash. In this way, millions of dollars of capital were accumulated through personal, informal relations within Islamic networks. Similarly, formal labor-market regulations were to be discouraged in favor of Islam-prescribed relations of cooperation, solidarity, and mutual trust between workers and employers.[9]

What ultimately differentiated Welfare from other parties, however, was its emergence as the visible tip of a populist iceberg, a movement that appealed to different orders of people, across class and ethnic lines. The notion of a "just economic order" appealed to the working class and to marginal people in the squatter areas, as well as to small businessmen and entrepreneurs. Although other parties continued to represent themselves as populist, in the reshuffling of economic priorities during the 1980s they had lost either the ability to deliver egalitarian programs or interest in the paternalistic *himaye* support and protection of the masses.

The opening of the Turkish economy to the world market in the 1980s, and the state's abandonment of its previous role as guarantor of economic security through a controlled economy, created enormous economic dislocations and visibly exacerbated differences between rich and poor. The government began to privatize industry and dismantle the already threadbare social safety net. Despite improvement in the economy, unemployment and income differentials increased. Yet discussion of poverty, inequality, and injustice in politics and the media fell out of fashion, replaced by a focus on identity issues. Politicians enthused about progress and "leaping to a new age." The media and politicians dwelt admiringly on Turkey's transformation into a fully developed Western country. Istanbul, with its high-rises, Yuppies, and night-life, was touted as not being much different from New York or any major Western metropolis. (This view was later challenged by elite Islamists with their own non-Western version of a developed identity.) The segment of the population left behind by the economic transformation, and not interested in this kind of social transformation, found a voice in the Welfare Party, which emphasized issues like social justice, unemployment, poverty, and social security, while respecting the more conservative lifestyle of the masses.

The liberal economy of the 1980s and 1990s was not accompanied by political liberalism. In the 1980s, the Özal government made some concessions to various special interest groups in an attempt to integrate (and co-opt) them. The sale of alcohol in cafes was banned to appease Islamists. The ban on speaking Kurdish in public and recording songs in Kurdish was lifted; Özal spoke openly about his Kurdish grandmother. However, the economic needs and the political demands of these groups and of the masses generally were left unaddressed. Civil rights came under continual pressure as journalists and writers were jailed for discussing Kurdish demands for social rights. Public discussion of the violent conflict between Kurdish separatists (The Workers' Party of Kurdistan, known by its Kurdish acronym, PKK) and the military in eastern Turkey in any but government-approved terms could lead to arrest and imprisonment. State limits on freedom of expression reached an absurd pitch in

1999, when the Ministry of the Interior issued a list of terms that could not be used in the media, and suggested alternatives. For instance, the "objectionable" terms "rebellion," "Kurdish rebellion," "Kurdish uprising," "armed uprising" and "insurgency" were to be replaced by "terrorist activities."

Repression of Islamists intensified with the expulsion of Islamist officers from the army in December 1996, and the banning of the Welfare Party in 1998. In April 1999, the Constitutional Court opened a case against the Virtue Party on charges of anti-laic activities. Along with journalists, politicians, too, were prosecuted for thought crimes. Both Erbakan and Erdoğan were charged and jailed for the content of speeches they gave. In general, the resentment and discontent occasioned by the lack of economic security and civil rights had no effective vehicle through which to be expressed and affect government policies. In this climate, Islamist ideas about social justice and decentralization of state power proved attractive.

The Welfare Party platform was influenced by the new generation of Islamist intellectuals. Their ideas attracted members of the professional middle class, students, and intellectuals who were questioning Kemalism, nationalism, and even the modern, centralized nation-state, which some saw as totalitarian. Islamist intellectuals were writing in the context of a global rethinking of the basic tenets of the Enlightenment: rationalism, universalism, modernity, and the inevitability of human progress along a normative trajectory set by the West. This gave impetus and credence to attempts to develop models for a non-Western political order the principles of which were based on Islamic philosophy, rather than secular rationalism. Many Islamist intellectuals had graduated from secular universities and buttressed their radical ideas with references to such thinkers as Antonio Gramsci, Fernand Braudel, Immanuel Wallerstein, and Henry David Thoreau.

One much-discussed proposal was that of a "confederation of faiths" under which each community would be governed by its own belief system and by legal systems derived from it. Modeled on the Ottoman *millet* system, it was part of a still-developing set of ideas called neo-Ottomanism. The state's role in the confederation would be to guarantee each community's autonomy. This system was proposed as a multiculturalist alternative to hierarchical and bureaucratic Western political models (Gülalp, 1999a, 28). Kurds were attracted to this model as well and by the party's openness to ethnic diversity.

A number of prominent leftist intellectuals turned to Islam. One of the best known was Ismet Özel, who was a fiery left-wing poet in the 1960s. In the 1970s, believing the ideological alternatives of the 1960s and 1970s to have come to a dead end, he began in his writings to mine Islamic tradition for a response to contemporary problems by developing a morally grounded Islamic way of life (Meeker, 1994, 211–12). In the leftist magazine *Express,* several leftist journalists "outed" themselves as Welfare supporters. One of these, Sinan Hıncal, explained that, to him, Welfare was the only democracy movement in the political center:

> It knows how to give a voice to the poor. It knows how to carry its movement to the elites. . . . It knows how to carry its movement to the . . . side of Kurdish people. . . . And perhaps most importantly, Welfare knows to make central that Turkey's problems are systemic problems (Hıncal, 1994, 7).

When challenged by those who accused Welfare of hiding its true aim of imposing an Islamic state, Hıncal admitted that doubtless Welfare had "many faces," but that he believed the sort of "hoodlums" responsible for the fire in Sivas had no understanding of Islam as a belief system and were a decided minority. In a final soul-searching, he wrote,

> I'm not exaggerating the importance of a "democracy movement in the center." I'm all for giving it the importance it deserves. But maybe I'm exaggerating Welfare a little. We'll see [Ibid.].

Following his article, on the same page, was a response by a fellow journalist entitled, "It would be better if I threw my vote into the sea . . . " In fact, the left had lost so much ground that in the 1994 and 1995 elections left-of-center parties declined almost out of sight. In calling for economic justice, Welfare took over the role of the social democrats as representative of those who sit below the salt in the economy.

The ideological leap from the left to the chameleonlike left-right-center of the Welfare Party also was undertaken by small businessmen and local activists, who sought freedom to express a religious lifestyle in the political arena. Some, like Ahmet Akkaya,[10] managing director of the Ümraniye Service Foundation, moved from left to right without changing their basic ideological orientation. Mr. Akkaya was a dapper man with a round Islamic beard, passionate about his beliefs. He had once belonged to the Party of the Revolutionary Left *(Dev Sol Partisi)*, a party he described as "socialist." By the mid-1990s, he had become an active Welfare Party member and directed an Islamic foundation that worked in tandem with Welfare municipal officials in Ümraniye, assisting the poor.

> Now, being a member of a socialist party, then becoming a Welfare Party member seems interesting to many people, but if you research socialism, you'll see that in Islam's principles, its main principles, you won't find any aspect that is contradictory. . . . Socialism, in short, is economic freedom, a just sharing, human rights, democracy. . . . Not one of these concepts is contrary to Islam, that is, to an Islamic lifestyle. But there is one single point on which they differ. It's not possible to be politically active in a [socialist] party while you are living your Islam. I remember very well that when it was rumored that one of our [Republican People's Party] members of parliament had gone on the pilgrimage [to Mecca], party members went on and on denying it.

Mr. Akkaya's newfound party allegiance, however, was clearly instrumental.

> The Welfare Party's mission is Islam? No! I am in the Welfare Party because [it] is the only party in which you can live an Islamic lifestyle and do politics at the same time. Now, I'm a member of the Welfare Party; I wasn't born into the Welfare Party; I didn't grow up with it. If the Welfare Party is no longer a party in which I can act and live on the basis of my ideas, then I'll leave it. We're not bound to anything; if I can't live my beliefs in any party, I'll leave politics.

The appeal of Islam in the 1980s was not only a result of the fading international profile and ideological exhaustion of the left and its distance from the more conservative and religiously inspired lifestyles of much of the population, but also of the military's repression. In a 1997 interview with the author, a Republican People's Party official heatedly decried the government's oppression of the left and kid-gloves approach to the Islamists.

> After the 1980 coup, a scythe cut across the leftist movement, across leftist organizations, even social democratic

parties like the Republican People's Party. With their arrogance from above [the rulers] silenced the left in Turkey and freed the religionists *(dinciler)*. And now those religionists have managed to pull the saddle out from under us. . . .

Even if Welfare isn't in power right now . . . it doesn't mean we've left all this behind us, that the Turkish Republic has been saved from the threat of political Islam or a yearning for a *sharia* state. In a country like Turkey that widely experiences such injustice, poverty, and inequality, people, the folk, the population seek a way out, because they're tired of being pressured in the mangle of life. Not being able to bring home bread, remaining unemployed, not being able to educate their children . . . to take advantage of health facilities—they want to be saved from all this. They'll turn to any party that seems to them different, convincing, that seems as if it will save them from the conditions they live their lives under. . . . This is one of the reasons why Welfare has become so popular. . . .

To save itself from this political organization that is threatening its own state and its own regime, it is not enough for [the government] to use political means or to lock Welfare headquarters and throw away the key. What has to happen is at the very foundation. Among the things that have to change, for one thing, it is necessary to bring an end to this injustice and poverty. It is necessary for people to be able to feel a little confidence that they'll be able to provide the basic needs of life.

Despite evident anger at "religionists," the politician admitted that Welfare addressed issues of importance to voters: the need for political change to deal with the enormous numbers living under the poverty line, reducing inflation and unemployment, rebuilding faith in the state and judicial system, and saving the educational system from its crisis.

The movement away from the left, unable to bring new ideas to the table, continued through the 1999 elections. That election saw the Republican People's Party, the party founded by Ataturk himself, unable for the first time in the history of the Republic to garner enough votes to be represented in parliament. Support for the center-right parties also slipped, from almost 50 percent in the mid-1990s to 20 percent in 1999.

Old Problems, New Actors

The political and ideological space between Islamic groups and Kemalist laicists is occupied by a large number of intermediate groups, ranging from radical to conservative to liberal in their beliefs, and from confrontational to pragmatic in political style. Thus, any discussion of an Islamist movement must acknowledge the sheer variety of positions and motivations inherent in this heterogeneity.

Islam is an important element of Turkish social and political life. Islamic affiliations are intertwined not only with various political positions and parties, but also with national and international financial and political interests. Since the 1980s, there has been an extraordinary increase in political activism centered on Islamic principles and lifestyle. It has drawn new social groups into the political process across class and ethnic lines, including large numbers of working-class women. In other words, despite the diversity of Islamist institutions and organizational styles, a discernible social movement has arisen, with new actors mobilizing around issues and desiring reforms. The Islamist movement has benefitted from the decline of the left and has taken over, although in different form, some of the issues the left had championed.

In other ways, contemporary Istanbul repeats the patterns of early Republican days. Economic circumstances are favorable to some, nearly unmanageable for others. The customs and mores of the *varoş* are kept at a distance by the Kemalist elite, especially those categorized as Islamic values. But the "bell jar" is irretrievably cracked. Customs and ideas seep from one side to the other. Power is slowly settling into new configurations, despite continual efforts by the military and the government to shore up familiar channels. Simple dichotomies are breaking down as the new landscape of power and status takes shape; new fractures beset this still-heaving political ground. When Kemalists support Welfare, when leftists become Islamists, when Islamists are Yuppies, environmentalists, and secularists, the ground slips away from any simple division of society into Kemalist secularists and Islamist radicals. Other divisions remain, or take up residence in new terrain: rich and poor; sectarian and racialist; moderate and pragmatic versus confrontational styles of doing politics; and generational differences.

4

GENERATION X AND THE
VIRTUE PARTY

While Istanbul's population is pulled toward opposite political and social poles, boundaries blur between the lifestyles, beliefs, interests, goals, and fashions that are meant to represent these poles. Differences in Islamist religious beliefs, political styles, and relations to supporters and to institutions are given a further twist by generational differences. Within the Virtue and Welfare Parties, power struggles over the direction of the party were played out between younger Islamists committed to a populist, integrationist style, with a power base in urban networks, and older leaders whose political style fit within the rigidly centralized, authoritarian, top-down political mold of Turkish political culture. The younger, populist leaders were better able than old-style politicians to dissemble social-class differences within the movement, in part through the inclusiveness of vernacular politics and in part by contrasting their populism with the class arrogance attributed to centrist parties.

The Welfare Party was a political party defined by its relation to Islam. Its successor, the Virtue Party, represented itself as a Muslim party defined by its relation to politics. These differing aims and constituencies were already apparent within the Welfare Party. Erbakan himself was a pragmatist, moving from more radical preelection rhetoric about changing the system (to a "Just Order") to moderation and

*Member of the Virtue Party's Youth Commission greeting
Mayor Recep Tayyip Erdoğan at a rally.*

compromise once he was in power. Erbakan's main constituency, inherited from National Salvation Party days, was made up of conservative followers of religious orders and provincial conservatives, although these had been to some extent co-opted by Özal's Motherland Party.

The Islamist Generation X, on the contrary, was invested in current political issues, not loyalty to regional patrons or religious brotherhoods. Many were urban youth in their twenties and thirties, educated in shabby secular institutions or theological (*imam-hatip*) schools, desiring upward mobility and economic security, but with few opportunities to participate in the global economy and booming service sector. They were open to new ideas and models of society that would incorporate these aspirations, while retaining an Islamic lifestyle and moral values. Some of the youngest Islamist activists were among the most radical, in the sense of desiring systemic change. A survey found that 45 percent of those who would support an Islamic government were between the ages of fourteen and thirty. By contrast, support for social democratic parties came primarily from voters between the ages of thirty-five and forty-five (Gülalp,

1999a, 35). In other words, while an older generation dissatisfied with the system looked to a social democratic model, Generation X had a great deal more tolerance for a radical Islamist solution. This was particularly true of those locked into an economically disadvantaged class, who were receptive to ideas about social equity, but sensitive to expressions of hierarchy on the part of the messenger. A decentralized, horizontal approach, neighbor to neighbor, held greater appeal than the top-down hierarchies of the political status quo.

Erbakan's preelection speeches were notoriously tailored to suit different audiences, but often contained radical promises and suggestions. His repertoire ranged from bread-and-butter issues like pensions and housing, to support for Kurdish linguistic and cultural rights and environmentalism, to plans to ban the charging of interest and replace the Turkish lira with an Islamic dinar. His proposal for a "Just Economic Order" called for the elimination of social inequality and corruption, state withdrawal from economic activities, and the promotion of individual small enterprise. He pledged to withdraw Turkey from NATO and the European Union's Customs Union agreement signed in 1996, in favor of political and economic alliances with other Muslim countries. He planned to cultivate a brotherhood of Muslims around the world, thus replacing Turkey's ties with and reliance on the West. He railed against the new military cooperation agreement with Israel. Much of this was a kind of knee-jerk religious radicalism and populist pandering that had little in common with the more sophisticated critiques of the social and political order by Islamist intellectuals which informed the radicalism of the party's younger members.

After he became prime minister, Erbakan tried to implement some of these ideas. At an assembly of diplomats, he praised the Iranian revolution. In February 1996, he dined with Louis Farrakhan, the American Nation of Islam leader who had been visiting Muslim countries, including Iraq and Libya. But he was soon slapped in the face by the reality of unbrotherly relations in the Middle East. On a state visit to Libya, its leader, Muammar el-Qaddafi—in front of the joint Libyan and Turkish press—lambasted Turkey for its foreign policy, which he said was "wrong from A to Z," and criticized Turkey for its treatment of the Kurds, suggesting that a "Kurdish nation" should be established. Erbakan slunk back to Ankara and was almost thrown out of office by an outraged parliament. He eventually broadened Turkey's agreements with Israel, thus further alienating the Arab states. Turkey's control of the water on the Tigris and Euphrates Rivers through its massive South Anatolia Project of over twenty dams had already strained relations with downstream Iraq and Syria. Although stillborn, the project of Muslim brotherhood had made for good radical election propaganda, but also stirred up fear and anti-Islamist activity among secularists.

On other issues, Erbakan's vision was informed by Islamist intellectual currents. In a neo-Ottomanist version of the Ottoman *millet* system, he envisaged a decentralized, pluralist political system of "multiple legal orders" under which each community of believers could live under laws corresponding to its beliefs. In other words, "pluralism" would respect the rights of both majority and minorities by replacing "democracy," which Islamists have tended to define as the rule of the majority over the minority (Gülalp, 1999b, 39). Given the diversity and shifting nature of beliefs and lifestyles and the overlapping of identities in Turkey, the drawbacks of such a system are immediately obvious. Who is to determine a person's "identity" or those of the separate "communities" and the laws that should govern them? Where would a nonreligious identity reside?

In practice, however, once in power Erbakan was a pragmatist who moderated the party's platform, worked within the system, and tried to keep the more radical members of his party in check. Indeed, at a party convention in 1996, at the height of his participation in government, he stood before a Turkish flag and a portrait of Ataturk and claimed that if Ataturk were alive today, he would be a member of the Welfare Party. The Islamist daily newspaper *Yeni Şafak* grumbled that the Welfare Party's new image was nothing more than an Islamic version of Kemalism (Gülalp, 1999a, 38).

Despite Erbakan's pragmatism, the Welfare Party was closed down in 1998 for allegedly threatening the laicist nature of the state. It was replaced almost immediately by the Virtue Party, which had been founded preemptively in preparation for a negative outcome in the Constitutional Court case against Welfare. The case against the party was a litany of questionable accusations and anti-Islamist innuendo. Many of the activities of which they were accused were not illegal in any strict sense of the word; others were unproven (for instance, that the Welfare Party collaborated with leftist groups and foreign terrorist organizations seeking to overthrow the Turkish state by exploiting fundamentalism). They included such things as the Welfare–True Path coalition government's decision to readjust working hours to suit the breaking of the fast during the holy month of Ramazan; the decision of the Ministry of Education to increase the number of *imam-hatip* high schools (theological schools that train Islamic preachers and that had developed into a parallel school system); and a fundraising film in which Erbakan called for donations to the Islamist television station Kanal 7 for the sake of a jihad (holy war or endeavor):

> A state cannot be founded without a TV. It is difficult to operate a state without TV. . . . It is not possible to wage the jihad without a TV. You can describe the TV as an air force or if you like as a tank force. . . . This is the meaning of the money you will give for Kanal 7. (Erbakan, quoted in *Turkish Daily News,* October 24, 1997, A5)

Welfare Party officials explained that jihad also meant a struggle for good and justice, but the overtones of militant Islamism were difficult to explain away, given Erbakan's fiery speeches in other fora.

The actions of more confrontational radicals in the party who had slipped Erbakan's leash gave the government grist for its anti-Islamist mill. Since Özal opened the political door to Islamists in the 1980s, radicals had infiltrated ministries and state bureaucracies. For instance, Welfare Party radicals within the system tried to move hundreds of secular-minded judges to posts in rural districts and replace them with Islamist judges who would stretch the interpretation of Turkey's secular legal code, especially in the area of family law. This prompted a public outcry and the move was blocked by a government supervisory council. In order to fill civil service positions with likeminded activists, radicals shifted non-Islamist civil servants (who cannot be fired) to unpleasant, absurd, and even dangerous jobs in an attempt to induce them to take early retirement. Some unfortunate civil servants were sent to stand all day in the middle of traffic at busy intersections, choking on fumes, to count cars. The press kept a watchful eye on the party's actions, and civic organizations and the public were quick to mobilize and demonstrate their displeasure. Many of the party radicals' more egregious attempts at undermining the political and cultural dominance of secularism were ultimately unsuccessful, but the pressure for systemic change remained strong.

The eye of the press was less focused on working-class areas like Ümraniye, and public pressure less effective there at blocking the actions of the more authoritarian and intolerant elements of the party. For instance, after winning local elections, Welfare Party activists closed some community libraries and educational centers for women by withdrawing municipal funds and rooms, often replacing them with Quran courses. Where the Welfare Party did not hold the purse strings, as in the case of private foundations and organizations, activists tried harassment. Clumps of veiled women sat all day in the halls and public rooms of women's occupational training centers or libraries, praying loudly, so that none of the usual activities could be carried out and participants were intimidated into staying away. Eventually, the organization would close or move to a new location.

However, the activities of Welfare Party mayors in other municipalities came under intense scrutiny. Early in 1997, the mayor of the small town of Sincan just outside Ankara came under fire for hosting the Iranian ambassador, who gave a speech in which he called for an Islamic state. (The military responded by "just coincidentally" directing a column of tanks through the town.) The mayor of a southern city was discovered to have three wives. (Polygyny is illegal, but the law can be bypassed if the other wives are married only in religious, rather than the required civil, ceremonies.)

Any comment or action that could have been interpreted as anti-laicist or critical of the government or the military was used against the party. The more radical and confrontational elements in the Islamist movement and the Welfare Party gave the court some ammunition and heightened public anxiety. However, judging by the tone of the chief prosecutor's hostile public pronouncements, the outcome was clear from the outset. The party would be closed, regardless. Although, in his indictment of the Welfare Party presented to the Constitutional Court, chief prosecuter Vural Savaş asserted that laicism was a legal, rather than a religious, term, his definition blurred the lines between law, religion, and society. The separation of the affairs of religion from the affairs of the world, he wrote, means more than just separating religious and worldly authority in the state, but "at the same time, the separation of fronts like social life, family, economy, law, rules about good manners, clothing, and so on, from religious rules" (Savaş, 1997, 14, author's translation). In the end, the Welfare Party was banned not because it violated the Constitution, but because it was "against the essence of the Constitution." Necmettin Erbakan was banned from political activity for five years.

The Welfare Party's experience of persecution pushed the Virtue Party's platform and rhetoric decidedly in the direction of championing democracy and human rights, political freedom, and pluralism.

The Virtue Party presented itself as a moderate, modern meritocracy, as populist, environmentalist, and open to women and minorities in its organizational echelons. Kemalists, however, were cynical about the party's sudden discovery of democratic principles and saw it as self-serving, given the party's precarious legal state. It was also perceived to be yet another example of *takkiye*, of hiding one's true nature and purpose in the interest of survival and achieving one's ultimate goal, in this case presumably to remake the Turkish state into a religious one.

Changing of the Guard: Virtue and the New Generation

In the Welfare Party, Erbakan attempted to control the tension between moderates and radicals by keeping the radicals in check. At the 1969 party convention, when a group of delegates began chanting "God is great!"—the slogan of militant Islam—Erbakan stopped speaking, looked sternly in their direction, and warned, "Do not let yourselves be provoked." There were no further disruptions. The reins slipped from his hands, however, when the Welfare Party was closed down and he was banned from politics. Although he continued to try to run the new Virtue Party from behind the scenes through the mild-mannered, grandfatherly, figurehead party leader, Recai Kutan, power moved inexorably into the hands of younger, populist, charismatic leaders like Istanbul mayor Recep Tayyip Erdoğan.

Erdoğan appealed to the new Islamist constituencies: young, middle-class professionals (Islamic Yuppies), students, and intellectuals who were radical in their ideas but moderate in approach. Erdoğan's populism bridged the gaps between conservative religious culture, the rising aspirations of disenfranchised youth, and the new ideas and ideologies of educated Islamists. He led a group within the Virtue Party that called itself the *Değişimciler* (those for change) or, simply, "the Young Ones."[1] Although he entertained Islamist ideas, he pulled the party further away from religion and toward politics as its engine.

Recep Tayyip Erdoğan was the rock star of Turkish politics. A former soccer player, university graduate, and married father of four, he attracted crowds of starstruck young people wherever he went. Receding chestnut hair, a slightly pudgy face, and prominent brown eyes gave him a permanently quizzical look that softened the edges of his urbane, professional manner. He tended to unassuming suits or polo shirts in his public appearances. His relaxed, patient manner put people at ease.

Born in 1954 in Istanbul's Beyoğlu district, he attended a theological (*imam-hatip*) school and then studied at Marmara University, where he earned a degree in accounting and management. He worked as a private-sector consultant and manager, and for sixteen years played soccer with local teams. He became interested in politics at an early age, winning his first election at age twenty-one as head of the National Salvation Party's Beyoğlu youth branch. The following year, he moved up to head the Istanbul province youth branch, then won a spot on the national youth branch General Management Committee. In 1984, he became head of the Welfare Party's Beyoğlu branch, then of Istanbul province, and in 1985 entered the party's inner management circles. In 1994, he was elected mayor of the city of Istanbul.

Where Erbakan was perceived as the patriarchal leader, Erdoğan was the guy next door. "He's just like us," was the common addendum to a description of the mayor. Sightings were reported in local barbershops, restaurants, and streets. "He lives just like us, not in a fancy government-supplied house." Where a politician of the old school, like Erbakan or Demirel, acted as *baba,* pater familias to the nation, Erdoğan was the neighbor. Where Erbakan exhorted voters to support and help the party, Erdoğan encouraged them to *be* a certain way, and then, as good Muslims, good neighbors, to help the party. Erdoğan's populist style moved the party away from the clientilistic politics of previous parties and the reliance on hierarchical ties of obligation between voters and brotherhood sheikhs, landlords, and political overlords. Instead, he embraced a culturally embedded network politics, that is, a vernacular politics that mobilized nonhierarchical horizontal ties among neighbors and relied on civil society for its organizational motor. Clientilism remained intact in the Virtue Party, as in all Turkish parties, since the principles of *himaye* (responsibility for and protection of weaker members of one's entourage), reciprocity, mutual obligation, and the return of favors were powerful mediators of interpersonal relations at all levels of society. Nevertheless, the Virtue Party's mobilization of horizontal networks on the basis of *imece* (mutual assistance among community members) was an important element in its appeal and will be taken up in a later chapter.

Erdoğan's actions were guided by firm Islamic beliefs and a pragmatic, seat-of-the-pants management style, with little recourse to religious dogma. One leftist journalist who knew Erdoğan personally admired him because he was known to hire people who knew their jobs well, in a kind of expert technocracy, rather than following the usual practice of repaying debts by placing cronies in top positions. "He's not an intellectual; he hasn't read all the literature on democracy, but he is *learning* to be democratic. He learns fast. He does the right things. . . . His yeast is very clean [*Mayası çok temiz*]." In fact, despite his support for some of the more radical ideas of the new Islamist intellectuals, in my conversations with Erdoğan he came across as a moderate politician more interested in making the system work justly for all its constituents than in overthrowing it.[2] "In terms of people management," he told me, " the management of the country is not in the hands of the best person for the job. Rather, the parties decide who will be at the head. We won't do this anymore. The system has degenerated. We want a humane system, with true roots. The state is not a chieftain; it is a servant to the nation."

This did not mean he was uninterested in systemic change. For instance, he said he favored a secular system "like the American system" instead of Kemalist laicism. Kemalism, he argued, was a form of religion. Secularism, on the other hand, would give people the freedom to found an Islamic university—or wear a head scarf in parliament. He expressed moderate views on a variety of issues ranging from women working outside the home (which he supported) to Islamic *sharia* law (which he believed to be merely a metaphor for a just society). He had no interest, he insisted, in changing Turkey's laws, just in making sure that the laws already on the books were actually enforced. He seemed to have little patience for the extreme radicalism of *sharia* legalists and those who wanted to paint curbstones green or close down the Istanbul ballet as obscene. "There are four kinds of *sharia*. There is the definition of *sharia* you find in the dictionary—*sharia* as a kind of order [*düzen*]. This could apply to all countries. Then there is *sharia* as law. The only country in the world today that is governed by *sharia* is Israel. Not Iran—Iranian Islam is more of a bureaucracy and very different. We don't envision anything like that. Thirdly, there is *sharia* as a person applies it to his or her own life and defines it for himself or herself. And fourthly, sharia is a metaphor" for a just society, for peace of mind and freedom from anxiety (*huzur*).

Beneath Erdoğan's soft-stepping populism was an agenda and an iron will to implement it. This was demonstrated quite clearly on the evening of October 10, 1997, when he was a live guest on the popular political interview program *Minefield,* on Kanal 7, the Islamist television station. For days, billboards around Istanbul had carried an announcement of "a conversation with the mayor" and listed the telephone number residents could call to ask questions about Istanbul's problems. Invited to observe, I arrived several hours ahead of time. The station studio was a two-building complex high on a hill in a middle-class neighborhood on the European side. One building was an old house, barely recognizable as such under the structural accretions, including a small, glassed-in cafeteria where male staff gathered to watch the programs. Someone remarked that the building used to be a church, although I could see no signs of that. Across the narrow street, another building housed the makeup room, control center, and set.

The urbane, unflappable station director, Mustafa Çelik, the two anchors, and a technician gathered to discuss strategy for the show. The technician was a slim young woman with sharply angled features and short hair, wearing jeans and a scruffy, loose turtleneck. The two *Minefield* anchors were Davut Dursun, a pale, sandy-haired man with a nervous manner, and Ayşe Önal, a fiery, dark-haired, left-wing journalist. Önal had been blacklisted by the mainstream press under government pressure for her writings on government corruption. Unable to work as a journalist, Önal was hired by Kanal 7 to host the controversial *Minefield* program. Despite her radical past and leftist views, the Islamist station had given her a great deal of freedom in choosing guests for the show and leeway in the questions she asked them. This (and a well-researched news and interview show hosted by Ahmet Hakan Coşkun) was one reason for Kanal 7's popularity, even among Kemalists who would excoriate the station in public as a pawn of the Welfare Party, but avidly watch the news and interview shows in private.

Because Kanal 7 had been accused of being the mouthpiece of the Welfare Party and accepting financing from the party, the station was particularly sensitive about appearing to be simply promoting the mayor. The director wanted the station to be seen as supportive of political Islam, but also independent of the party. For this reason, the show with the mayor had to be carefully planned. Station staff had shot three videos of interviews with the "man in the street." We watched the first tape. It consisted entirely of people praising the mayor. After some struggle with the director, it was cut out entirely.

On the next tape, the people seemed to have been asked to evaluate the mayor's work, but again the result was one-sided praise, so Önal asked for the tape to be cut. On the third tape, people talked about Istanbul's problems, mostly about traffic and the environment. Önal was exasperated. Again, the praise was overwhelming, and everyone started their statement with "Dear Mister Mayor," clearly coached by the television crew. A fourth tape summarizing his accomplishments had been submitted by Erdoğan himself. There was no argument about leaving that tape out. In the end, it was decided to use clips from tapes two and three and to try to balance the comments so that they did not look too sycophantic.

Although the show, scheduled for two hours, was meant to be a call-in interview, the mayor had requested twenty minutes to make a presentation. No one believed it would be only twenty minutes long, and the two anchors discussed how to keep the mayor from running away with the show. As it turned out, the anchors barely got a word in before Erdoğan said he wanted to make a statement—and proceeded to give a highly political speech for one-and-a-half hours. He spoke at length about the lack of true democracy in Turkey and his vision for Turkish society. He also defended Kanal 7 and denied reports that it was financially linked to his party. He then took another hour or so to coach a thirteen-member "team" of dark-suited, bearded officials, each responsible for a different facet of the administration of the city, in reciting their lines about progress made under his administration. The anchors managed to get in a few faxed-in questions, which Erdoğan promptly used as springboards for his own message. The anchors even had trouble getting him to stop talking long enough to run commercials. The first live call-in questions were taken after one in the morning, and the show stumbled to a close around 2:30 A.M., several hours later than planned. The mayor had been an irresistible force.

After Erdoğan left, the staff and several visitors met in the manager's office over a 4 A.M. breakfast of tomatoes, cucumbers, bread, cheese, olives, and tea to rehash the evening and to discuss Kanal 7's programming. At issue was the station's image as an organ of the Welfare Party, decidedly underscored by that evening's events and the appearance on past interview shows of a number of controversial figures. An Islamist intellectual visiting the station told those assembled that they were treading very near the edge. He warned that if they went beyond a certain line, they could be prosecuted, adding,

"We are now at that line." The press syndicates, he pointed out, were hounding Kanal 7; there was a concerted campaign against it because Kanal 7 was seen as an official organ of the Welfare Party, which was also under attack. A staff member demurred, arguing that while Kanal 7 was philosophically Islamist, it was politically independent. At this, Önal turned to the director and quipped slyly, "Is that why you wouldn't let me do the show on Alevis?"[3] The director looked nonplussed. "Did we do that?" Yes, she reminded him. Someone else broke in, truculently, "What difference does it make who we put on? We're independent. The other stations do it." Önal and the Islamist visitor tried to convince him that it did indeed matter, Önal stating, "It makes a difference because we're under attack and walking a fine line." There was a contemplative pause as those present gloomily drew on their cigarettes or chewed on cucumber slices. Finally, the director broke the silence and asked plaintively, "If we do the Alevi show, will that fix things?" The room broke out in laughter at the absurdity of the proposed Band-Aid, given the magnitude of the danger.

Erbakan, too, was a strong politician, tempered by decades at the political helm, but he approached leadership without Erdoğan's velvet populist glove and image of the can-do politician busy with his team of experts adjusting the nuts and bolts of city life. Erbakan's old-fashioned style of elite leadership contrasted starkly with Erdoğan's populism and the image among his constituents that he was and lived "just like us." Unlike Erdoğan's "everyman" image, Erbakan increasingly gained a reputation as an elite politico.

Erbakan was born in 1926, on the third anniversary of the founding of the new Republic. His family wandered Anatolia's cities, wherever his father's duties as a judge took him. These duties undoubtedly extended to enforcing Ataturk's draconian changes in those early years of the Republic. Erbakan himself was sent to secular Republican schools. There were no Quran courses in those days, and the one hour per week lesson in religion added to the grade school curriculum in 1927 was removed again in 1930. According to a somewhat tongue-in-cheek 1994 biography, the young Erbakan loved the cinema, especially Laurel and Hardy movies and *Frankenstein* (Yalçın, 1994, 16).

Erbakan studied engineering at Istanbul Technical University. In his graduation yearbook, his friends described him as "devout, religious and industrious. He occupies half his life with prayer, the other half with projects" (17). One of these classmates was Süleyman

Demirel, later to become president. Erbakan was the son of a bureaucrat, Demirel of an illiterate villager. Both profited from the educational opportunities of the new Republic. Both future leaders were influenced at the time by racialist (*ırkçı*)[4] Turkic or Turanist writings that stressed the Islamic and Central Asian Turkic heritage of the new Republic's citizens (rather than its multiethnic Ottoman roots). In 1948, Erbakan moved to Germany and earned a Ph.D. at Aachen Technical University, then returned to Istanbul to teach, with an interlude from 1956 to 1963 spent managing an engine factory. His election to head the Turkish Chamber of Commerce began Erbakan's political journey. It was here that he incubated his defense of small Anatolian businesses and earned a reputation that could be traded upon politically. Refused a place in Demirel's Justice Party, he won his first seat in parliament as an independent candidate from Konya in 1969 and soon thereafter formed a political party.

On January 10, 1967, Erbakan married twenty-four-year-old Nermin, a secretary at the Chamber of Commerce. The wedding party reportedly was held at Istanbul's Çınar Hotel, with jazz, dancing, and alcoholic beverages. Although initially his wife did not cover her head, she later began to veil and quit her job to stay at home (Yalçın, 1994, 33). Neither Erbakan nor his wife were strangers to the Islamist yuppie lifestyle. One of Erbakan's trademarks was his penchant for tailored suits and expensive, showy Italian ties. When he threw a lavish wedding for his daughter at the Istanbul Sheraton Hotel in 1994, the conspicuous consumption made national news and outraged some of his followers. The scandal may have been responsible for the party losing the 1994 local election in Fatih, one of Istanbul's most conservative neighborhoods. It was reported in the newspapers that a Nakşibendi sheikh in Fatih had ordered his followers to vote instead for a more down-to-earth centrist candidate with Nakşibendi ties.

Even in Ümraniye, people who had voted for the Welfare Party criticized Erbakan for wasting money. Several people pointed out that, although the pilgrimage to Mecca is only required once in a lifetime, Erbakan had gone several times, all televised. Füsün asked, "How many times does one have to go? What is he trying to show—that he's a better Muslim than we are? And when he goes, he takes his whole entourage with him, his family, and once he even took his grandchild. What is a baby doing on the pilgrimage? Do you know how much money that cost? There are a lot better things he could have done with that money. Like help the poor."

Istanbul mayor Recep Tayyip Erdoğan greeting constituents.

By 1997, some young party supporters in Ümraniye were referring to Erbakan as a "dinosaur" and a "creature of the state," no different from the leaders of Turkey's other parties. One put it in the
language of a popular saying about politicians: "They're going to
build a port in [landlocked] Konya." Füsün's husband Zafer, a devout
Muslim and supporter of the Islamist movement, explained that
"Erdoğan comes out of a more democratic tradition than Erbakan.
Erbakan does old-style politics, like the other parties. He controls

everything, appoints everyone. Erdoğan is more one of the people (*millet*). Although as prime minister we don't know how he'll actually behave. But he's very popular with everyone—Welfare or not—because he's such a good mayor." His visiting nephew chimed in, "Last month Erdoğan went to Trabzon and had twice as many people in the audience as [Motherland Party leader] Yılmaz when he went the following week." In a national poll, over half of respondents familiar with the party (including one in three Republican People's Party supporters) thought Virtue needed a new leader and that it should be Erdoğan. Only 4 percent supported Erbakan (Çarkoğlu and Toprak, 2000, 60, 63).

Under Erbakan's leadership, the party operated in many respects like any other Turkish political party: tightly run from the center and ready to make deals with other parties and politicians. This also struck a sour note in Ümraniye, where the local municipality was dependent on the largesse of the government in Ankara and the goodwill of party leaders for much of its operating revenue. Local governments were not allowed to raise their own revenues, except in the form of fees for local services. Residents were unhappy when the Welfare Party municipality began charging fees to park on main thoroughfares, for garbage collection, and for such services as filing a deed. One jaded resident put it in perspective, noting, "Under the previous administrations, you used to have to bribe the civil servants to get anything done. Now you get a receipt for your bribe." To deal with this kind of fiduciary strangulation and consequent opportunities for corruption, the Virtue Party "Young Ones" agitated for decentralization and more local political and financial control.

Although Erbakan found himself more and more isolated within the Virtue Party, he continued to try to maneuver party activities and policy from behind the scenes, including orchestrating Merve Kavakçı's ill-fated confrontation with parliament. In 1999, a veiled Merve Kavakçı, newly elected on the Virtue Party ticket, tried to take her seat in parliament. The chamber broke into a pandemonium of outraged shouts, accusations, and counteraccusations. When she refused to unveil, she was not allowed to take the oath of office and was escorted out. She was later stripped of her Turkish citizenship when it was discovered that she had taken out United States citizenship without informing the Turkish authorities. One Virtue Party member of parliament, Aydın Menderes, resigned from the party in disgust. Erbakan's Islamism also had a Turkish racialist (*ırkçı*) complexion, an interest since his university days, that was at odds with the party's evolving inclusiveness and multiculturalist (*çok renklilik,* multicoloredness) policies. The party's confrontational style was denounced in Ümraniye even among those committed to change. As Zafer's son Ahmet put it, "I like [True Path Party leader Tansu] Çiller; she's pro–headscarf. She's a better politician than the Welfare leaders—they went too far. They're too conservative [*tutucu*] and got in trouble. Erbakan couldn't manage it successfully."

Erdoğan's "Young Ones" faced another faction within the Virtue Party, a group of émigrés from the centrist Motherland Party and ultranationalist Nationalist Action Party, conservative nationalists uninterested in the party's Islamic ideology. Under their influence, the party would move to the center-right, closer to existing centrist parties. A member of this faction, Nazlı Ilıcak, scandalized the party by not veiling and by holding parties at her home for Virtue Party officials where she served and consumed alcohol. Her response to criticism was swift and pugnacious. She bluntly pointed out that, if the Virtue Party wanted to present itself as a party with a broad constituency, that is, as a Muslim party interested in politics, not a political party representing Islam, then it should be able to incorporate someone like her. The front page of a national newspaper printed a cartoon of a smiling Ms. Ilıcak perched languorously in a martini glass, legs dangling over the side, challenging the Virtue Party to accept her. The Virtue Party's changing profile, veering between moderation and showdown, and its new interest in democracy were attributed by some to an attempt by the party to accommodate itself to the military's limitations, for fear of being closed down. Given the diverse bases of support and the restless factions fighting for direction and control of the party, inconsistencies in policy and action could be more readily explained as resulting from internal accommodations and pressures from the ranks.

In January 1998, Erdoğan met the same fate as Erbakan and the Welfare Party: he was banned from politics. The National Security Court, a military-backed tribunal that tries cases related to subversion, accused him of having "provoked religious hatred" and of having called for religious insurrection when, during a campaign speech in 1997, he read a verse from a poem written in the 1920s by the nationalist hero Ziya Gökalp: "The mosques are our barracks, the minarets are our spears, their domes are our helmets and the faithful are our army." By this time, the military's lack of appreciation for poetic metaphor was well established. His supporters demonstrated and signed petitions, to no avail. Sentenced to a ten-month jail term and banned from politics for life, Erdoğan continued to manage party affairs from his jail cell and struggled to remain in the political game. "This song is not yet over," he promised his supporters. In the meantime, the courts were busy preparing a case against the Virtue Party.

The leadership of the "Young Ones" was taken up by Abdullah Gül, a forty-nine-year-old former economics professor from Kayseri. Although not as charismatic as Erdoğan, Gül is widely respected for his integrity and intelligence. From his youth, Gül was exposed to nationalist and Islamist politics and ideas. In 1973, his father, a retired tire factory worker, stood unsuccessfully for election as a National Salvation Party candidate. Gül pursued his interest in Islam in student organizations and in his studies; his doctoral dissertation was a study of economic relations between Turkey and Islamic states. In the course of English-language studies and eight years as an economic consultant to the Islamic Development Bank, Gül spent time abroad. In 1991, he won a seat in parliament as a Welfare Party candidate. When Erbakan became prime minister in 1996, Gül took the post of secretary of state.

Gül was a leading figure in the restructuring of the Virtue Party, moving it further away from an "Islam-referenced" party to what he called a "new politics" based on a "more universally understood democracy . . . [of] basic rights and freedoms of which one is freedom of belief." Insisting that the party had changed even from the days of Erdoğan's tenure, Gül supported tolerance of different lifestyles, arguing (in response to an interviewer's question) that such issues as whether or not a woman wore a bathing suit in public were personal decisions and of no interest to the party. He supported gender equality and expressed an interest in attracting the support of what he called "contemporary modern women who accept a lifestyle like that found in developed countries." When the interviewer referred to these as "urban women," he pointed out that, while his wife was born and lived in a city, she lived a quite conservative lifestyle. The party, he said, was against any kind of discrimination.

These differences in political style and ideological direction were expressed in fierce internal battles over party leadership in 2001. At this writing, the fate of the party is unclear, but the continual attacks by the military and the Kemalist government on Islam-oriented parties and their most popular and experienced leaders have taken a toll.

In the 1999 elections, many of the Virtue Party's votes moved to the Nationalist Action Party, surprising even seasoned election watchers. The Nationalist Action Party, with a history of pro-Turkic racism and antiminority violence stretching back to the 1960s, won 18 percent of the vote. The Virtue Party dropped from 21 to 15 percent. For many voters it had become clear that the military would not allow an Islamist party to stand, and that their votes might be put to better use in supporting another outsider party that shared some of the Virtue Party's respect for religion and Turkish nationalism, albeit in a more virulently racist form. The election came at a time of high nationalist feeling, on the heels of the capture of Abdullah Öcalan, the leader of the separatist Kurdish PKK, after a dramatic, intercontinental chase. This undoubtedly helped hoist both Bülent Ecevit's Democratic Left Party and the Nationalist Action Party, each heavily nationalist, to power.

The Nationalist Action Party also shared with the Virtue Party a respect for conservative cultural norms. Like the Virtue Party, it emphasized solidarity and national unity against class-based or ethnic cleavages in society. While the Nationalist Action Party was not anticapitalist, it took a position against get-rich-quick speculation in real estate, currency, and the stock market—which the Virtue Party, too, criticized as being morally wrong. Both parties supported individual enterprise and, in particular, the small entrepreneur. They took stands against poverty, corruption, economic injustice, and moral erosion, blaming the latter on the West. They supported credit for small business, public housing, an independent judiciary, clean government, and a powerful but just state. Both parties claimed Ataturk for their cause. For the Nationalist Action Party, Ataturk was a nationalist. Within the Nationalist Action Party, a faction centered its racialist, pan-Turkist ideas around a common Islamic core—just as, in the Virtue Party, one faction espoused a conservative nationalist discourse that represented Islam as a native Turkish tradition. Erbakan himself had an affinity for Islam-centered, pan-Turkist ideas. At this level, the two parties had moved very close to one another (and thus shared a voter base), even though the liberal-democratic discourse and emphasis on ethnic pluralism ("multicoloredness") in the Virtue Party platform in general contradicted the racialist basis of the Nationalist Action Party.

Politics and Class:
Have You Had a Face-lift?

Social class was an implicit and explicit factor in defining the Virtue Party in opposition to entrenched and powerful centrist parties like the True Path and Motherland Parties. On a sunny June morning in 1998, the journalist Ayşe Önal, her daughter Şafak Pavey, two of their friends, and I crowded into Ayşe's scuffed white Fiat and inched through traffic toward a pleasant suburb to attend the official opening of an ice cream salon belonging to the daughter of a Motherland Party parliamentarian.

The store was a franchise in a rented two-story building that the young woman and her partner, her brother, had repaired. It was in a prime location on a busy corner several blocks from the promenade beside the Sea of Marmara. The glass front faced a patio studded with wrought iron tables and chairs. A dozen waiters hovered in attendance on the ever-arriving stream of well-heeled guests. In front of each guest, a waiter placed a plate of vanilla ice cream and pistachio-crammed baklava pastry. The proud father greeted the stream of men arriving with their well-groomed wives. The customary congratulatory flower arrangements, large medallions of blooms on high wooden stands like battle standards, were placed in thick, colorful layers out of sight along one side of the building. Each medallion was draped with a ribbon announcing the sender, revealing an impressive array of professional and political well-wishers.

We peeled the aluminum tops from our pre-packaged, plastic glasses of water and sipped, nibbled, and watched the crowd. Plates of fresh noodle and cheese pastries appeared and, later, tiny china cups of fragrant Turkish coffee. The member of parliament came over and greeted us effusively. Ayşe and her daughter teasingly remarked that his son had a romantic interest in Şafak. Şafak was a lovely young woman of twenty with azure eyes and naturally blond curls, who walked with a cane after having fallen under a train in Switzerland, losing both her right arm and leg. Despite her prostheses, she had made a name for herself as a talk-show host on a cable television channel, written a book about her experiences, and even modeled fashions in a popular magazine. The parliamentarian's son was in his late teens, a shy, presentable young man with black hair slicked straight back from his forehead in a fashionably stark wave. He sat with us for a while, but didn't say much, obviously embarrassed and clearly somewhat starstruck by Şafak. His sister, her dark-blond hair bobbed, was more chatty. She wore a stylish beige suit and white nail polish. It was her store, she explained to us proudly; she was the manager, although she admitted apprehensively to having no experience in running a business. She illustrated this by pointing out that she seemed to have hired too many waiters and would have to let some of them go. Her brother added quietly that he and his sister were actually partners. Smiling, she explained that he was under eighteen and therefore couldn't officially be a partner yet. He seemed unconcerned.

The parliamentarian joined a group of five men for a serious conversation at another table. Ayşe leaned toward me and whispered that they were all Motherland Party members of parliament. His wife took his place at our table. Like her daughter, she was carefully and professionally coifed and wore an understated but obviously expensive suit. Her nail polish was the same pearly white as her daughter's. She appeared to be in her mid-to-late forties, her face slightly lined beneath the understated makeup. She spoke carefully, as if keeping her face immobile so as not to crease it, as Ottoman ladies are said to have done. The other wives came over one by one to greet her. All were immaculately coifed and made up, wearing expensive but conservative suits. As each approached, the hostess stood and greeted them. Compliments were exchanged. One of the most common of these was, "You're looking wonderful. Have you had a face-lift?" Ayşe had asked this of the parliamentarian as well, so it appeared not to be gender-specific, or perhaps only Ayşe was brazen enough to get away with the cross-gender usage. After yet another such query, the parliamentarian's wife touched her hand tentatively to her cheek and responded, "Maybe it's that new cream I bought. I started using it a few months ago. You know, one of those new European blends for the skin after age forty." She wandered off to another table.

Everyone made a point of coming to greet Ayşe, a well-known journalist, the men more effusively than the women. Ayşe was an anomaly for this class of women: a handsome, passionate woman up to her neck in the work of politics; a risk-taker, a muckraker, a woman who had lived for a month in the Bekaa Valley in a guerilla training camp; a woman who had been in jail; a woman treated as an equal and a confidante by their husbands; a woman who did not appear in the least concerned about her clothing, coiffure, or wrinkles. A young woman dressed in *tesettür* passing by on the sidewalk leaned over the bushes dividing the sidewalk from the patio and greeted Ayşe, who turned and exchanged pleasantries with her over the hedge. When she turned back to the table, the parliamentarian's wife came over and asked, "Who was that?" "Who?" "The veiled woman you just spoke with." "Oh," Ayşe shrugged, "a woman I know through my work at Kanal 7." The parliamentarian's wife nodded acknowledgment and returned to mingling with her guests. After another half-hour, Şafak began to tire and we set out on the excruciatingly long and tedious trip home, directly through the central maelstrom of Istanbul traffic.

Later that same evening, Ayşe, a journalist friend, Figen, and I planned to attend a Virtue Party rally in Izmit, a small industrial city near Istanbul. I wasn't sure that the clothes I wore to the ice cream salon opening—a short-sleeved, white silk blouse, a long, narrow linen skirt with a modest slit front and back, high-heeled black open-toed sandals, and bright pink nail polish on my feet and hands—would be appropriate at a Virtue Party rally. But Ayşe assured me that some wives of the Virtue Party politicians also wore nail polish and open-toed sandals and slit skirts, along with their head scarves. So off we went, battling traffic. As we entered Izmit, we asked for directions to the sports stadium, and finally spotted it by the side of a dark road. The road was lined with vehicles; guards were waving cars away from the entrance. Several rows of soldiers and policemen stood at attention at the front of the building.

Ayşe showed her press pass and caught the attention of some of Erdoğan's assistants, who immediately ran over and waved us in. We gave someone the key to the car to park it and entered the stadium through a back door. We were about an hour late and the proceedings had already begun. According to the printed invitation, we had missed some folkloric entertainment, but it turned out that the entertainment had been canceled in sympathy with the victims of the Adana earthquake that had occurred that morning. In response to Ayşe's anxious apologies and queries about whether we had missed the mayor, our guide, one of the mayor's staff, a slim, well-dressed man with a friendly face framed by a round, neatly cut, ebony beard, whispered that the mayor hadn't arrived yet. He had been delayed and was, in fact, arriving that very moment. We hastened down a gray-walled back corridor and were guided up an entrance into the stands.

I emerged into a dazzling, disorienting kaleidoscope of sound and color that drenched the senses. The covered stadium, about the size of a stadium at a midsized college, was festooned with flags—

Virtue Party flags alternating with Turkish flags. Strings of these large, red flags were draped tentlike from the center of the roof. Giant Turkish flags draped the walls. Within this startling, blood-red atmosphere, phalanxes of people massed in the stands. The side of the stadium facing me was entirely populated with women in *tesettür,* a palette of pastel coats and glinting, gold-flecked head scarves. The stadium was completely full. A dull but expectant roar filled the air. It was very bright and very hot.

I was handed over to a young, veiled woman who guided me past the knees of a row of older, bearded men sitting on broad, plush, upholstered seats rather than the plastic stadium seats I could see further up the stands. Ayşe, in linen slacks, T-shirt, and a crumpled linen jacket, and her friend Figen, in jeans and short-sleeved flowered top, sweater tied to hide her bare midriff, sat at the end of the row behind me. I came to rest between the veiled woman on my left and a middle-aged, unveiled woman in a warm-looking brown suit on my right. Whenever I moved my hand to take notes, I nudged one of the women. I was sweating profusely.

My seat was directly behind Recai Kutan and Recep Tayyip Erdoğan, so all the television and press photos would show the two party leaders with three women behind them, two of them unveiled. A long shot would show the three women in a sea of bearded men. As I moved to my seat, Kutan and Erdoğan turned and smiled, extending their hands to be shaken. Recai Kutan was a kindly-looking, white-haired old man, sitting quietly by as Erdoğan, the star, was continuously besieged by autograph seekers. Starry-eyed young, veiled women and girls flocked around his seat, clutching albums to be autographed and passing cameras back and forth so that each could have a picture taken with the smiling, patient mayor.

The veiled woman to my left introduced herself as Serap, Virtue Party press liaison for Izmit. She had a pleasant, round, lightly freckled face with delicate features and was obviously proud of her local organization's success in setting up this event. We talked in snatches over the noise of amplified announcements and the muted roar of the crowd. She indicated the stands of women across the stadium and pointed out a distant figure in a white suit and orange head scarf. "My daughter," she shouted proudly in my ear. "She's sixteen. She decided on her own to join the Virtue youth group."

A small stage was set up at the front of the stadium. Next to it loomed a square of twenty video monitors stacked together like pieces of a large puzzle. Serap took my hand and whispered that the local Virtue Party representative (she pointed him out to me, a young man in a beige blazer) had spent two entire days setting up this video presentation. It had been very difficult to get it to work properly. "But doesn't it look wonderful now?" she beamed. The lights dimmed. Every cube in the video puzzle showed a different part of the picture, making a single large "screen." On this screen images appeared of well-dressed men and women sitting at dinner at a fancy reception, clinking wine glasses. There was some scuttling about around the stage and Serap leaned forward anxiously. Finally it became clear—the sound wasn't working. "Too bad," she commiserated, "all that work. . . ." But the video itself had a clear enough message, even without the accompanying soundtrack.

One of the guests shown at the reception was Prime Minister Mesut Yılmaz of the Motherland Party. Whenever his image appeared on the screen, the silent crowd exploded into a disparaging boo. For ten minutes we watched the elegantly dressed matrons of the ice-cream-parlor-opening set, this time at a reception, wining and dining on sumptuous displays of food amid silver and crystal on patios and in ornate rooms. Wine flowed; a décolleté bride made a grand entrance through palatial doors. If there had been sound, we might have heard the women leaning close to one another and asking, "You look wonderful. Have you had a face-lift?" As it was, the only sound was an occasional groundswell of boos as Yılmaz appeared, lifting a glass, shaking a hand. Suddenly, the image changed to a desolate place that appeared to be a garbage dump. Small figures approached from the distance, winding among the hills of garbage, bending low to examine the refuse, occasionally sorting out a piece and secreting it in the plastic bags they carried. As they approached, it became clear that they were children, heads close-shaven against lice, in torn slacks and frayed sweaters that no longer showed their original colors but had faded to muddy greens and browns. A garbage truck pulled up and spilled its load. The children sprinted over to examine the new material. As they came closer, they noticed the camera and lined up, grinning and jiggling their feet.

The video screens winked out, the lights came on and the host on stage announced the next speaker, Recep Tayyip Erdoğan, mayor of Istanbul. When Erdoğan took the stage, the hall of supporters rose to its feet and greeted him with an ebullient roar. Virtue Party flags were swung lustily back and forth. (The stylized staff of wheat gracing the Welfare Party flag had transformed into an abstract shape cradling an "I ♥ New York"–style heart.) There was a sense of triumph and jubilation. A chant broke out: "Turkey takes pride in you."

Erdoğan began his speech by referring to the film, to the outrage of having both of those scenes occurring simultaneously in a country. The crowd roared its agreement. The rest of his speech was straightforward, setting out the Virtue Party platform. But his delivery was masterful. He thundered, then lowered his voice to an intimate growl. He paused to let his words take effect. He pivoted and addressed all sides of the stadium equally. Once again, the overwhelming impression the mayor gave was that, regardless of whether one was part of the stadium audience or standing next to him while he signed an autograph or shook one's hand, he was entirely, intimately there with the viewer. When he spoke, his words had a steely conviction, whether the listener agreed with them or not.

The content of his talk was more prosaic and reminiscent of his hijacking of the Kanal 7 interview. He recounted his successes as mayor in reshaping and improving the city. This was followed by a description of the five goals of the Virtue Party: human rights, democracy, freedom, economic progress, and a state based on law. As evidence of the party's respect for human rights he listed price decreases, the provision of water, and the year-round, rather than merely seasonal, operation of the Sea Bus, Istanbul's hovercraft commuter service. These were services for everyone, he pointed out. "Not making distinctions—this is the mark of Virtue." Human rights were economic rights. Democracy was equated with respect. "Mesut Yılmaz is not a democrat. He has no respect for people. . . . Either [democracy] will come, or . . ."—and he held that moment, playing with the implied threat, before finishing his sentence—"or we will continue our struggle for democracy." Freedom, he went on, meant that people have their rights protected. The centerpiece of this argument was the right to attend university wearing a head scarf. His discussion of economic progress focused on the threat by big business to environmentally sensitive land that the mayor believed was held in trust for the people by the government. He was referring to recent incidents in which a large Turkish holding company sought to obtain rights to build a private university on forested land in Istanbul. Finally, he urged the creation of a state in which laws that are on the books are actually implemented. He emphasized, as have Virtue Party activists in other conversations, that for the most part the present laws are not in need of change but rather need to be implemented equally and fairly. The mayor ended his speech to wild applause, flag waving, and chanting.

By contrast, when the bespectacled, gray-haired Recai Kutan, the nominal head of the party, rose to speak, the crowd buzzed with its own affairs and people began to leave, revealing patches of empty seats. Kutan spoke mildly and slowly, with little inflection. He was explaining the symbolism of the heart in the Virtue flag. "We need love. We need tenderness. We need affection." Virtue, he intoned, stood for progress. "They ask, are you left, right, mid-left, mid-right? These are artificial differentiations. We are neither. We want democracy and we are exactly in the middle of democracy." The party that recognized the needs of the people and met them, that was the party that would succeed. "The most central party is the Virtue Party."

Afterwards, I sat with Erdoğan and members of his entourage in a tea garden attached to the stadium. It was nearly midnight. The tables were pushed into a long row, the mayor at one end. I was given the seat to his right. Along the length of the table, two rows of bearded countenances, local Virtue Party mayors and members of parliament, looked expectantly in our direction. Waiters in pink shirts scurried about. We were offered ice cream pops, soda, tea, coffee. Before long, a line of waiters and staff had formed, each young man clutching an album or piece of paper to be autographed. Mayor Erdoğan patiently signed each one, handed it back, smiled, and spoke a few words or shook the hand of the anxious young man hovering before him. Although party members, dignitaries, and I were waiting, he gave every comer his full attention, as if signing the books of these young admirers for half an hour was the most important task he had to accomplish that day. When the long line of autograph seekers was dealt with, he turned the same intense focus on me, and I was able to chat with the mayor at my leisure in the same patient, one-on-one manner, despite the rows of anxiously attending bearded faces. The charismatic Erdoğan attracted the goodwill and interest of his audiences by projecting a combination of intimacy and powerful resolve. As we prepared to leave, a simple, inexpensive cardboard box of Turkish delights, of the kind commonly available at roadside gift shops, was placed on the table before each visitor.

5

POPULISM: DEMOCRACY
IS PEACE OF MIND

The Welfare (and later Virtue) Party's populism derived not only from the characteristics of its leaders, but from the manner in which the party situated its ideological message within local cultural norms. This was accomplished informally through interpretation by activists and formally by municipally sponsored events at which the party's principles were "explained" to local residents. To explain social justice and the party's economic platform, for instance, activists and party leaders shuttled back and forth between cultural and religious domains, between *imece* and hadith. The Quran and the hadith, or sayings and example of the Prophet Muhammed, enjoin neighbors, whether related or not, to actively support one another and to observe equitable distribution of resources like food and water. Principles like democracy and Islamic law (*sharia*) also were transmitted and apprehended within a cultural idiom. Not surprisingly, the hybridity of the Islamist movement infected these interpretations as well. As we have seen, Islamist activists and supporters were embedded within a particular economic and cultural context that conditioned their goals and the meanings they assigned to the party's ideological statements. Thus, democracy, like *sharia*, had many meanings. Indeed, sometimes one was used to define the other. This chapter examines the intersection of norms, values, and political motives in the activities of the local Welfare Party administration in Ümraniye.

On a brisk fall day, I visited Halil in the municipal building where he worked. Nefise and Sevgi, Halil's wife and sister-in-law, accompanied me. We jumped out of the *dolmuş* and, dodging traffic, pushed against the wind toward a large, gray concrete building on the other side of a busy intersection. Inside the swinging glass doors, we walked through a metal detector. The alarm brayed as I went through, but no one took notice. A guard sitting at a small table waved us over, asked our business, and clipped our identity cards to a rotating holder. The lobby had an air of efficient bustle. We climbed the broad, carpeted stairs. The walls of the municipal offices were decorated with framed prints of Ottoman sultans. Halil was not at his desk, so we stepped down the hall to meet Nefise's former co-workers and friends. Two young women sat behind a boomerang-shaped desk arrayed with computer equipment: two late-model computers, scanner, fax, and several complicated-looking telephones. The only decoration was a magazine cutout of a baby taped to the file cabinet in the corner. One of the women was Makbule. The women's faces lit up at the sight of Nefise, and they greeted us effusively. We sat and chatted in a colorful group, the four young women in pastel *tesettür* coats and scarves, my dark skirt and sweater a somber contrast. A wiry old man in a white shirt brought us tea and coffee and left, wordlessly.

Nefise admired the new computer her former co-workers had acquired since she left. The young women showed me the annual report they were putting together. All the slick graphics were their doing and they were justifiably proud. Nefise explained to them who I was and what I was interested in learning. She had grasped the nature of my research so well, and articulated it so clearly, that I brought her with me to my first meetings with municipal officials (who, of course, all remembered her) to introduce me. What I had initially judged in her as timidity was simply politeness and reticence, masking a keen intelligence and strong will. The young women were eager to help and sent male assistants off to collect relevant publications and materials. They were obviously in charge of this realm. Another young woman with long, brown hair entered the office, wearing a calf-length skirt, sweater, and makeup. She, too, joined in the effusive greetings. Her former co-workers had not seen Nefise since she'd left her job to marry Halil several months before. The woman with uncovered hair was an administrative assistant; in later

Peace of Mind Conversation. Women sit behind the bookcase at the back.

interviews, several male officials referred to her as proof that the Welfare Party was not intolerant of women without head scarves.

Halil stuck his head in the door to let us know he was back, and retreated to his cubicle to wait for us. After a while, I left the young women to chat and moved to the chair in front of Halil's desk, a seat where, over time, I grew to feel comfortable and in the company of a friend. This was my first visit, though, after the tense confrontation at his brother Hasan's home. He sent for tea and, between phone calls, we chatted a bit about safe topics like the weather and family events. I told him how well Nefise had explained my project and asked whether we could take her with us to my first meeting to do the introduction again. He looked pleased at my account of Nefise's skill and agreed readily. After a while, he called Nefise and we went together to the office of the municipality's Minister of Cultural and Social Work. Nefise introduced me and explained my project, then went back to her friends. Halil stayed, clearly anxious and curious about what I might say. Although he said little, as the interview progressed, I could sense him relaxing.

The minister was a published poet and an artist and quite clearly wanted that part of his image in the forefront. His pictures, impressionistic landscapes in oil, filled one wall of his office. We spoke for some time about the cultural and educational programs put on by the municipality. Halil excused himself to see to his work, leaving the door to the hall open. Every so often, he stuck his head in the door to see how we were progressing. Eventually, he came in to say that the mayor, Mehmet Bingöl, was waiting to meet me. Halil and the head of municipal publicity, Ilhan Polat, led me into the mayor's office, trailed by a young photographer. I had asked beforehand whether I, too, could take photographs and they had agreed. The object of this initial visit, I discovered, was to have a photograph taken of me together with the mayor. This was the first of many uneasy moments when I felt I was being inserted into the Welfare Party's well-oiled propaganda machine: the photograph probably appeared in one of their many publications. Yet, I supposed it was only fair for the municipality to use me, as I was using them for my own work. The meeting was short. We shook hands. I sat and stated briefly what I was doing there. Other people in the room were waiting to speak with the mayor, so I said I would come again at another time. The photographer posed us and his bulb flashed.

The publicity office was a small, cluttered cubicle on the ground floor, just behind the guard collecting identification. The office was somewhat public, walled in glass, the door always open as if to eliminate any barriers, even spatial, that might impede news and information finding their way in and out. Mr. Polat showed me their various publications, newspapers, magazines, and leaflets, and explained the rationale behind their design. "There has been a loss of memory, as a result of which people have become ignorant about citizenship. People have rights as citizens, but don't know what they are, and forget what they're told. So we design these flyers to be fun and memorable, like this announcement." He held up a flyer designed to look like a gilded scroll. It announced a "Garbage Chronicle," playfully using an Ottoman formulation: *Çöpname*. The Garbage Chronicle was a long poem exhorting residents to dispose of their garbage properly and to pay their garbage taxes. If residents were dissatisfied, they were informed in rhyme, they could call the appended telephone numbers.

Don't say, "Let's throw it away. Anyway, someone will pick it up."

Don't neglect your duty to your neighbor [*kul hakkı*]; let the watchword be affection.[1]

Even in the Garbage Chronicle, communal responsibility was

evoked and put in the context of neighborly obligation set within a religious idiom. The term *kul* means slave, and also human being in relation to God. The relation of human being to God, and thus of God's creatures to one another, ideally is one of duty and service. People have rights (*hak*) to their neighbor's service and assistance. The term *hak* means justice, right, and one's due. The roots of the Turkish term can be traced to the Arabic *haqq,* meaning "claims upon." It appears prominently in ritual verbalizations of mutual assistance and obligation.[2]

Mr. Polat also showed me a colorful, detailed map of an Ümraniye neighborhood that included all the streets and street names, and marked the road, sewage, and other projects the Welfare Party (through the municipality) had completed in that area. These were distributed to the local tradesmen with the idea that they would find them useful to help people find their way around the neighborhood, while at the same time becoming informed about what has been accomplished there by the municipality. Just then, a middle-aged, veiled woman walked into the office and announced that she had been sent there with her problem. Mr. Polat, looking pained, asked what her problem was. She answered, "Water is leaking in the bathroom and the landlord won't fix it." While Mr. Polat directed her to another office, I excused myself and went back upstairs, lugging a plastic bag emblazoned with the municipal logo (hands cradling a factory, an apartment building, and a tree bearing hearts) and containing several pounds of magazines, newspapers, and flyers documenting municipal projects. The salt-and-pepper-bearded face of the mayor appeared often in these colorful publications, sometimes in the presence of a smiling Recep Tayyip Erdoğan or thin-lipped Necmettin Erbakan. The municipal actors in these publications were all men. (When women were portrayed as participants in municipal projects, they were invariably veiled and appeared in separate photographs.[3])

Between visits with various municipal officials, it became my habit to sit with Halil and chat or just observe his work. After I became a familiar face, people dropped by to join us, briefly, in an ever-circulating salon of those wishing to discuss issues and those who were simply curious. Those clustered around Halil's desk were invariably men: Mr. Polat and some of the other civil servants, even the chauffeur who had ferried me several times to other parts of the neighborhood for interviews. Makbule and the other women met in their own offices, so I joined them there, ordering fresh tea. Although Halil rarely lost his serious expression and coiled-spring intensity, I enjoyed these visits. In the evenings, when he came from work, he sometimes would find me at his parents', along with Nefise and several of his siblings, or nearby in the apartment of his brother Hasan and Sevgi, where I stayed overnight. Although Halil's assistance had initially been granted as a family obligation, helping me understand the Welfare Party in Ümraniye soon became a communal project. People offered information and analyses, told stories about their experiences, and commented on the latest news.

One evening after dinner, as we lounged with glasses of tea on the green-flowered couches in the sitting room of Halil's parents, Hasan told me, "The Welfare [Party] is service. Service to the people. Service to your neighbor." People have a responsibility to help the less fortunate, he explained, with the caveat that this assistance should be done without expectation of return. This was in the spirit of *imece,* the traditional system of open-ended mutual obligation, as when villagers help one another at harvest time. "There is a saying, 'What the right hand gives, the left hand shouldn't know.'"

Nefise added, "Another saying is, 'Do a good deed, put it under a stone.'"

"And you should give new things to people in need, not used things that you no longer want. 'Whatever is the best you have, give that to your friend.' I think that is a saying by Celalledin Rumi."[4] Hasan pulled a religious calendar from the wall and began to leaf through it. "'Service to the people is an act of worship.'"

The calendar contained quotations from the Quran and the hadith, the record of the tradition of deeds and words of the Prophet Muhammed. Hasan read from several of the pages, casting about for quotations that supported the Turkish sayings enjoining obligation to one's neighbor. "Justice," he read, listing another concern of the Welfare Party in its call for a Just Order, "is one of the ninety-nine names of Allah."

Peace of Mind Conversations

One day Halil suggested I attend the municipality's Conversations, events sponsored by the municipality to discuss moral issues. Unstated but understood was the additional goal of explaining the Welfare Party's principles to local residents. In effect, at these meetings, the Welfare Party linked its ideological message to religious ideals as well as cultural norms governing interpersonal behavior— much as Hasan had done that evening. Once or twice a month, the Ümraniye Welfare Party municipality sponsored a lecture and discussion about topics like "the roots of loss of conscience," "why we live," and "human relations in the Quran." Some of these Conversations were held in a public park, others in a public room. The latter were called *Huzur Sohbetleri,* Peace of Mind Conversations. *Huzur* refers to a state of peaceful repose, free from anxiety. In a neo-Ottoman double entendre, a *huzur dersi* (*huzur* lesson) was the name given in Ottoman times to a lecture in the sultan's presence or in a mosque. In fact, in our conversation, the culture minister had used the term *huzur dersi* to describe the events and explained that they were modeled on the Ottoman function. "*Huzur dersleri* are a means of imparting a lesson that originated in the Ottoman era and have a long history. In those days, at the sultan's order, his bureaucrats, administrators, intellectuals, and scholars met in the manner of an assembly [*meclis*]. . . . We said, let's update this and bring it into the present; let's have a monthly *Huzur Sohbeti* [Peace of Mind Conversation]."

Invited speakers explained philosophical principles to local citizens, who were able to ask questions afterwards. The talks were rarely directly political (although the talk on "why we live" was given by the mayor), but their messages corresponded to the party's ideological platform. On a cold, rainy evening in October, I arrived at the municipality and waited in Halil's outer office for the event to begin. Someone came by and informed me that the evening's speaker had been canceled and was replaced by the retired prayer leader (imam) of a well-known mosque. The topic was to be, suitably, "morality and peace of mind." Halil rushed in shortly after eight and told me they were starting late. We ran through the rain to a building across the street, puffed up several flights of narrow stairs, and entered through an apartment door into a large, blindingly pink room. On a table just inside the entry were ranged paper plates on each of which nested a small cardboard box of fruit juice with attached straw and a handful of sweet cookies. This was for the reception after the presentation, Halil informed me. We entered a large room with serried rows of comfortable metal chairs upholstered in leatherette. The only decorations on the walls were several framed prints of Ottoman sultans and a bulletin board on which were displayed clippings from Islamist newspapers announcing the anniversary of the death of Cahit Zaferoğlu, an Islamic poet who died of cancer in 1993 at the age of fifty-three. One headline announced that an Ümraniye library had been named after him. In a niche at the back of the room was a tiny library, with just enough room for a heavy wooden table and chairs. The library was surrounded by bookshelves that screened it from the rest of the room.

The room filled with men of all ages, but most were middle-aged, a few with the rounded beard of the Islamist. Many looked like fairly prosperous local businessmen, some still in suits, toting brief-cases. The only woman in the main part of the room, I sat next to Halil, who positioned himself protectively between me and the male audience. Taking to heart the Welfare Party's rhetoric of openness about veiling, I had not covered my hair, but I did not unbutton the wide navy blue coat I was wearing. Two young, veiled women listened to the speaker from behind a bookcase at the back of the room, sitting in the dark at the library table. Three men moved around the room, their heads obscured by giant television cameras. A photographer also roamed the room, documenting the event.

At half past eight, the culture minister introduced the speaker. The imam, his friendly face fringed by a round beard, began with a blessing in Arabic. From behind dark-framed glasses, his eyes sparkled with intelligence and humor. He wore a gray suit over the round-collared shirt common among Islamists. His voice vibrated with warmth and concern, like a loving uncle with one's best interests at heart. He spoke without notes, pronunciation perfect, each syllable clearly voiced, pauses expertly timed for effect. Smiling often, he related colorful fables and stories in a friendly, humorous, and sincere manner, punctuating them with broad, illustrative gestures. The audience was rapt.

His message was mainly about economic justice. Were he not waving a Quran in his hand, in another time and place, he could easily have been taken for a socialist firebrand. "It is not only stealing a wallet that is morally wrong," he expounded. "It is stealing the money a man makes and sweats for. This is oppression." The audience murmured assent. "There are people in this society," the imam continued, "who charge interest, amass capital, engage in dirty business. . . . There are lots of people around filling their pockets, their stomachs, their cash registers. Even in Turkey, there are now people with a million dollars—millionaires! Yet in a country like this, there are also people who don't have enough to eat. A civilized world is not possible [under these conditions]. After the sun goes down, savagery rules. . . . In this country, there is oppression by guns, by capital, by organizations. The big fish eats the little fish. . . . Rage is growing!"

In suggesting solutions to the audience of small businessmen, the imam focused on their responsibility to their employees, telling them to pay their workers what they were entitled to. "They're not angels, that they don't have to eat and drink! . . . You don't have to be the Prophet to have morality," he intoned. "You can do it by not oppressing your fellow man economically. What follows is peace of mind." He then went on to link general principles of oppression and justice to local, religiously justified, culturally embedded principles of personal responsibility. "OK, let's have morality. But how?" he challenged. "In a modern world, in an ideal system, an ideal regime." He raised the Quran in his hand. "This is how you can achieve morality." He spoke about the obligation to help one's neighbors and reminded the audience of the importance of selflessness and anonymity in rendering this assistance. The giver must be free of ulterior motives. "If even the word 'hello' has in it something you want to get out of someone else, then there is no morality." People have a moral right to this assistance. "Don't say, 'Give him his salary.' Say, 'give him his *hak* [his due].'"

The bond of obligation was represented not as between family members or between citizens, but between neighbors. "If someone eats and goes to sleep while his neighbor is hungry, the Prophet Muhammed says he's not a Muslim." The imam's prescriptions were coded in religious terms. "If you take the Quran seriously, even if you go hungry, you don't rape the rights of others."

He briefly covered several other topics, alluding to government corruption and criticizing the government's ban on women wearing head scarves in schools. He ended earnestly, "There is a saying, 'Instead of cursing the darkness, light a thousand lights instead.' It's much more useful. . . . One of God's names is 'Light.'" There was no clapping at the end of his talk. Some members of the audience muttered a standard invocation, "By the will of God." The culture minister asked if there were any questions. A scruffy young man in the back of the room stood up and was handed a roving microphone. He asked a long, rambling question about prayer. Halil, often scolded by his brother for coming home so late and leaving Nefise at loose ends, was anxious to get home, so we left.

The rhetoric at the Peace of Mind Conversations and other local Ümraniye events contrasted sharply in both style and content with events sponsored by the Welfare Party–run Greater Istanbul Municipality. These regular, city-level events were held in major cultural centers and addressed highly abstract intellectual topics, such as "Islam and aesthetics," "critiques of modernity," and the "Islamic philosophy of science," in an attempt to replace secular-elite high culture with an Islamist high culture (Navaro-Yashin, 1998, 9–10). Meanwhile, in Ümraniye the Welfare Party message was translated into local cultural codes, in a bid for populist esteem, rather than elite esteem. Much of the party's interaction with Ümraniye residents was face-to-face through neighbors involved in civic or party-related activities. The party's message was phrased in the language of moral principles (stated in cultural and religious terms) that governed face-to-face interaction, whether personal or political. The new social networks on which the Welfare Party's fortunes rode were not civic organizations relying on membership of individuals with common interests, but rather a collection of neighbors and relations with a variety of interests, joined by trust and a common expectation and history of mutual assistance.

Thus, the party platform at the national level did not necessarily reflect local explanations of what the party stood for. This ideological promiscuity opened the way to the support of the party by a variety of constituents, regardless of educational, cultural, class, or gender differences. On the one hand, the party's populism and shared Islamic symbols created a common discursive field that obscured competing motivations and interests. On the other hand, differences in its political message and bases for legitimacy (in universal principles, religion, or local cultural norms; in a bid for populism or for elitism) imported into the party potentially active fault lines. The imam's discussion of workers' rights is instructive in this regard. While the Welfare Party platform promised economic justice, in Ümraniye this was defined in moral terms, based on local custom and religious moral principles. Employers were to give workers their rights because it was the morally just thing to do. They were to be treated as family, with mutual trust creating solidarity between a just, affectionate employer and respectful, hardworking employees. Although the Welfare Party did not have a well-articulated economic program, it was clear that they did not favor labor unions as a means for workers to gain their rights, despite the quite different position of the labor confederation, Hak-İş, representing the religious right (Buğra, 1999, 28, 41).

Indeed, despite the party's rhetoric about inequities between rich and poor, social class was not acknowledged as a factor. Rather, the inequity was perceived to be a moral problem, thus one with a moral solution. Party activists avoided references to identities forged on the basis of economic position (like *alt tabaka*, "lower class") or shared work experience (like *işçi sınıf*, "working class"), preferring terms like poor (*fakir*) and "the victim sector" (*mağdur kesim*). We have seen that other fault lines, such as those between radicals and moderates, have had consequences in struggles over leadership and direction of the party. The implications of another fault line, that between the interests and motivations of women and men activists, will be taken up in a later chapter.

Sharia Is Democracy

Democracy, *sharia,* local cultural expectations, and peace of mind became inextricably linked in the cultural logic of Islamist politics. In his Kanal 7 speech on October 25, 1997, Recep Tayyip Erdoğan spoke at length about his vision of democracy. Democracy, he said, was based on free elections and the supremacy of the elected government (implying that in Turkey the military had supremacy over the government). Civil disagreement and nonviolent demonstrations were important components of democracy. The government corruption that had come to light was not democratic, nor was the banning of head scarves from schools. He took the opportunity to defend a much-criticized statement he had made that "Democracy is not an aim, but a means." He stood by his statement: "Democracy is a means, but not for totalitarianism, not for undemocratic aims. We are seeking a moral, ethical [*ahlâki*] basis" for governance. He explained that he was using the word "means" in its everyday sense, as a "means" to give people peace of mind. "The purpose of democracy is to give people peace of mind. To give people peace of mind, you need ethics." This was a departure from the Islamist definition of democracy as a flawed system that supported the rule of the majority over the rights of the minority. The "flawed democracy" model required a change in the system of governance, while the "ethical democracy" model allowed for change within the system.

In other words, arguments for reasserting the Islamic cultural practices deemed necessary for an "ethical" society were represented as arguments for democratization. Laicism was represented as anti-democratic because it impeded freedom of religious expression by controlling it. Many Islamists espoused secularism, the separation of religion from state, which they believed would allow religious expression in public arenas. There is no terminological equivalent for the laic/secular differentiation in Turkish. The only available Turkish term is *laik*. Thus, Islamists use modifiers like "American rules" or "European laicism" to refer to a separation between church and state under which they envision the freedom to open religious schools and wear religious clothing. It is not clear to what extent they would be willing to embrace certain other consequences of playing by "American rules," such as giving up national religious holidays and excluding religious instruction and prayer from public educational institutions.

The equation of Islamic cultural expression with democracy has emerged in heated debates about whether Muslim dress may be worn at university. The government has a contradictory record on this issue, first banning Muslim dress at public institutions, then leaving it up to each individual school—tightening the ban or looking the other way depending on the prevailing political wind. In 1998, under Turkish law, female employees could be fined up to one-fourth of their salaries for wearing head scarves in public offices or schools. At the same time, parliament was deliberating new measures imposing prison terms of up to one year for laymen wearing Islamic headgear in public.[5] This issue in the 1990s became one of the most divisive, resulting in massive demonstrations every Friday after prayers by men spilling from mosques all over the country and by women marching in the streets and converging in buses on the capital. Nursing school students were not allowed to wear Muslim dress on ostensibly hygienic grounds. Veiled medical school students were refused admission to final exams unless they uncovered. Graduates were barred from graduation ceremonies if they were veiled. A university professor told me that she had once come to class to find several Islamist women students wearing green wigs instead of head scarves. Since there was no provision for wigs in the ban, they were allowed to continue. Demonstrations, on occasion, degenerated into violent clashes between laicist and bearded Islamist students. Newspapers reported police tearing off the head scarves of women demonstrators.[6]

However, when universalist themes that appeared in national party rhetoric, like democracy, freedom, social justice, equality, and pluralism, were set into local cultural codes, different sources of legitimacy were brought to bear. This was apparent in the greater emphasis on *sharia* law and cultural norms in local activist discourse than at the citywide or national level of party rhetoric. The explanatory emphasis was on the Quran, rather than on democracy. This corresponded with the belief that *sharia* law was necessary to be able to live the requisite moral principles fully and that this was not possible under the present system. This perception, in turn, lent support to the radical and confrontational elements of the movement. In Ümraniye, the party emphasized the moral requirements of the Quran (buttressed by local cultural understandings of morality) as the rationale for change, rather than issues, which were presented merely as the outcome of an immoral versus a moral system.

It was perhaps for this reason that in Ümraniye one often heard the terms democracy and *sharia* used interchangeably when people talked about what needed to be done for there to be a morally just system. People listed issues, like the ban on head scarves and Islamic schools, to demonstrate the lack of democracy under the present system, but then added, "What we need is *sharia*." Ahmet Akkaya, for instance, Welfare Party activist and managing director of Ümraniye's Islamic charity foundation, argued that

> Whatever you choose to call it—let it be Islamic or laic or American rules—let's bring its law to Turkey, American rules included. Ninety percent wouldn't be contrary to Islam, nor to *sharia*. Why? Because aren't human rights, basic freedom, economic independence. . . social rights and democratic rights—aren't all of these necessary?. . . Anyway, we don't believe that the rules existing in Turkey are contrary to Islam, just that they aren't applied justly. When those rules are applied justly . . . we accept that they aren't contrary to *sharia*. . . . That is, of Turkey's laws, there are maybe on the order of three percent that are contrary to *sharia*. . . . We'd even be resigned to that. . . . If these were justly applied, it wouldn't matter if you called that *sharia* or if you called it law.

From the highest party leaders, such as Recep Tayyıp Erdoğan, to the street-level activist, as well as those who simply voted for the Welfare Party, there was a general disaffection with Islamic law as it was applied in Iran and Saudi Arabia, not to mention the Taliban in Afghanistan, who were often characterized as having nothing whatsoever to do with Islam.

For many in Ümraniye, *sharia* was understood less as a system of law—everyone had a different version of what it would require legally—than as a template for moral action. The proponents of *sharia* explained it as much by reference to the Quran as to cultural values of interpersonal obligation. Mr. Akkaya:

> "He who sleeps satisfied when a neighbor hungers is not one of us," says our master, the Prophet [Muhammed]. If our master, the Prophet, hadn't said it, someone else would have said it. A person who sleeps satisfied when a neighbor is hungry isn't a human being. . . . Someone may work, like I said, to make the Prophet's saying a reality. Another works not because of any Islamic dimension to the work, but because of the human dimension. But the service they both perform is the same. For me, there is no difference at all.

The concept of *sharia* law itself was reinterpreted within a cultural idiom and came to represent a range of meanings representative of the diversity of backgrounds that characterized Islamist activists and followers. This included vast differences in the understanding of *sharia* by male and female activists. Some male activists in Ümraniye who were in favor of *sharia* law emphasized that, along with introducing justice, *sharia* law would mean the legalization of polygyny and would protect women and reaffirm their central place in the family and household. Even Mr. Akkaya, despite his support for human rights and avowal that he would never accept being labeled a reactionary, supported polygyny. On the other hand, the head of the Welfare Party Ümraniye Women's Branch laughed at the thought of introducing polygyny. "What woman would consent to anything like that nowadays?" *Sharia,* she believed, was a metaphor for a just society and was practiced on a personal level through one's choice of lifestyle, clothing, and prayer. She insisted that "living *sharia*" included, indeed required, women leaving the home to get an education and to work. Radical Party leaders and Islamist intellectuals presented yet another range of ideas about "living *sharia*," including the proposal for multiple legal orders. *Sharia* rule also was made equivalent to civil society as a vehicle for liberating the interests of the people from an undemocratic state (Gülalp, 1999b, 40).

In contrast to the fine distinctions between religion and political and social practice drawn by intellectuals and activists laying out their own programs, in the homes of poorly educated Ümraniye voters the edifice of religion, law, and politics was cemented by authority—and voting was seen as a means of ushering in different eras of authority. One afternoon in Nefise's apartment, we were having tea with several visiting women. The women had been trying to convert me to Islam, and I reminded them that the Christian Bible was accepted as legitimate in Islam. One woman explained the difference to me this way: "The Quran is like Demirel. Like Erbakan. Like Yılmaz. When Demirel is in power, his law is in effect. When Erbakan is in power, his law is in effect. Just like when Yılmaz is in power, his law is in effect." The other women nodded. Her point was that the Bible had been superseded as law, but it also indicated an understanding of both religion and political rule in terms of authority, and a lack of differentiation between religious and laicist parties in this regard. The other interesting implication of her remarks was that, while all regimes were legitimate while in power, they were replaceable by the voter.

Municipal People's Days

The Welfare Party's basic principle as expressed in Ümraniye was, "Service to the people; service to justice" (*Halka hizmet, haka hizmet*). The practical consequences of this emphasis on service were visible in all aspects of the workings of the Ümraniye municipality. Stenciled on the back of the municipal garbage trucks was the motto "Cleanliness is a part of faith" (*Temizlik imandandir*). This was a far cry from advertisements put out by the national party and the Welfare-led Greater Istanbul Municipality in 1997, which rarely mentioned religion, but urged voters to say "no to rentiers," "no to all kinds of imposition," and to remember "those who closed the schools." A billboard and poster campaign by the Greater Istanbul Municipality in 1998 showed a collage of modern Istanbul with a smiling, clean-shaven businessman pointing to the municipality's Internet address. The caption: "Istanbul is finally in your hands: http://www.ibb.gov.tr."

The Ümraniye municipality's service to the community was embodied in the mayor's weekly open-office session, when residents could air grievances and make requests. The mayor and his assistants gave personal attention to constituents' problems, their one-on-one interaction with constituents another manifestation of the party's populist political style. Every Wednesday was People's Day (*Halk Günü*). The mayor of Ümraniye, Mehmet Bingöl, spent the remainder of his day after 2:30 P.M. hearing personal petitions from citizens; the day did not end until the last petitioner had been heard. Mayor Bingöl was a tall, massive man in his fifties. His receding white hair and round, salt-and-pepper Islamist beard gave him an air of solidity. In his spotless white shirt and brown suit, he embodied both prosperity and probity. His large office was dominated by an imposing polished wooden desk. Colorful popular prints of Ottoman sultans decorated the walls. Arrayed before the desk were two rows of low, black, leatherette easy chairs, facing each other about five feet apart. To speak to the mayor while seated in one of these chairs, one had to turn one's body sideways in a way that felt oddly supplicative.

On People's Day, I was told, no one was turned away and no one left without seeing the mayor. On the day of my visit, there were fewer visitors than usual because of the torrential rains. Still, there was a continual stream of petitioners. They were seated in the anteroom and given tea. When someone left the mayor's office, a new person was ushered in. The ten chairs in the office were continually full. The person in the chair nearest the mayor's desk presented his or her case, received an answer, and finished his or her glass of tea. When the person stood to leave the room, the remaining supplicants rose and moved over one chair to edge closer to the mayor. Those in the two chairs closest to the mayor took turns presenting their cases, sitting on the edge of their seats, twisting around and up toward the mayor, who loomed above them behind his enormous expanse of desk. An assistant hovered beside the mayor, ready to advise on legalities and to take any action the mayor indicated. When one assistant left, another silently and efficiently took his place. The image was of a well-oiled, efficient administrative machine with overtones of both populism and paternalism. The mayor's face invariably expressed concern for the supplicant, even when he delivered unwelcome news.

The first exchange I observed was with an elderly woman in threadbare coat and polyester head scarf (not the full *tesettür* style). Perched at the edge of her seat, speaking slowly and formally, she presented her situation: she needed TL 100 million (about $500) for a kidney operation. She wondered whether she could get the money she needed here. The mayor, looking at her kindly, said she should have herself transferred to "our clinic here" and have the operation done there. (There was a clinic attached to the municipal offices, a relic of the previous administration. The clinic was rented out to a private contractor, the rent going to the Ümraniye Service Foundation, a local Islamist foundation.) The woman looked unhappy. She insisted that she had been seeing this same doctor for years; she had an appointment with a specialist who was a leading expert in this disease and she didn't want to come to the clinic instead. The mayor was calm, but inflexible, and repeated that she should have the operation at the clinic. The woman began to plead and explain. The mayor listened patiently, but always repeated the same advice. Finally the woman thanked him and left, frowning.

The line of supplicants rose, moved over, sat again. Next was a scruffy young man who complained that he wasn't able to find a job with the municipality. The mayor, in a terse, commanding voice, asked him, "Did you meet all the requirements?" Well, actually, the young man admitted, he hadn't. The mayor told him to go to ISKI (the municipal public works office), that they would find something for him. He looked briefly aside at his assistant and told him to arrange it. The assistant wrote in the notebook in his hand. The young man stood, thanked the mayor profusely, and, back bowed in obeisance, left the room. The line rose, moved over, sat.

Next was a man with a day's growth of beard and a distraught air. The mayor turned his full attention to him, his face floating like a distant moon above the man in the low chair. This time the assistant, speaking in a low, respectful, but efficient voice, filled the mayor in. The man's house had been flooded and was unlivable. He wanted permission to rebuild on the same spot. The man confirmed that he had submitted a petition for this purpose and reminded the mayor that he and his family had no place to live. They were staying with relatives and were at the end of their rope. The mayor asked the assistant what the situation was. The assistant, who had obviously done his homework, responded that there was an ISKI plan for that area—a sewage project which would ease the flooding but also displace homes—and that within a couple of years ISKI would be building and he would have to leave his house anyway. In any case, the assistant added, it would flood again and again until the ISKI project was completed. The mayor repeated this to the man, who looked pained and asked what he should do. The mayor recommended he move elsewhere or rent. The man made another halfhearted attempt to regain his property, but soon left, looking defeated and worn.

Next was a black-haired woman in her thirties who said she was there to represent her father, who was ill. The mayor told her to proceed. Her father wanted permission to build a house. She had handed in the appropriate petition. The mayor looked to his assistant for confirmation. He nodded. The mayor asked if she had a deed and the appropriate permissions. "I think so," the woman said, rummaging in her handbag. "He gave me these papers. Must be here somewhere." She handed over a wad of documents to the assistant, who flipped through them and then nodded assent to the mayor. The mayor granted her permission, since the deed was in order. The woman thanked him, sipped the rest of her tea quickly, rose, and exited. As she went out, another woman came in and sat in the chair nearest the door. The line rose, moved over, sat.

A thin old man with a white mustache and prominent Adam's apple leaned forward and asked plaintively for permission to build another story on his house for his son, since his own apartment was too small to have his son's family live there as well. He wanted his son near him. The mayor looked at his advisor quizzically; a whispered conversation followed. The mayor turned back to the man and advised him to have his son rent an apartment nearby, that they could not give permission for another floor because of zoning. Disappointed, the man left the room, back bent in resignation. Next was a shabbily dressed, dark-haired, middle-aged man with a black mustache. The assistant whispered to the mayor. The case had already been discussed. The mayor asked the man how it had worked out. The man replied that he still did not have a place for his store. The mayor instructed his assistant, "For now, give him the unused store in the municipal bazaar. They're going to tear it down, anyway." The man thanked the mayor profusely and exited. The supplicants rose, moved over, sat.

I finished my tea and left the room as well, having taken up one of the seats nearest the mayor for some time now. The chairs were still occupied, all by men now, save for one old woman in a head scarf. Outside in the waiting room, Halil was trying to calm down several veiled women who felt they had been waiting too long. He suggested they sit and ordered tea to be brought to them. While waiting for the tea, he told me in a low voice that most people come to get permission to build, for which they have to show their deed, but that people had even come to ask permission to build illegal squatter houses. "Can you imagine! That is always denied, and if the squatter houses are built, they're torn down."

Navaro-Yashin describes the People's Parliaments held by the Welfare Party mayor of another Istanbul squatter area. These were similar in structure to the Ümraniye People's Days in their patron-clientilistic and paternalistic overtones, although they seemed less inclusive of women and nonparty residents than in Ümraniye. Navaro-Yashin suggests that the squatter-area mayor in her study tried to legitimate his claim to political power by allying himself with "the people" through God (1998, 12–14). In Ümraniye, the administration allied itself with "the people" by means of powerful cultural norms obtaining between people in local urban social networks, as well as through patronage and paternalistic *himaye*.

A comparison with the style of People's Days under the previous left-of-center Republican People's Party administration also is instructive. During a visit to a Republican People's Party event in Ankara in December 1997, I had an opportunity to spend several hours with Şinasi Öktem, mayor of Ümraniye from 1989 to 1994, first under the Socialist People's Party, then the Republican People's Party. (Previous Ümraniye administrations were under the Justice Party [1977–1984] and Motherland Party [1984–1989]. With the victory of the Welfare Party in 1994, the neighborhood had elected mayors from across the political spectrum.) While we were waiting for a much-delayed car to take us to the event, I took the opportunity to ask Mr. Öktem about the Ümraniye municipality under his administration.

The Republican People's Party had held People's Days for three years, he explained. Like the Welfare Party, they set aside one day a week to hear constituents' requests and complaints. However, unlike the Welfare Party mayor's meetings with his constituents over tea in his office, Republican People's Party People's Days were held in the municipal auditorium at the back of the building. The mayor sat on stage with his assistants and people in the audience below raised their hands and asked questions. Most of the questions and requests, as with the Welfare Party petitioners, had to do with people requesting permission to build. They also requested paved roads in their neighborhood or complained about lack of water. If people needed jobs, they were placed in municipal positions that had become free through retirements and attrition, much as I had seen the Welfare Party mayor assign an unemployed young man without skills to an ISKI job. Mr. Öktem explained that every year about forty positions would become available that could be filled by constituents. Others were sent to big firms whose owners the mayor knew. Women also came, the mayor said, sometimes one or two hundred of them at once, to complain, for instance, about not having water. He would listen to their requests and then tell one of his assistants to take care of it and give him a report the following week. The municipality, he added, stopped the People's Days when they realized the event was becoming "professionalized." "There were always the same people in the audience," he complained, "only RPP party people or people wanting building contracts."

Personalizing Rights

The Welfare Party's organization and mobilization strategies in Ümraniye drew on principles of communal interaction that characterized migrant and working-class communities, both hierarchical, modeled on the family, and horizontal, based on reciprocity. Welfare Party mobilization in Ümraniye was not based on common interest among citizens so much as on the metaphor of the family, paternalistic care (*himaye*) and mutual obligation (*imece*). The metaphor of family and its associated responsibility and obligation were carried over to the neighborhood, where they meshed with cultural and religious norms giving fellow human beings (in the form of neighbors, employees, etc.) rights to assistance and just treatment. Human rights and citizens' rights were made personal obligations. People were exhorted, as their religious duty, to feel personal responsibility for their neighbors. Activists carrying out charity and other services described their activities in terms of interpersonal obligation. This personalization extended even to conceptions of foreign affairs. As one local activist put it, "We are for solving [foreign relations problems] in a friendly, brotherly, comradely manner, within the law of neighborliness." Then, he added, there would be no more need for NATO, the European Union, or the Warsaw Pact.

The previous, Republican People's Party administration, on the other hand, had a different political style premised on the responsibility of the state and of the neighborhood administration to assist its citizens. This was undergirded by universalist rhetoric about human rights and women's rights. Some of the Republican People's Party administration's projects were designed to develop networks among residents based on face-to-face interaction and meetings in homes for women. However, after initial contact, the women were encouraged to leave their homes and attend central, public places for lectures, classes, and other politically relevant work. This was a conscious policy to get women out of their homes and into the political sphere, away from the influence and authority of their families. Welfare Party activists, on the other hand, encouraged women to participate by bringing politics into their homes, and, through veiling, symbolically extend *himaye* protection into the political sphere. Such engagement with public life through the limiting lens of male approval and protection, however extensive, carried a penalty in terms of full engagement on a formal institutional level. There were no women in central Welfare Party bureaucratic circles at the time. Republican People's Party activists, on the other hand, paid a price for their inability to situate their ideological message within local cultural norms. While networks of Ümraniye women developed around particular Republican People's Party activities, once those activities ended, the networks fell apart. (Ümraniye's secularist activists will be discussed in chapter 8.)

Different political styles have different consequences in popular mobilization. Through its populist style, institutions like the Peace of Mind Discussions and People's Days, and the participation of civic organizations, to be discussed in the following chapter, the Welfare Party translated its ideological message into a culturally embedded, personally transmitted message that partook of the trust and mutual obligation inherent in the relationships among neighbors. The resulting party-mediated relationships among neighbors or people acting "as neighbors" were more vibrant and enduring than relationships based on direct contact between socially distant party representatives and groups of citizen residents, as under the Republican People's Party administration. This was so even though most of the requests for assistance during People's Days were denied by the mayor, and the mayor's populism ("The mayor is just like one of us") was belied by the hierarchical and paternalistic setting.

Principles of mutual aid and obligation can be found in Turkish village culture and also are demonstrably important in urban life. The Welfare Party built on these principles, but it was not clear exactly how this was done. What observers noted was the Welfare Party's tight neighborhood organization, its ability to cross class lines, and its seemingly different messages to different audiences. It was also noted that the party was not homogenous. It contained moderates interested in social issues, as well as radical Islamists, those who wished to change the system to make it conform to a just order for which *sharia* provided a metaphor. Others wanted to replace the system with some instantiation of *sharia* law or neo-Ottoman social and political models. When, in the interests of mobilization, political action is embedded in the cultural matrix of daily practice, party ideology becomes embedded in local cultural values as well, leading to heterogeneity and potential conflicts. Nevertheless, the personalization and popularization of the Welfare Party's message and organization created an appearance of homogeneity and common purpose among the activists, despite these internal divisions.

The Welfare Party mobilized the masses one by one, mediating and controlling the party's relationship to the masses through an elaborate structure involving civil-society organizations that will be the subject of the next chapter. I began this book with an account of the grounding of vernacular politics in relations among people in urban networks. Above, I have described the institutions to which vernacular politics connected these networks. In the next chapter, I discuss the role of civic organizations in linking institutions to the masses.

6

CIVIL SOCIETY:
IN WHOSE SERVICE?

Civic groups provided arenas within which Islamist activism was coordinated. In Ümraniye, neighborhood cells supported party–related associations, an Islamic charity foundation, and the municipality. Although they worked closely together, the foundation insisted upon its autonomy from both party and municipal administration. The foundation directors and activists clearly wished to impress upon me that they were not linked to the party except by sentiment and membership. Since it was illegal for a civic organization to be directly linked to a political party, this insistence upon autonomy was not surprising. However, they explained their claim to autonomy differently. They considered themselves to be participants in a social movement to which the party was important, but ultimately inconsequential. What the party provided for the movement was a national framework, reinforced and orchestrated by intricately detailed computerized data banks on individual neighborhoods like Ümraniye. The Islamic foundation itself had limited resources, but coordinated the activities of Islamist businessmen as donors and board members, of Welfare Party officials, members of party-related associations, and local Islamist activists and their neighborhood networks.

In other words, civic organizations like the Islamic charity foundation cannot be described simply as formally autonomous of a political party or informally co-opted by it, but must be seen as linked in practice to both a party and a social movement rooted in the community. This presents the seeming paradox of an autonomous civic organization engaged in grassroots mobilizing while also participating in a project of social monitoring and control by a political party. This paradox dissolves if civil society is seen not as a form of organization, but as part of a larger picture, that is, as part of a political and cultural process that extends beyond the organizational boundaries of any particular institution. Civil society, in this broader rendering, incorporates personal, kin, and ethnic relations on the one hand, and civic and political institutions on the other, linking them in practice, rather than artificially separating out "cultural," civic, and political domains.

Foundations have played a particularly important role in Islamist mobilization in Turkey, even though, in terms of numbers, associations have grown at a more rapid rate. The long Ottoman history of foundations and their relatively low profile over much of the Republican period have given them a cachet of respectability and the advantage of less state supervision than the more recent associations. Since their implication in the violent ideological factionalism of the 1960s and 1970s, the state has tightly controlled the activities of associations. Nevertheless, they have proliferated. The numbers, however, may be misleading. Polls show that working-class people, especially women, tend not to join associations. How, then, do they participate in civic and political life? Foundations, while numerically less common, nonetheless serve a bridging function between people as they are situated in their personal networks and civic and political activities. Thus, foundations link and mobilize people whose involvement would not be apparent in "membership" counts.

Setting foundations and associations within this broader framework of relations also requires a reexamination of claims of autonomy. If civic activity involves informal and unacknowledged links with personal and party networks, examination of the organization's formal structure and activities alone may not reveal the broader ideological context within which it operates. Much as foundations may support and facilitate implementation of an Islamist ideology, the middle-class bias of associational life in Turkey may point to a pervasive Kemalist, feminist, or other ideological bias.

Director of an Islamist foundation speaking with a local activist in his office.

Welfare's Web

The Welfare Party presided over a network of independent, inter-locking support groups that was the envy of all other parties. In addition to the party's formal representation at the provincial, municipal, and neighborhood levels, informally linked associations and groups of activists rooted the party in every block, in every street. This organizational level had been achieved in almost every province of the country, so that Welfare Party activists could boast that there was no place they could not reach with their election message (Seufert, 1997, 333). It is important to note that this organizational network was independent of religious orders and religious communities, just as much of it was structurally independent of the Welfare Party itself, although personnel, activities, and, in some cases, financial support were coordinated or shared. (It was illegal for a political party to directly fund a civic organization.) Information about local needs and activities and the people involved were centrally collected in a national Welfare Party database. So much information was gathered for party records, including such details as blood group, that the police reportedly called Welfare Party headquarters to ask for possible blood donor matches after accidents (332 fn). Seufert notes that voter registration information was added to the Welfare Party lists, thus expanding the Welfare Party "membership" count to include voters that "just [weren't] aware yet" of their support for the Welfare Party (332). To this database was added a continual flow of personal information gathered by neighborhood activists. This allowed

Welfare representatives to send congratulations to newly married couples or sympathy cards in the event of a death in the family, assist old people or people living alone, and even intervene in family arguments.

The party motto, "Service to the People," was put into practice in Ümraniye by a corps of associations and an Islamic foundation (*vakıf*) that operated in tandem with the Welfare Party and the party-run municipality. All claimed autonomy from municipality and party, although they worked with both. These groups, in turn, organized fleets of volunteers who formed cells (*hücreler*) among their neighbors and took individual responsibility for seeing to their needs. Residents' needs were relayed to the foundations and the municipal government for resolution. The foundations, municipality, and party shared the task of charity and other assistance.

The foundations were run by local businessmen, the cells by activists drawn from the neighborhood, bridging differences in income, education, and even gender. Islamist businessmen donated time and materials and presented an alternative picture of an Islamic-style prosperity as a viable alternative to the secular, Westernized lifestyle that had characterized upward mobility and economic success in the modern republic. There is no ethic in Islam that dictates that one should not enjoy one's wealth, although there are Islamic and cultural injunctions against displaying one's good fortune. Money, Islamist businessmen are fond of repeating, has no religion. Rather, the onus is on ensuring that one's profits are morally just (for instance, not based on speculation) and that one's wealth is shared with the less fortunate. Thus, assistance to the poor by Ümraniye's civic organizations, despite intensely bureaucratic record-keeping, to a great extent was personalized, neighbor to neighbor, person to person, and hedged about with cultural prescriptions fortified by religious ideals.

On a bright fall day, Halil arranged for me to meet Ahmet Akkaya, managing director of the Ümraniye Service Foundation, a local Islamic foundation founded in 1994 after Ümraniye acquired a Welfare Party mayor. The Welfare Party had been accused by its opponents of "buying votes," particularly through its well-publicized charity work, carried out primarily by formally independent foundations. I wanted to take a closer look at how Ümraniye's Islamic foundation was organized, its relationship to other associations, the party, and the municipality, and the extensiveness and effectiveness of its work. Hugging my coat against the chill, I followed Halil out of the municipal building, across the street and up a dark, narrow staircase into a cramped apartment converted into an office. In the stairwell, Halil warned me that Islamists sometimes didn't like to shake hands. What he meant was, shake hands with a woman. I told him I understood, and didn't extend my hand when Mr. Akkaya met us at the door to his office. He was a dapper man in his late thirties, with a self-confident intensity. He was clearly used to being in charge and being listened to when he spoke on any subject, which he did easily and volubly. The small room was crammed with shelves of neatly labeled black binders. Halil and I sat in brown leatherette chairs while Mr. Akkaya retreated behind his desk. Halil evidently had prepared the ground and explained that I was interested in learning about the foundation. After asking the man in the alcove outside his office to bring tea, Mr. Akkaya leaned back in his chair and elaborated on the foundation's activities.

He began with a recent event concerning a woman who had run away with another man, leaving her children with her husband. He had been unable to care for them properly and their plight had come to the attention of the foundation. "We told him, divorce her and we'll help you remarry." But just as the man was about to file for divorce, his wife returned. She brought with her the child she had borne the other man. Her husband took them both in. As a result of the scandal, they could no longer live on the same street, so they sold their home and moved to another district where no one knew them.

> This man had no work, so we placed him in a job. Now he is working. In fact, we explained his situation to his place of work, because we wanted him to be treated a little differently. That is, we help people not just economically, not just materially, but also from a moral [*manevi*] direction. . . . When there are families living in such terrible conditions, the lives we ourselves lead seem wrong. We should give what we have, do what we can and not be at ease until we can save them from those conditions. This work has a human dimension that can't be measured in money.

Mostly, the foundation's assistance was in service and in kind: used clothing and furniture, food, heating coal, dormitories, transportation, help in finding a job or a spouse, or in getting school fees waived. The foundation placed men in jobs found through firms connected with the foundation, through the municipality, and by word of mouth through personal connections. It gave modest monthly scholarships ($30) to about three hundred high school and university students, both girls and boys. Education, however, was not a central area of foundation activity.

> First we want to feed those who are hungry and have fallen on hard times; hungry people aren't in a position to think about education. But there are other Islamic foundations that do work related to education. Some do nothing but education. . . for instance, the foundations of Fethullah Hoca [Fethullah Gülen]. . . . We'll fill their stomachs; they can educate them.

Some cash assistance also was given. For instance, if someone was unable to pay hospital fees and therefore was not allowed to leave the hospital,[1] the foundation would pay the fees so the person could be released. However, the foundation, like the mayor, encouraged people to use the municipality's subsidized medical facilities whenever possible. If a local resident needed money, perhaps after an accident or flood, the Welfare Party's neighborhood administration might provide a cash gift. They did not ask for the money back, Mr. Akkaya explained. If an individual was truly in need, they were assisted without expectation of return.

> But something like this might happen. . . . Let's say we helped a family today and tomorrow that family became wealthy. . . . If they remember today and come and give us money, that is both very welcome and very nice, and at the same time that person would be absolved of carrying that load.

In other words, it was against the foundation's principles to help a family in dire straits and then expect repayment, but people might relieve themselves of the resulting burden of reciprocal moral obligation by donating money when they were able. "It makes us happy, and it makes them happy."

The foundation did not make loans. A loan was something given only to people one knew personally, with whom one had a history of trust. This made sense, if one considered that money lent to friends or family was money freely given, adding to a history of mutual exchange that intensified social bonds, rather than endangering them by introducing the possibility of default. Although family and friends might expect to be repaid, repayment was voluntary, without time constraint, and might not be in currency, but rather in kind, in services, or simply in loyalty. Money lent to strangers was without the alchemy of reciprocity and mutual obligation that transformed debt into social ties, and thus had to be demanded back, a form of coercion that went against the foundation's religious and cultural ideals.

The foundation, while not formally connected to the municipality and the Welfare Party, acted in concert with them. Mr. Akkaya, a Welfare Party member, was quite firm about the lack of connection. This, again, may have been simply because a formal connection would be illegal, but Mr. Akkaya also made a philosophical differentiation.

> This work has nothing to do with the Welfare Party. Whatever you do, don't draw a connection! . . . I'm a person with a Muslim identity, but it's wrong to say that just because I have a function in the Welfare Party that Welfare is the Muslims' party or that Welfare's mission is Islam. [It's also wrong] to say that if a member of the Welfare Party has a function in a foundation, that it is Welfare's foundation. It's important to really consider the meaning of separation of powers. . . . I'm simultaneously a member of the Ümraniye Association to Build and Maintain Police Stations; that is, something having no connection at all to the Welfare Party.

Despite their formal independence of one another, the municipality, party, and foundation shared personnel and roles in the identification of those needing assistance and in the rendering of it. Generally, it was a neighbor who noticed that someone was poor or in need of assistance and reported it to someone they knew who was a Welfare Party member, to the municipality, or, more rarely, to the foundation directly. Another method of ascertaining need was to send party members canvassing door to door, saying, "The Municipality is carrying out such-and-such assistance campaign. Do you need anything?" A person in need was reported through party channels to the municipality, which then authorized a party member in the neighborhood to ascertain whether the person or family was truly deserving of assistance. Party members also checked discreetly at the family's local grocery store, or with neighbors. The family was asked to obtain a "certificate of poverty" from the local headman (*muhtar*). The family brought the certificate to the foundation and a file was opened in a family member's name (male or female) in one of the binders on Mr. Akkaya's shelves.

Once party members verified that the person or family was indeed poor, they brought food, coal, or other assistance to the home. They did this discreetly, so as not to embarrass the recipient. Or the family was given access to a depot of donated used clothing, furniture, and appliances. Assistance generally was given only once. Mustafa Dikmen,[2] administrative director of the Ümraniye Service Foundation, explained that they did not want to make people dependent on assistance. Every effort was made to find the male head of the household paid employment, often by finding him municipal employment, as the mayor had done with some of the supplicants on People's Day. Mr. Dikmen pointed out the scarcity of resources compared with the enormity of need in this very poor neighborhood with over two hundred thousand residents. Only in rare cases, he explained, could assistance be given continually, for instance, if a woman was widowed and had no male relatives to care for her. Mr. Akkaya had made the same point. When I asked him whether the foundation had any programs that tried to implement long-term solutions to the neighborhood's problems, in addition to such stopgap assistance, he replied, "It's not possible to make long-term investments in this economy. . . . We have the money we've managed to collect and with that money we help certain families. For instance, at present we're paying the dialysis costs for twenty kidney patients; we take them back and forth to the hospital."

The municipality and party also were active in charitable giving. During Ramazan, the month of daylight fasting, the municipality served free food from special tents set up in a central plaza, as a service for the poor and so that working people away from home could eat immediately at sunset. In the evenings there was free public entertainment, such as a puppet show for children. In the winter of 1995, the Welfare Party mayor of a suburb of Istanbul distributed 1,500 tons of coal free of charge; during Ramazan gave away thirty-five hundred 250-kilogram packages of groceries; provided clothing for a hundred college students; and paid for the circumcision ceremonies of a thousand children (Akinci, 1999, 77). Since circumcision ceremonies, like weddings, require new clothing, gifts, and entertainment for the circumcised boy and his guests, many families could not afford them. Municipalities subsidized mass circumcision ceremonies for local families to spare them the expense. Party and foundation activities reached well beyond their own neighborhood. Activists collected used schoolbooks, shoes, bookbags, and other useful items, had them cleaned and repaired, and distributed them free in the poorer areas of the country like the southeast. In 1996, the Welfare Party carried out a door-to-door campaign to collect unused medicines sitting around in people's cabinets. The medicines were screened by doctors and then sent to Chechnya.

Akinci reported the figures cited above to make the argument that the Welfare Party bought votes with its services. However, "buying votes" through preelection largesse is widespread in Turkish politics and engaged in by all parties. The preelection distribution of deeds to squatter homes was so entrenched that building in squatter areas intensified just before elections, and one such neighborhood, to celebrate the manner of its formalization, took the election date as its name. My own observations of Welfare Party and related charitable activities in Ümraniye spanned pre- and postelection periods. While such activities intensified before elections, they continued afterwards as well, although, as Mr. Dikmen and Mr. Akkaya both pointed out, they were hardly sufficient to deal with the poverty of the neighborhood.

Helping the Official Poor Help Themselves

To make an appointment with Mustafa Dikmen, I called the telephone number listed on his Ümraniye Service Foundation business card. Much to my surprise, given the pains foundation officials took to differentiate themselves from the municipality, the municipality's central switchboard answered. I checked Mr. Akkaya's foundation business card. The numbers were the same. Clearly, this was the main contact number for the foundation. After some suspicious screening, the operator put me through to the foundation. Undoubtedly thanks to Halil's good word on my behalf, I was given an appointment to see Mr. Dikmen that afternoon.

He occupied a small office in a building around the corner from the municipal building. (Mr. Dikmen, also concerned to keep his distance from the municipality, volunteered that the building was not owned by the municipality, but that the foundation rented it.) I climbed the narrow stairs to the first-floor landing. A glass partition screened the landing, but its door was open and I entered. Several people were crowded onto the landing outside Mr. Dikmen's office, waiting to see him. The people were middle-aged to old, but uniformly down and out. The women wore shabby, faded peasant dress, not the more expensive *tesettür*. The men leaned against the wall in worn pants, scuffed shoes, and homeknit sweaters. Feeling a bit guilty at queue jumping, I was ushered into Mr. Dikmen's office. The office, a small, gray cube, was sparsely furnished with a desk, three chairs, and a bookshelf containing ledgers. On the wall by the door hung a calendar displaying a picture of the Kaaba, Mecca's holiest shrine, the foundation's logo printed beneath it. The logo bore a striking resemblance to that of the municipality. The same stylized blue hands enfolded a flower, instead of the factory, apartment block, and tree in the municipality's logo. The same large, red, sun-like sphere blazed over the blue hands. A reproduction of a portrait of the Ottoman Sultan Mehmet hung on the wall behind Mr. Dikmen's desk.

Mr. Dikmen was a short, compact man with a round, black beard, closely cropped in the Islamist style. Under his jacket he wore a blue striped version of the collarless shirt favored by Islamist men. Seated in a chair before his desk, I explained that I wished to witness some of the foundation's charity activities. He agreed and, after some further conversation about the foundation, suggested we visit the foundation's charity store, which was nearby. He took along the people who had been waiting by the door and we walked in a loose group several blocks to a pink apartment building next to a mosque. A large sign over two doors on the ground floor announced "Ümraniye Service Foundation Help Market." He led the people trailing us through a pink iron door into a used clothing depot, tidy and well organized, where they fanned out to examine clothing hung neatly on long racks. One woman tried winter coats on her young daughter, another pondered a selection of children's shoes. In the next aisle, a man tried on shoes.

Mr. Dikmen led me back outside and unlocked the adjoining door. Inside, neat lines of vacuum cleaners, irons, and washing machines stood sentinel amid a jumble of furniture stacked in the gloom. The people coming here, he said, were required to have a "poverty certificate" issued by their headman. Then the foundation checked them again to verify that they really were in need. They generally were helped only once. Otherwise, he explained, the people would become dependent on outside help. "For instance, if a family is poor because the father isn't working and we find out that the father isn't working because he sits in the coffeehouse all day, then if

Activist fitting a poor child in the Ümraniye Service Foundation used clothing depot.

we help that family, we are just supporting him in his bad behavior. But if someone is ill or is alone, a widow or someone with an elderly sick relative living with them, then we help them regularly." In support, he recited a Turkish saying, "Instead of giving a person a fish, teach him to fish."

The foundation relied on other individuals or organizations to tell them who was poor. For instance, referrals might come from the associations set up in almost every neighborhood to assist people who had migrated from a particular region of the country. Welfare Party members were another source, particularly the neighborhood "Observers," assigned to keep track of residents on a certain set of streets. (Welfare Party organizational structure will be examined below.) Their referrals were routed to the foundation through the municipality, by way of the public relations office. Mr. Dikmen was very insistent on this line of communication and, like Mr. Akkaya, anxious that I make no other connection between the foundation, the municipality, and the Welfare Party. These are three separate things, he insisted, and their activities and properties are distinct from one another, even though they may be working for the same goals. For instance, he pointed out, the People's Education Center belonged to the municipality. (The Center held classes, much like the preceding Republican People's Party administration's People's Schools.) The Foundation for National Youth, on the other hand, belonged to the Welfare Party.

We returned to his office, accompanied by an old but lively woman in a simple head scarf who had been minding the used clothing shop. She introduced herself only as Neriman and, on the walk back, confided that she had lived in Ümraniye for over thirty years, and had been one of the very first migrants. She was now a local activist and worked to identify and help people needing assistance. She knew everyone, she commented dryly, and everyone knew her. The crowd outside Mr. Dikmen's door had disappeared, so we took seats in his office. Neriman began to chat with Mr. Dikmen, who clearly knew her well. He asked about her medical treatment and commiserated with her about her family. Then they got down to business. Neriman showed him documentation of a new "poor person" and they discussed his case for a while. Meanwhile, I leafed through a file of poverty certificates that Mr. Dikmen had handed me. Each document, neat in its own plastic sleeve, contained a passport photograph and such identifying information as place of birth and father's name. There was no mention of party affiliation, as Mr. Dikmen had pointed out. The Welfare Party and the Islamic foundations had been accused of helping only Welfare Party members, a charge denied by everyone involved in these activities in Ümraniye. He called my attention to the fact that some of the photographs were of unveiled women.

I asked Mr. Dikmen about long-term assistance for families, such as helping women learn skills that would allow them to bring an income into their families. The foundation, he countered, put on occasional fairs (*kermes*), small-scale public events at which women could display and sell their handicrafts to other women. These fairs are a common means of assuring women an income, but they rarely provide more than a few lira. Put on intermittently as special events by all manner of civic organizations, both Islamist and secular, they could not be relied on for a steady income. The Welfare Party Women's Branch, for instance, held occasional fairs at which they sold handicrafts to raise money for needy families. At other fairs, the women kept the money they earned from selling their embroidery or handmade ornamental knickknacks. The Foundation for the Support of Women—one of the more successful civic organizations, run by a group of educated secularist women, that carried out charitable activities in neighborhoods like Ümraniye—had introduced an innovation upon the *kermes*: a permanent shop in the Westernized heart of Istanbul, where people with discretionary incomes would have access to handicrafts and food products made by women in poor neighborhoods. The producers received a commission for their work and the foundation retained a share to cover costs.

Neriman jumped into the conversation and said eagerly that she knew about the program of the Foundation for the Support of Women and thought it was a good idea. She began to press Mr. Dikmen to set up something like it. He appeared thoughtful as Neriman leaned forward expectantly, waiting for his answer. When he spoke again, he did not address the idea of a shop at all, but mused instead that he knew some people from whom he could get some parts that could be assembled at home. The foundation could bring the parts to families at their homes. In other words, he was suggesting piecework, with the foundation as middleman. Piecework , a low-paying form of assembly work for businesses, a kind of factory without walls and without benefits, became widespread in urban areas during the economic transformation of the 1980s. While it did bring in some income to the family, it was highly exploitative and took advantage of the cultural undervaluation and consequent low cost of women's labor.[3]

Given the inability of the foundation to do more than scratch the surface of the area's widespread poverty, I suggested to Mr. Dikmen that providing women with money-earning skills and opportunities seemed to me a way to help families and alleviate poverty in the long term. But despite the poverty of the area, the foundation had no plans to expand family income through women's work. Even Mr. Dikmen's suggestion of home-based piecework most likely would never be put into practice. As he and Mr. Akkaya both had explained, the ideological emphasis of the foundation's activities was to solve families' problems through the male breadwinner. This also was the position of male Welfare Party activists and municipal officials in Ümraniye (although not of the female activists, as we shall see). While many Welfare Party activists were women, and the party did sponsor computer courses for (usually unmarried) female students, no courses were offered to teach married women or housewives skills that would allow them extra income, even income from work at home. There were only handicraft courses available, and the women sold what they made at the *kermes* fairs set up for that purpose. The policy of the previous Republican People's Party administration was the exact opposite. The People's Schools subsidized by the RPP municipality taught women typing, sewing, hairdressing, literacy, and other skills with the express purpose of making the women financially more independent from their families (not only to add income to families). The secularist associations working in the neighborhood, like the Ümraniye Women's Center that rose from the ashes of the local People's Schools (the subject of chapter 8), shared these goals.

For many families, occasional income from *kermes* sales was not enough to make a difference, and they supplemented it by doing occasional work for relatives and neighbors and sending their children to work. One day, Sevgi paid her neighbor, Melek, to make *gözleme* for us, a thin, unleavened bread folded like a piece of cloth around a small quantity of white cheese or ground meat. Melek herself came over to eat it with us at the table crammed into a corner of Sevgi's parlor. Afterwards, we settled ourselves in the sitting room. I made myself comfortable on the cushion-backed bed next to Melek, who chatted while stitching patterns onto a tablecloth bound for the trousseau of a niece. Melek was a hearty, red-cheeked woman, chubby and pleasant, with a big, open smile and easy manner. She told us that her eldest daughter wanted to attend high school, but that she couldn't afford to send her. Melek had six children. Her husband was a bus driver. They would have to pay registration money as well as for books and school supplies. She complained that even in school they expected you to pay extra. For instance, her daughter's school had hired an English teacher privately and had asked the parents to bear the cost. "They have eight janitors for the school building, can you imagine, one for each floor. That's too many. They should use that money for other things." Her daughter came from next door and joined us. She was a thin girl, poorly dressed, with a slim, pointed face and a large pleasant mouth. Eyes demurely lowered, she sat on the bed next to her mother and crocheted. The daughter, like her mother, was rarely to be found without crochet work in hand. Later that day, when I asked Sevgi about Melek's daughter's prospects, she told me that the daughter was working in the basement of the house across the street, in a workshop where they sewed T-shirts. "But I think they have her doing cleaning work because she doesn't know how to sew. Most start with that kind of work."

I told Halil about the girl's situation and asked whether the Welfare Party, the municipality, or the foundation could help her. I pointed out that Mr. Akkaya had boasted that the foundation could help parents get their children into school by negotiating a lower tuition with school officials. Halil diligently noted the details in his notebook and said he would check into it. At my next opportunity, I explained the family's situation to Mr. Akkaya and asked whether the foundation could help the girl attend school by paying some of her fees. Slightly exasperated, he responded, "Now look, the work we do is normally work that ought to be done by the state." But what the foundation could do, he said, was go to the school principal and explain the family's situation and try to convince the school to waive its fees. Most principals, he claimed, would agree, and if they didn't, the foundation would pay the school fees. But when I mentioned this possibility to Halil, he just shook his head and explained carefully that Melek's husband would never accept that kind of help. "He's too proud. After all, he has a job, a real job, even though it doesn't pay enough. He won't accept help." I told him that the foundation gave other kinds of assistance to the poor, but Halil shook his head again. "They probably only give aid to people who really need it. For instance, if they don't have a job, if they're alone, or if they have an older relative living with them." I had to admit that Halil was probably right.

Thus, while the social welfare functions of Islamic foundations had been revived as civic adjuncts to the political process, their effectiveness in easing poverty and providing welfare services was questionable. It might be argued that some assistance was better than none at all for poor families, but the level of assistance I observed was well below that provided, say, by churches and food banks in the United States. Some of this obviously reflected lack of resources, but it was also related to a philosophy of the family that emphasized men's roles as breadwinner and rejected women's roles as potential economic providers. The perceived shamefulness of charity and the implication that a man receiving charity was unable to support his family also stood in the way of easing the plight of families that were poor, but not desperate. Non-Islamic associations, on the other hand, emphasized women's work opportunities and sought to maximize them. However, they, too, generally did this by training women in "female" trades like hairdressing, or within the same paradigm of women as home-based craftworkers, selling their wares at occasional *kermes* fairs, rather than as potential contributors to Turkey's expanding technological base and service economy. Even the Foundation for the Support of Women's craft shop was merely an extension of this principle.

In a creative addition to their array of charitable activities, the Welfare Party and the Ümraniye Service Foundation had revived what they presented to me as an Ottoman custom whereby rich families in effect adopted poor families. If a wealthy family expressed an interest in this form of charity, the Welfare Party, through its activists or the foundation, brought a member of the wealthy family together with a poor family, generally over dinner in the poor family's home. The visitors brought the dinner and they would all eat together. The relationship between the families was construed to be a personal one and the donor family undertook the long-term economic assistance, and perhaps education, of the poor family's members. I was unable to determine how widespread this practice was, or how successful and sustained over time. Members of wealthy families engaging in this form of assistance tended to be women, I was told. This was true to the long tradition of elite women's charitable activities in Republican, as in Ottoman, times. "Adoption" (*evlatlık*) of individuals by wealthy families also was still practiced. A friend's elite, secularist, and staunchly Kemalist family had brought a young village girl to live in their household. She had her own room and was responsible for cooking, cleaning, and other services. The family took full responsibility for her upbringing, safety, some education, and, eventually, her marriage. The elite family's elders found her a suitable groom, stood in for the girl's natal parents during the marriage negotiations, supplied the dowry, and paid for the wedding. This was not true adoption by the family, of course, in the sense of equality with the wealthy family's children or rights to inheritance. Rather, the wealthy family took the young girl under its protection (*himaye*) and carried out the basic duties of a family toward its members: providing a social identity, a place to live, protection, food, and a good marriage. In other words, the custom of "adoption" of the poor, like other Islamist charitable activities, reflects cultural traditions and widespread political strategies as much as Islamic values.

Formal Autonomy, Shared Duty

Although formal links between party, neighborhood associations, and foundation were absent, informally these were linked, coordinated, and harnessed to the party's agenda. When I asked Mr. Akkaya what would happen to the foundation's activities if the Welfare Party did not win the next election, he pointed out that the foundation was unrelated to the Welfare Party, and that there was no connection to the municipality either. "The mayor just gave the impetus for this work to be begun. He is our elder, otherwise he has no legal authority within the foundation. But, of course, if our mayor . . . says, 'this family's situation is as follows; help them'—well, that is our duty anyway, to help people who are in need."

Mr. Akkaya claimed to receive no pay for his work with the foundation. Funding for the foundation's work, he explained, came from local Muslim businessmen along with in-kind donations from businesses and large companies. The foundation received the rent charged by the municipality for its health center, which was run by a private company on municipal property. Another financial connection between the municipality and the foundation was through the company owned by Mr. Akkaya. When I asked him what he did professionally, Mr. Akkaya did not answer directly, saying, "Oh, this and that. I do business." But enthusiasm about his work overcame his reticence. "We are making the house numbers that will be used by the municipality in all of Ümraniye." He had designed them himself, he said, and proudly showed me blue plastic numbers that popped in and out of a yellow frame. These would be required of all households in Ümraniye, he added. Indeed, I had seen them pictured in one of the municipality's publicity magazines. I silently estimated the profit such an undertaking would generate in a neighborhood of over two hundred thousand people. He was working on a computerized overview of the entire neighborhood, he added, also for the municipality. While there was no obvious quid pro quo, it was clear that, while Mr. Akkaya's work for the foundation was voluntary, his business profited from municipal contracts. It was nothing unusual in Turkish political life for close associates and ideological bedfellows of those in power to reap profit and gain influence, nor was it necessarily illegal. But it added fuel to reports of cronyism in a party that had billed itself as free of favoritism. In fact, by the following year, Mr. Akkaya had moved his foundation activities to his business office in a different district of Ümraniye, quite a few *dolmuş* stops away from the municipal offices. "People kept misunderstanding the relationship between the foundation and the municipality," he explained when I asked him about the move.

Akinci (1999) presents evidence that the service foundations of Islamist-run cities were involved in municipal and party-linked corruption and cronyism. For instance, anyone submitting a proposal for municipal tenders was required to make a mandatory "donation" to the local service foundation. Akinci also argues that many of the service and welfare improvements made by Islamist-run municipalities were, in the end, subsidized by the state treasury when the municipalities defaulted on payments, and by hikes in unit prices of water, natural gas, and public transportation. Whenever possible, unemployed people were given jobs on the municipal workforce, padding the workforce and passing the cost on to the taxpayer. In effect, Akinci argues, the consumers ended up paying for the improvements through taxes and rate hikes. However, local governments in Turkey have their fiscal hands tied in ways that encourage unorthodox accounting and deal making to bring in resources. Under a heavily centralized system, municipal governments are held hostage to the fiscal and ideological requirements of their party leaders and the central government in Ankara, which tends to be relatively unresponsive to local needs. Municipalities have limited control over their budgets and facilities, few funds, and lack authority to generate revenues from local resources. They often do not control much of the land or infrastructure that they wish to impact or the resources they need to do so; these are under the control of the central government. Thus, there are few resources to target local needs and little continuity between administrations. This situation, in combination with common patron-clientilistic practices, tends to blur the fine line between teamwork and cronyism.

Flyer informing people that the Ümraniye Service Foundation takes in and distributes used goods. Caption: "'I didn't know' is no excuse. Now you know what to do." The figure at right exclaims, "Kindness [or humaneness] is not dead."

When I asked Şinasi Öktem, the former left-of-center mayor of Ümraniye, whether he knew where the Islamic foundation in Ümraniye was getting its money and what its relationship was with the municipality, he was predictably vituperative and incensed at what he perceived to be the corruption of the Welfare Party administration that had replaced his own. (Although his own administration had been accused of many of the same things.) "They claim they are doing this without pay, but it's not true," he thundered. "For instance, in Ümraniye the contract for collecting garbage was given to" a certain company (he named the company and its owner). The compact, energetic former mayor lit another cigarette. The Welfare Party, he continued, was supported by big Islamic holding companies and businesses. He rattled off a list of some prominent companies known to be owned by Islamists. "Welfare has had campaigns where, for instance, they tell their supporters not to buy from certain companies" that were competitors or associated with leftist causes.

In fact, under both administrations, the municipality, party, and associations like the Service Foundation and the People's Schools were connected, acted in tandem, and exchanged financial support.

At the time Mr. Öktem was mayor, his sister worked for the municipality and, later, ran the People's Schools with municipal support. At some People's School events, Mayor Öktem gave speeches and encouraged party support. Municipal jobs and contracts were handed out to supporters who used People's Days to lobby for them.

Mr. Dikmen showed me the municipal clinic. This was the clinic to which the Welfare Party mayor had referred the woman who petitioned for help with her medical expenses. It was located next door to the municipality offices, on the ground floor of a municipally owned building. According to Mr. Dikmen, it had been fully equipped by the Ümraniye Service Foundation, then rented out to private doctors, the rent going to support the foundation. The clinic looked very clean and modern. Mr. Dikmen claimed that under the Republican People's Party administration, it had been dirty and badly run, with old equipment. (An acquaintance who had been a patient at the clinic in Republican People's Party times had told me the same thing.) "We equipped it new ourselves." They charged patients on a sliding scale, poor people receiving free treatment and medicine. Even so, he pointed out, it was inexpensive, even for people who weren't poor. "An examination that costs several million Liras elsewhere, here costs only 900,000 liras." We sat with a white-smocked caregiver in his office and ordered tea. Mr. Dikmen demurred, as he was fasting, although Ramazan was over a month away. Some Muslims, he explained, began the fast early and did a three-month, instead of a one-month, fast.

According to Mr. Akkaya, in the future the foundation wished to found a large hospital in Ümraniye. "There are a lot of *vakıf* hospitals in Istanbul and they're giving very good service these days. A lot of them are seeing patients without charging fees; these are great blessings. In part, the reason for there being so many of these kind of foundations in Turkey derives from the state's insufficiency in these matters. The state does help [the poor] . . . but it's not enough. In any case, the state's budget really doesn't permit it." When I had left Mr. Akkaya's office, conscious of some Muslims' strict observance of custom and of Halil's warning, I did not extend my hand. Mr. Akkaya, however, smiling broadly, extended his and we shook farewell.

Welfare Party Organization

The foundation's activities slotted neatly, though informally, into an intricate network of party-related associations and activities. At the neighborhood level, below the official Ümraniye Welfare Party representative, was a Neighborhood Management Commission (*Mahalle Yönetim Kurulu*). Below the commission were the Head Observers (*Baş Müşahidler*). Each Head Observer was responsible for about 250 to 300 people in his neighborhood, assigned according to voting districts, each district comprising about 300 people. In addition, every Head Observer had under him four Observers (*Müşahidler*). In effect, in every neighborhood, for every voting district, there was at least one Observer for every seventy-five people. These were generally people who lived on the same street as the people they "observed." An exception was made if someone of a particular regional or ethnic origin was needed in another part of the neighborhood because they were thought to be more effective in making contact with residents of the same origin. Between 160 and 180 people worked for the Welfare Party in the Ümraniye district of Çakmak alone, almost one per street. This differed from the local organization of other political parties, which assigned only a few persons per voting district, generally active only around election time.

The job of the Observers was to keep track of everyone's needs. They kept detailed written records that were then entered into a computer. This information was located not only on the municipality's computer but could be pulled up by a central Welfare Party computer in the capital, Ankara. Other than the party delegates and their teams, the rest were ostensibly volunteers. One activist described his work as "without pay; associational work." Another explained his involvement in terms familiar from Peace of Mind Discussions: "If someone is uncomfortable, you should be, too." While these sentiments are likely true reflections of activists' motivations, it is also important to remember that economic and political benefits may accrue to active Welfare Party members through their networking and the awarding of work contracts.

The Head Observer sent holiday cards to the people under his care. If a person was ill, he sent a car to take them to the doctor. He went to weddings and funerals. The Observers observed their neighbors continuously and unobtrusively, noting if anyone needed assistance, then referring that information upwards in the hierarchy of associations. For special campaigns they went door to door, generally on weekends when the men were at home. It would have been inappropriate for the male Observers to speak to women home alone.

The Women's Commission (or Women's Branch, as it was also called) was tied to the neighborhood organization, but informally. During the week, activist women visited neighbors or went door to door. They were not bound to any particular streets and, unlike the men, could knock freely on the doors of women they did not know.

Delaney has suggested that women in the Turkish village she researched were socially interchangeable, while men carried socially bounded identities. Before marriage, women's essential value was in their virginity, the guaranteed purity of the soil in which the seed of the husband's patriline would be planted. Women also were expected to leave their natal families and join the family and household of their husbands. The interchangeableness of virgins and expectation of interchangeableness as brides bonded women in their shared physicality, regardless of other characteristics, such as place and family of origin. Men, on the other hand, as carriers of a social identity linked to and reflecting on a particular family and place of origin, always represented and acted on this identity, specific man to specific man (Delaney, 1991, 150).

Thus, women activists could range more widely than men. They held "conversation and lessons [*sohbet ve ders*]" about Islam with women in their homes, and, like the Observers, referred upward any problems they noticed in the families they visited. Women acted as volunteers for the foundation and, in their capacity as Welfare Party members, worked within the Women's Branch and Youth Branch, formally unincorporated into the Welfare Party, and in street-level cells. More so than male activists, they were able to create and penetrate women's networks throughout the neighborhood and, thus, were instrumental in expanding the Welfare Party's voter base. However, formal party representation was largely male, as was leadership of the foundation.

Foundations: The New Political Arena

An important implication of the informal links between the Welfare Party and civil society is that party-related activities were independent of the fate of the party itself. At the time of my research in fall 1997, the Supreme Court of Appeals was considering closing the Welfare Party for violation of the constitutional separation of politics and religion. (It was closed down in February 1998.) When I asked Welfare Party activists what would happen to their organization if this were to occur, I was told that it didn't matter. An activist working for the municipality put it succinctly: "If Welfare is closed down, about fifteen hundred elected politicians will lose their jobs. The others are unofficial and will continue." Responding to my question, Mr. Akkaya commented that, in any case, they thought of their activities as part of a movement, not a political party. This would be unwelcome news to Kemalists and members of Turkey's armed forces who believed that if the Welfare Party were closed, it would not be able to reorganize in time to win in the next elections—which it was widely expected to do.

In fact, when the party was closed down that winter, another party, the Virtue (*Fazilet*) Party, had already been founded by members of an Islamic foundation (*vakıf*) that claimed it had no links to the Welfare Party. The Virtue Party magnanimously invited members of the former Welfare Party to join its ranks. A wary government watched the Virtue Party carefully to make certain it was not simply a replacement for the Welfare Party. As we have seen, despite some of the same faces, the Virtue Party did change its message, if not its strikingly effective means of mobilizing support—its reliance on vernacular politics. A central element of vernacular politics is civil society. In Turkey, that role is played by Islamic foundations.

Foundations (*vakıflar*) are particularly important in the Islamist organizational network, despite the fact that there are many more associations than foundations in Turkey. Foundations, which have roots in the Ottoman Empire, have made a comeback over the last two decades as a major conduit for charity work, particularly Islamic foundations. They are legal corporations founded on the basis of continual use of proceeds from a reserved form of property, such as a house, land, or shop. This differs from an association, club, or union in that foundations do not have members or partners. Associations comprise groups of people as members or, in the case of companies, as partners, joined to participate in a particular activity. A foundation, by comparison, is an association of property, not people. Its participants are "those who profit from the foundation," rather than members or partners (Zevkliler, 1996, 1438). During the Ottoman era, foundations were established to assist the poor and indigent and to furnish members of a particular family or profession with social, economic, or educational assistance. Some provided public services, such as road construction or the distribution of food and drinking water.

After the founding of the Republic, a new entity, the association (*dernek*), was given legal place next to foundations. During this period, associations were established for various purposes, including charity, once the province of foundations. While associations may be founded to pursue activities similar to those of foundations, they cannot be established for the purpose of financial profit, while foundations may. All contemporary foundations are under the control of the General Directorate of Foundations, which sends an inspector at least once every two years to ascertain that the foundations are using their property for the declared purposes. Every year, nonexempt foundations are taxed up to five percent of their net income. Other foundations, those doing a public service, for instance, are tax-exempt. Like associations, foundations found to be supporting a particular ideology, political party, or religious community can be dissolved by the court, but oversight of foundations has been less stringent than that of associations. Associations, however, were easier to set up and, unlike foundations, they could be established without setting aside property sufficient to achieve their goals. As the number of associations increased in the early Republic, the number of foundations decreased. However, the popularity of associations was curtailed at various times during the ensuing half century, and foundations gained new life as a result.

The Secret Life of Associations

In its present usage, the Turkish term *dernek* means association, society, or club, forms of civic association that arguably developed in the West. However, the term *dernek* has a long history and was used in Anatolia to mean the organization of villagers around the discussion and planning of an event, such as a wedding (Toksöz, 1996, 367). In its modern civic manifestation, a *dernek* is a group of individuals formally organized around a common purpose, idea, or interest. It is an individual enterprise not under the control of the state. In principle, associations may include everything from economic associations to political parties. However, in its modern, legal definition, *dernek* excludes political parties, associations organized by the state or whose membership is involuntary, and organizations that have profit making as their primary goal.

The first legal associations were founded after the 1908 Constitution gave Ottoman subjects the explicit right to freely congregate (although illegal associations had existed prior to that). Associations were permitted as long as they did not contradict the Constitution, state law, or public morality. Most associations of the time were concerned with social work and social welfare, filling service niches, such as care of the old, protection of indigent children, and education of the handicapped, that only later were taken over by the state. In the early Republican era, some associations were dedicated to implementing the path of nationalist, modernist social change decreed by Ataturk. These included the *Halkevleri* (Folk Houses), which encouraged a national culture, and the Turkish Historical and Turkish Language Associations, which were instrumental in creating a new national historiography and language, respectively. Despite lingering suspicion of the right to free assembly, the founders of the Republic were well aware of the power of associations and used them to spread acceptance of Republican values and ideals. In the 1990s, many associations, such as the influential Society for the Support of Modern Living, still have as their raison d'être the guardianship of Ataturk's social revolution.

The 1924 constitution did not specify particular limitations on associations, but rather left regulation to the legal system. This left the door open to cycles of restriction and liberalization as different governments enacted applicable laws. A 1953 law, for instance, imposed heavy fines on anyone using public meetings for religious purposes. The 1961 constitution expanded and liberalized associational freedom by allowing public demonstrations and marches. Only general restrictions were placed on freedom of association—for instance, that it not endanger public harmony or general morality. However, it was still required that authorities be notified before a public meeting was held, and the courts were given the right to close down associations that behaved contrary to societal rules and laws. Labor unions and political parties were dealt with separately. In the 1960s, civil servants won the right to organize unions.

Compared to previous laws, the 1972 statutes were quite specific in the strictures surrounding associational life. Among the types of associations forbidden were those based on religion, religious sects, and orders; those based on family or race; secret organizations; organizations promoting regional separatism or the domination of one region, race, social class, religion, or denomination over another; those inciting religious feelings and using them to attempt to overthrow the state or social order; attempting to change the constitution;

derogating Ataturk, his actions, his memory, or the Turkish state; supporting a political party, working with a political party, or supporting (or hindering) candidates in an election; undermining human rights and freedoms; and intending to commit a crime. Because of widespread student activism, student political activity came under particular suspicion. Student members of political parties were forbidden to also join student associations and, in some cases, student associations were banned. In a harbinger of events to come, the Constitutional Court was given the power to close down political parties. A 1972 law stipulated that a member expelled from a political party or who caused a party to be closed down was prohibited from forming or leading an association for five years. Similarly, those who founded an association banned for illegal activities were forbidden to establish another association.

Despite these restrictions, the numbers of associations continued to grow, from 205 in 1938 to 40,170 in 1971, and 53,657 in 1981 (Toksöz, 1996, 373). The state's anxious reining in of the associations was, in part, a response to inflation in their numbers. They increased only slightly from 1938 to 1946, a period marked by economic stagnation and the dislocations of the Second World War, but burgeoned in the relative stability and openness after 1950. This was a time of increasing pluralism, as the economy diversified and the social class structure became more complex, and as the rural population began to flow en masse into the cities. Along with the voting booth, associations provided avenues of self-representation to emerging groups. The steep growth in associational life was not just a matter of increase in numbers, but also in variety. There was a particular increase in social and cultural organizations, but also in the number of religious associations, as they stepped in to fill the gap left by the state in dealing with the needs of urban migrant populations.

After the introduction of multiparty politics in the 1950s, special interest groups formed around Islamist, liberal, and nationalist agendas, while a nascent market economy gave rise to professional associations. Three times since then, Turkey has experienced political gridlock and army intervention. The first time, in 1960, was to allow parliamentary opposition to what the military perceived to be an increasingly authoritarian ruling party. The 1960 coup resulted in a new constitution, expanding and guaranteeing rights of free speech and free association. Thereafter, the number of political parties, interest groups, and civic associations grew tremendously.

The next two coups in 1971 and 1980 were, in a sense, an effort to rein in the autonomy of these alternative social forces that had proliferated, some violently, since 1960. Between 1960 and 1980, several human rights organizations were established, as well as organizations representing nearly every occupational group. Student groups and women's groups emerged in educational institutions and in political parties. Strong trade unions formed. Many associations, however, became highly politicized and were oriented toward gaining ideological supremacy and even overthrowing the state, rather than representing group interests. This led to the intergroup violence and polarization that brought on the 1980 coup. In 1982, after the 1980 coup and under the stern eye of the military, which wanted to prevent a recurrence of the violent social unrest of the 1970s, a more restrictive constitution replaced the former, relatively liberal, document. In the decade after the 1980 coup, as constraints were put on associations with ideological and social aims, the balance moved again toward foundations as the means for implementing these aims.

Ironically, the staunchly Kemalist military had set the stage for the expansion of Islamist civic activity in this period. In an attempt to find a means to counter a perceived threat of communism and to reunite a country torn by the ideological divisions of the 1970s, the military had encouraged the public expression of Islam and allowed Islamic publications. They repressed the most radically ideological of the Islamic groups, but encouraged groups that represented ideologies they thought would have a unifying effect on society or that did not represent a threat. The military also crushed associations with leftist views, leaving the field open for others, like the Islamists, to take up the message of economic and social justice. In fact, as we have seen, a number of leftists joined the Islamist ranks.

Another important factor in the spread of civil society after 1983 was the connection to the global communication network though the Internet, cable television, and the spread of telephones and televisions to the most remote corners of the country. Deregulation of until then government-controlled television and radio led to an explosion of stations representing a variety of political and religious views, and multiplying sources of information and forms of entertainment. The publication of periodicals and books increased and research institutes and private universities sprouted like mushrooms.

In this ferment, Islamic groups and points of view were particularly well represented. Islamists of varying stripes controlled a number of radio and television stations and published newspapers and journals. Their intelligentsia was respected, their ideas widely debated. Graduates of schools giving religious education, both male and female, were increasingly entering the universities. Conservative Muslims had their own labor confederation (Hak-İş) and business association (MÜSIAD). Islamic civic groups were among the most organized in Turkey. The groups, however, were by no means unified, given the vast range of positions and practices that characterize Turkish Islam and the equally diverse motivations for political and civic mobilization that we have discussed in previous chapters. MÜSIAD members, for instance, did not necessarily vote for the Welfare Party or agree with the Hak-İş labor confederation on the issue of workers' rights.

Civil society became more differentiated. New political actors entered the scene: women, businessmen, environmentalists, urban migrants, Islamic engineers, Yuppies, and members of Generation X. Voluntary associations proliferated, organizing around every conceivable issue. When Turkey switched from a statist economy to a neoliberal export-led economy in the early 1980s, this created new opportunities for upward mobility and demands for a better political and economic climate for business, and encouraged the strengthening of business and professional associations. Women's groups lobbied successfully for changes in the legal and criminal codes. Feminist groups moved away from the state feminist model that cast women as moral role models for the nation and began to agitate for individual freedom of expression. The best-selling novel *The Woman Has No Name* by Duygu Asena, published in 1985, was a harbinger of this new feminist ground. In the novel, which caused a sensation in Turkey, a professional woman revels in sexual freedom and, to safeguard her own career and personal freedom, refuses marriage.

By 1993, there were about 65,000 civic organizations in Turkey. Most of these were associations; only 2,500 were foundations. (Gönel, 1998, 21). With their traditional Islamic affiliation, history of involvement in charity and public works, and relative freedom from oversight, foundations experienced a renaissance as an Islamic response to the inequalities and economic dislocations of the new economy. Unlike associations, tainted by involvement in antigovernment activities in the 1960s and 1970s, foundations have a long and honorable history. This was played up by Islamists who pointed out that their present-day foundations did much the same as *vakıflar* under the Ottomans, providing civic services that the state was not expected or was unable to deliver. Consider the issue of schools. State schools may have ninety to a hundred students per class. Facilities are poor, teachers underpaid, and, as we have seen in Ümraniye, parents are required to pay fees many cannot afford. Girls and boys are expected to sit together in classrooms, much to the consternation of religiously conservative families. One response by parents has been to hijack the services of alternate schooling, like theological schools, supplied by the state. Another response has been to rely on civil society, especially Islamic foundations, to provide or subsidize education.

State-run theological (*imam-hatip*) schools increasingly were seen as an alternative form of education by conservative families. These schools were originally designed to prepare students for entry into theology training programs that turned out government-approved laicist religious specialists appointed to mosques and other religious institutions. After the 1980s, the schools came increasingly under the control of nonlaicist-minded officials and expanded their brief to educate boys and girls of conservative families who wished segregated classrooms and a religious component to their children's educations. The schools were perceived as providing better quality education, with curricula that covered religion as well as subjects taught in other state-run schools.

The government, however, in its drive against what it perceived to be Islamic fundamentalism, tried to weaken or eliminate use of these schools as an alternative form of education. The raising of mandatory school attendance in 1997 from five to eight years was perceived by many to be aimed as much at structurally undercutting the Islamic schools as at improving children's educational achievement. The decision resulted in a scramble to train enormous numbers of new teachers in time to implement the new requirement, but did little to address the conditions which made the Islamic schools so popular in the first place: cost, quality, a curriculum perceived to be morally guided, and a segregation of male and female students that made it more likely for parents to send girls to school. (Despite the previous five-year schooling requirement, 28 percent of women were illiterate in 1990, compared to 11 percent of men [SFYDP, 1995, 24]. That number was even higher in eastern and southeastern Anatolia, where 48 percent of women could not read or write [TESEV, 1997, 29].)

Islamic foundations set up legal and illegal Quran schools. Islamist activists pleaded with public school principals to waive fees for poor children. While the Welfare Party and the Service Foundation in Ümraniye did not provide direct financial assistance for grade school education, they did supply donated books and used school clothing; for university students, they also offered a small stipend and subsidized segregated dormitories. The Fethullacılar set up a network of foundations that ran high-quality, subsidized middle and high schools in Turkey and Central Asia. Like the foundations associated with the Welfare Party, the Fethullacılar were organized as individual foundations with no formal interconnection, although they all took their ideological direction from the charismatic preacher Fethullah Gülen. The reemergence of civil society to take over state functions coincided with the decline of Turkey's statist economic policies in the 1980s and the resulting lack of confidence in the state's being able to deliver development to its people.

Present-day foundations have other advantages. Unlike associations, which must obtain permission from the police for every move they make, foundations can operate relatively freely. Although establishing foundations is more difficult because it requires dedication of capital or property, once founded, they operate with minimal government oversight. This appealed to more than just the Islamists. A Republican People's Party official at the opening of a party-sponsored women's center in Ankara volunteered that he wished this and other planned centers could be part of a foundation instead of an association. Use of the building in which the women's center was housed was donated by a wealthy female party supporter. If it had been a foundation, the official pointed out wistfully, the supporter could have donated the building, with all the profits from the building going to the foundation in perpetuity. An association, he complained, had to get permission for everything. "Associations had a bad image before; they were left-wing, armed. The state came down on them very hard." But with a foundation, "you gain an identity, a personality and more respect in the eyes of the people. . . . They're something with historic roots, fitting to the Turkish makeup. They have a tradition; they're an example of Ottoman civil society. . . . Until recently, there were no left, left-democratic foundations, only Islamic ones. Now there are also left foundations." A final advantage, he added, was that "if the army takes over, they can close the associations but not the foundations."

While there are many associations in Turkey, the numbers do not tell one much about the quality of the membership or the purpose of the organization. It takes only a handful of members to formally register an association; twenty or thirty people in a neighborhood who get together regularly may decide to list themselves as an association. Even if they no longer meet, they remain on the books. In Ümraniye, Mahmure was a member of the Welfare Party Women's Branch, but had never gone to any meetings. She had once attended a Welfare Party–sponsored meeting and had called attention to herself by speaking up. "The Welfare women insisted strongly that I join, so I did, even though I told them I'd never be able to attend any of their events or meetings." Associations were allowed to serve alcohol, so people might register a regional assistance association, when actually they ran a cafe that served alcohol, like Osman's assistance association in Yenikent, which his wife laughingly referred to as a "gambling den."

Furthermore, formal membership in associations is class- and gender-biased. Only 5 percent of women and 28 percent of men in the squatter areas of Turkey's three largest cities belonged to an association of any kind, mostly unions and political parties. The men belonged also to professional associations and, to a lesser extent, religious and charity organizations and sports clubs (Gökçe et al., 1993, 315, 317). Three major confederations of about eighty labor unions represented more than three million workers, or 63 percent of the salaried labor force (Toprak, 1996, 104). But since union membership was not optional in many industries, this figure does not tell us much about the spirit of civic participation in squatter areas. Sports clubs, such as karate clubs, often were associated with political parties and served as party youth incubators.

The issues addressed by elite-run associations may have little resonance in the working-class and squatter areas, where people are more concerned about growing economic inequality, the spread of Western-style consumerism, and what many see to be a related decline in moral values. This message was taken up by the Welfare Party and Islamic organizations, along with other related issues: employment, protecting the environment, access to education, and the dispute about the right to wear a head scarf at university, closely associated with educational opportunity for women.

Since the 1923 founding of the republic, 4,157 new foundations have been established. By far the greatest number (1,267) list their aim as social assistance, 939 as education, and only 397 as religious

(GDF, 1997). Other religious foundations on the books date from Ottoman times. Many of these are now defunct, although still listed, and have been absorbed into the state-managed General Directorate of Foundations. From 1926 to 1967, when a new law eased foundation requirements, only around 50 new foundations were established (as against 28,375 associations) (DPT, 1983, 22). This means that the past thirty years have seen a veritable explosion of foundational life. But to write about civil society by itself—the number and type of organizations—is meaningless. One needs to ask how these organizations are attached to the social and political body.

Civil Society Reconsidered

Civil society recently has received a great deal of attention and occasioned impassioned debates among social scientists about the inclusion or exclusion of such basic forms of social organization as family networks and tribe. Cohen and Arato (1994), for instance, argue for incorporating a cultural component into civil-society analyses. However, the Middle East, long associated with tribalism and dynastic family networks, has been until recently a lacuna in the field of civil-society studies. This was rectified to some extent by Augustus Richard Norton, editor of two comprehensive volumes on the various modern and traditional institutions in the region that arguably can be considered to be acting as civic organizations (Norton, 1995, 1996). Nevertheless, the structural relation of culture, politics, and civil society remains undertheorized, with analysts focusing either on a single plane or on the intersection of two of the three, as, for instance, Diane Singerman's (1995) insightful analysis of the interplay of politics and culture in an urban Egyptian community.

A further lacuna has been in the area of social class, leading to an internally undifferentiated account of civic organization in countries, like Turkey, where there are thousands of civic associations, but where polls show that the working-class population tends not to join associations, although it is active in civic affairs and politically engaged. This reframes the question to be asked of civic activity, from one of structure and numbers to one of culture, and causes us to revisit the debates about the civic and political potential of culturally embedded forms of social organization. What galvanizes working-class people who do not have a history of membership in civic associations to become involved in civic activities, demonstrations, social movements, and political action? When they do become involved, what forms of social organization frame their participation?

In disenfranchised communities like Ümraniye, classical civil society had limited representation. Instead, culturally situated associational practices linked these communities to state institutions, like political parties. Some of these practices were directed by formally incorporated civic organizations, like foundations and associations, others by activists operating without a clear formal designation. The Welfare Party mobilized activists on the basis of informal, culturally defined forms of social organization that relied on face-to-face, personalized relations of trust and mutuality. While the Welfare Party's promise to be more responsive to local needs was part of its appeal, the extraordinary success of its mobilization of Turkey's working-class population and cross-class appeal can be traced to its particular structure, method, and message, all of which were framed in terms of local moral conventions and solidarities.

The structure of Welfare Party politics emphasized the local and was conducted as a well-organized and integrated triad of party, municipality, and local foundations, supported by a phalanx of male and female volunteers. Unlike other parties, the Welfare Party did not rely primarily on the media to get its message across, but worked face to face. Street by street and village by village, cells of activists were built on a foundation of personal relations. Activists also were matched to voters in their district by age, gender, and place of birth, taking advantage of preexisting loyalties. A Welfare Party member was responsible for attendance to people's needs at a personal level. On election day, every voter was brought to the polls, even the old and frail.

The Welfare Party strategy relied on building interpersonal trust, taking full advantage of neighborhood, regional, and other cultural bonds that tied people to one another in mutual assistance, as well as its flip side: mutual obligation. The party translated complex political ideas into local cultural codes, which included the practice of *imece,* or generalized reciprocity. Ideas were translated into a culturally embedded, personally transmitted message. Personalization of a political message constitutes a particular mode of mobilization: mobilizing the masses one by one. Welfare Party mobilization thus appeared to many supporters in the streets of Ümraniye to be a social movement of which they were in the vanguard, rather than a well-orchestrated campaign for party support. Indeed, because of the loose organizational structuring, local, personal transmission of the Welfare Party message, and filtering of contact through civic organizations, the relationship between party, activist, and local resident was complicated and often obscured. Personalization and popularization situated an ideological message, grown in the medium of national politics and intellectual debate, in the cultural matrix of everyday life, where its yeast could thrive. Class differences were obscured *not* because identity politics per se is blind to class differences, but because the structural processes of personalization and popularization bridged the gap between classes. In Ümraniye, civil society assisted this bridging function by providing the organizational framework within which personalization and mobilization could occur.

Despite the shortcomings of the Islamists' civic activities—too few resources to meet the needs of a large and poor population; the dubious nature of municipal and foundation income; the exclusive focus on men for income-production opportunities—civil society provided a powerful fulcrum for vernacular politics, coordinating Islamist ideology, populism, local culture, and political and human resources, and making these available to the political will of both social movement and political party. One of the most important resources put into play through civic coordination of neighborhood networks was the participation of working-class women. The contradictory place of women in the Islamist movement is the focus of the next chapter.

7

ISLAMIST ELITISM AND WOMEN'S CHOICES

Women's opportunities and choices are affected by the economic conditions of their environment, whether they view themselves as Muslim, Islamist, or secularist. Within the boundaries of economic possibility, there is a broad space of movement within which women can strategize and manipulate existing options and pursue new opportunities. The Islamist movement populated this space with a panoply of new options for women. This included opportunities to gain an education or professional training, work outside the home, and participate in political activism. As we have seen in the preceding chapters, in Ümraniye these opportunities were not open to all women equally. Unmarried young women were given access to different training and education than older married women. Furthermore, women often found that their aspirations and the Islamist promise of an alternative lifestyle were short-lived. At marriage or motherhood, women often found themselves pulled back into a more restrictive lifestyle. Middle-class and elite Islamists were more likely to be able to maintain an alternative lifestyle (indeed, develop their own version of middle-class Islamist chic). But even these women faced the dilemma at marriage of continuing their economic, educational, or political work outside the home, or focusing their energies on and submitting to the authority of husband and family. The primacy of women's duty to home and family is also a basic principle of Islamist thought.

Tesettür veiling is a key symbol of the Islamist movement, but, despite its centrality, *tesettür* is fractured by the same multiple, contradictory meanings as are other Islamist lifestyle choices. *Tesettür* bears a heavy symbolic burden. As we have seen in previous chapters, among Islamist followers it connotes egalitarianism, party populism, and resistance against the laicist autocracy. Göle (1996) has argued that wearers of *tesettür* are engaged in identity politics, that is, a bid to acquire elite status for an Islamic lifestyle that would put it in competition with a Western lifestyle in the definition of social status. Certainly, *tesettür* in Ümraniye was a "city look" that had developed its own momentum as fashion. This gave it a cachet of upward mobility. Islamist fashion also implied moral uprightness and other qualities residents found attractive, especially in the opposite sex. *Tesettür*'s association in the media and public displays with the Islamist social movement also added to its value within the community, at least among Islamist supporters.

However, there was no evidence that *tesettür* had any effect on the actual social status or economic position of its wearers in Ümraniye. Indeed, the relative freedom of action that the Islamist movement afforded women within the economic and social restrictions of Ümraniye might simply be part of the life cycle for young, unmarried women, or married women before they have children. This is quite a different image from that drawn by studies of Islamist elites—the editors, writers, intellectuals, middle-class activists, Islamist Yuppies—who are perceived to be engaging in identity politics.

The paradox of veiling lies in two sets of superimposed meanings: first, the Islamist challenge to the status quo; second, Islamist support for the principle that woman's place is in the home and her role is to take care of husband and family. Islamists have attempted to deal with this paradox by differentiating "Islamist" practices from those of the masses. Islamist practice is regarded as superior because it is "conscious" (*şuurlu*), unlike the unconscious adherence to tradition that is presumed to explain these same practices among the masses. Much like Kemalists who attempt to distance themselves from certain shared behaviors and values by attributing them to the "Other" Istanbul, Islamists attribute the restrictive, patriarchal nature of shared practices to the "Other" Muslims. This constitutes a kind of Islamist elitism quite distinct from the more neutral "elite status" envisioned in the discourse of identity politics.

Ümraniye Welfare Party activists.

This "enlightened" explanation of veiling, seclusion, and women's proper place in the family, however, does little to change the fact that women are subject to the constraints accompanying these practices. In many instances in Ümraniye, a practical seclusion at marriage was "chosen" because of a lack of other credible options for establishing and maintaining a family. Even educated women may have difficulty finding the resources to establish a professional life. The *himaye* of family life, also implied by veiling, is a powerful source of support, protection, and comfort, although it exacts a great price from women in the curtailment of their choices, activities, and movement outside the home. Not surprisingly, female and male Islamist activists in Ümraniye emphasized different sides of the paradox when asked about their own goals within the movement. Women were interested in the means by which the Islamist movement could allow them to challenge the status quo; men envisioned an ideal in which women were wives, mothers, and homemakers, and some wanted the possibility of a polygynous marriage (presently illegal under secular Turkish law). Below, I describe the lives of women in Ümraniye, their choices and constraints, and the role the Islamist movement played in these.

The Islamist Paradox

Halil was an Islamist activist. His wife, Nefise, had received training in computers and, before her marriage, had worked for the Welfare Party municipality doing secretarial and computer design work. She was interested in Islamist politics and knew some of the leading women activists in Ümraniye. The lives of Halil's extended family, in many ways, were typical of Ümraniye. Halil's parents lived on the second floor of a four-story structure on the outskirts of Ümraniye. It looked much like any other small apartment building in the area, a confection of slender iron rods in a concrete core, a wooden frame filled in with cement brick, walls painted a neutral color. There was no sidewalk and the street was badly paved and full of potholes. The neighbor across the street had taken the initiative and paved an area that exactly matched the size of his car, so he could park it without it becoming mired in mud. Halil and Nefise lived on the third floor, above Halil's parents. The fourth floor was slated for Halil's brother, Hasan, and his wife, Sevgi, who lived in a rented apartment a few streets away. Another brother and his family would occupy the ground-floor apartment. Neither floor was finished; at the moment there was not enough money to continue building. One of Halil and Hasan's brothers lived in the village and would not be joining them in the new structure. Another lived nearby and was happy to remain in his own domain; it was rumored that his wife did not get along with her mother-in-law.

Usually Nefise spent much of the day with her mother-in-law, Müşerref, downstairs in the latter's apartment. When I visited, that is generally where we sat and where people looked for us. The only telephone was in the parents' apartment. One day, however, Nefise had visitors in her own flat, some distant relatives who had come to keep her company. On a warm afternoon, the sun filtering thickly into the room through the broad, white, lace curtains, ten women settled onto the sofa, chairs, and thickly carpeted floor of Nefise's parlor. Their hands moved continually, knitting and stitching as they talked. On this slow, languid afternoon, time seemed meaningless. Tea was poured continually; food was served whenever it was ready. The women murmured to one another, their voices adding texture to the three-dimensional quality of the light. Threads of conversation spooled aimlessly, occasionally gaining everyone's attention and, for a while, spinning into discussion of a single topic.

The subject of women's freedom of movement caught everyone's attention. One woman, her face shadowed by her head scarf and indistinct in the diffuse light, commented, "It's hard to sit alone at home all the time." Another added wistfully, "If only I could travel somewhere." The women immediately muted their complaints by adding firmly that they knew it was right for women to stay at home. They agreed among themselves that unprotected women should be limited in their movements. "One never knows what can happen." They discussed what the Quran said on the subject, although one woman pointed out that, when it came to the severity of the restrictions, it was men's power that determined this, not the Quran. The women compared notes about the different limitations on their movements. Müşerref told them about Halil's restrictions on Nefise (who was not present; she was either praying in the back room or washing dishes in the kitchen with Sevgi, the other daughter-in-law).

I had first met Müşerref at another home in Ümraniye after a wedding party. The assembled women had been debating the proper way to treat a new bride. One woman, with two school-age sons, was adamant that "you shouldn't spoil them in the beginning. If you're too permissive they become spoiled and refuse to do anything. Look at my brother and his wife. She just does whatever she wants and doesn't treat my parents right at all. She's always gallivanting about. If they had put their foot down right at the beginning this wouldn't have happened." Müşerref, a large, formidable woman with strong features who had borne and married off four sons, disagreed and said she worried about her daughter-in-law, Nefise. She thought her son was wrong in his treatment of her. "Imagine, he won't even let her go out to go to the grocery store. Even to me he says I shouldn't go out. 'If you need anything, mother, just tell me and I'll bring it to you.' But I tell him it's not right to lock a young girl like that up in the house. She'll get bored and then who knows what will happen." The other women murmured agreement. "She used to work and wants to take courses, but he won't even let her out of the house to buy supplies. It's not good for a young woman to sit at home by herself all day long. What can she do? A bit of cleaning and housework. That's all.

The rest of the time she sits. This is dangerous. How long can this go on before something happens?" She lamented that he was never like that before he joined the Welfare Party. "Maybe I spoiled him as a child. One does that with the youngest. Maybe I did something wrong and let him have his way too much. It worries me."

Yet Nefise's situation was not unusual. Even after knowing some families for years, I had been unaware of the fact that the women were not able to visit each other at will. Visits, even to nearby relations, required permission from a woman's husband. There was some variation in the severity of this rule. Unmarried women in the family seemed to have somewhat greater leeway to move between homes to visit relatives or friends. Since I had always telephoned before visiting, arrangements to visit other people presumably had been made in advance or out of my earshot. This only became clear to me on the last day of my visit to a woman and her daughter-in-law, when I expressed a desire to pay an impromptu farewell visit to a family member who lived a few *dolmuş* stops away. I suggested we all go there together for an hour or so, then return. This was out of character; generally it was they who determined when and whom we visited. The women looked at each other in consternation. Obviously embarrassed, they explained that neither could go out of the house without the permission of their husbands. The mother-in-law managed to reach her husband on the telephone and quickly obtained permission, but the younger woman's husband was nowhere to be found. Grounded, we waited for the men to come home from work. Since it was evening, they joined us and drove us there in the car. It would have been unseemly for them to entrust us to a stranger driving a minibus after dark.

At Nefise's that sunny afternoon, one of the women turned to me and said, "A woman's life is very hard." Others muttered agreement. Müşerref scolded, "They're creating separate women's and men's quarters [*Haremlik, selamlık kuruyorlar*]!"—then added forcefully, "I wish I were a husband." One woman confided, a bit anxiously, that an acquaintance had once fooled her husband into thinking she was going one place and then taken the bus to the city of Iznik instead to visit a sick relative. The other women responded cautiously. Amazed, one repeated to herself, "And she went all the way to Iznik!" After an awkward pause, another commented, "When my son goes with me, it's okay. I can go out." But several women exclaimed, shocked, "He's just a child!"—in other words, an inappropriate guardian. The daughters-in-law brought in trays of small savouries, sweet pastries, and plates of cucumbers and tomatoes cut into bite-size pieces. As we nibbled, one of the women asked me, "Is America far away? How many hours' drive is it?" Nefise explained that there was water in between and one couldn't drive there. But the question illustrated just how narrow many of these women's horizons were.

Late afternoon shadows began to move around the room like uninvited guests. A strain of dissatisfaction had infected the group. "Men make our lives hard." "I wish we had more education." "I wish I could work. Earn some money. It's hard when you have to rely on your husband every day to leave money for you. And sometimes he forgets; then what do you do?" I had witnessed these problems myself. Just the week before, a woman I knew in Ümraniye went to a battered box on the kitchen shelf and looked in it for money her husband should have left for her to take to a meeting of her rotating savings club,[1] but there was no money there. So she had to borrow the money from a neighbor (she refused to take it from me, a guest). There was a lot of borrowing of small sums among neighbors, not only for household expenses, but also the expense of maintaining a network of relationships. When the women visited one another, they generally brought some small item as a gift, especially if they hadn't seen each other in a while or came for a special occasion, like a holiday or birth of a child. This activity was so important that, when her husband forgot to leave her any money, in desperation one woman used a small gold coin from her wedding portion to purchase a pile of cheap head scarves from a visiting relative so she would have something to take when she went out to visit. Her relative was engaging in one of the informal means by which women are able to earn some small amount; reselling inexpensive items bought at a discount; stitching, embroidering, sewing, or crocheting for money; or selling small items they have made.

Nefise had met Halil while they were both working at the municipality; theirs was a marriage of mutual attraction, not an arranged marriage. Indeed, although restrained in public, the affection and companionship between them broke through in the occasional unguarded word or look. It was said that Nefise knew Halil would require her to stop working after they married. Nefise herself told me that she stopped working at the municipality after they married because "problems emerged" as she was interacting with other men there. Although she was eager to keep up her clearly advanced computer skills, Halil would not allow her to take a computer course or to give courses herself. Halil also worked late hours, leaving her to her own devices for most of the day. On a day I was visiting Hasan and Sevgi, Nefise sat with us until Halil came to get her at 11 P.M. His brother scolded him for coming so late. "Your wife has been sitting here waiting for you. You ought to be at home." Halil replied matter-of-factly, "There's a lot of work to be done at the municipality."

In Nefise's sunny parlor, the conversation meandered from a desire for mobility to lack of money to the women's inability to earn money. Several women said they wanted to work but the men wouldn't let them. And, one added, we don't have an education—where would we find work? Another pointed out the problem of getting to a workplace. Her daughter worked, she said, but was brought to work and back by a company bus. "Otherwise it would be too long a way for her to travel by herself. You can't trust everyone." Underlying these women's ambivalence about work was not the desire to stay at home, but the anxious feeling that, to be safe, women must be protected, that is, be under a man's *himaye* when outside the home. Even among my college-educated secularist friends, there was a reluctance to take taxis at night because "something might happen." Everyone had heard stories about taxi drivers taking advantage of lone women passengers, yet no one actually knew anyone to whom such a thing had happened. The taxi stories were an urban myth that restrained women's mobility. In Ümraniye, the fear of "something happening" was more generalized.

At the other end of Ümraniye, Nurcan, her sister-in-law, and I had a discussion one day about why Nurcan's eight-year-old daughter needed to learn not to mix with boys and why she should begin wearing a head scarf. The conversation started with the new eight-year-minimum school requirement recently announced by the government, and the resulting expectation that boys would be together in classes with girls, their heads uncovered, for all eight years. That is, unprotected girls would be thrown together with boys after puberty. This would be a disaster for her niece, the sister-in-law insisted, because something was bound to happen. "People have no brakes. If you put them in a situation like that, something bad will happen." I explained that in the United States boys and girls were put together all the time in school and nothing happened (although I realized in retrospect that this was not entirely true, given the alarming numbers of students that complained about harassment by other students). I added that in the United States it was assumed that people have brakes inside—children were raised to acquire those brakes and were punished for not heeding them. They grew up knowing inside that something was wrong (internalizing that knowledge) and so not doing it, rather than growing up thinking some behavior was wrong, but believing there was nothing one could do to avoid it except avoid the situation.

For Nurcan and her sister-in-law, however, control came from the outside, not the inside. Thus, women could be blamed for bringing trouble on themselves by heedlessly being in the wrong place at the wrong time. People were assumed to have no brakes, and it was up to society to set the boundaries and keep people's behavior straight, through constant vigilance and social disapproval, ostracism, or punishment. If unrelated men and women were alone for any length of time for whatever reason, it was assumed that "something happened." It must have, because people had no brakes and society hadn't been there to keep them apart.

Managing Virtue

If the impetus to maintaining one's virtue is located in behavior, then behavioral signals become important markers of unapproachableness and inviolability. Ironically, it is the very act of covering the body, of veiling, that has allowed women like Nefise the first step across the threshold to a public life of work and political activism. Islamic foundations gave scholarships and funded gender-segregated dorms that allowed young women from conservative, poor families to pursue higher education. Veiling, itself, established a kind of mobile honor zone from within which young women could interact with male students and teachers without fearing loss of reputation. Islamic corporations established training centers and issued professional certificates for men and women. This allowed some women to establish professional footholds, however precarious.

I encountered one such woman in a shop behind the enormous pink fortress of the Istanbul Security Headquarters, where I had come to apply for my residence permit. Rows of shops catering to the needs of petitioners of the bureaucracy offered Polaroid photography, photocopying and typing services, lunch, stationery supplies, accounting and legal advice. Until the early 1980s, itinerant scribes with portable typewriters sat in small stands outside post offices and bureaucratic buildings, offering their services to the illiterate public. Those services have now moved inside storefronts.

I had waited in a maze of lines at Headquarters and now clutched the forms I needed to submit that afternoon. The forms had to be filled out, typed in triplicate, and a petition drawn up. I stepped into the nearest shop advertising typing services and was shown into a small, cool back room. Set diagonally across one corner of the room was a desk behind which sat a young, veiled woman with glasses, dressed in a sweater and long skirt, firmly pounding the keys of a manual typewriter. My first thought, perhaps as a result of my own society's prejudices, was that she must be the secretary. The room was filled with folding chairs on which sat several patient people. I took a seat as well and looked around to find the person to whom I should register my presence. The chubby, bearded, middle-aged man who had manned the store in front did not appear, so I settled back until the situation should make itself clear.

Before long, I noticed that the woman behind the typewriter was very self-possessed. Whenever she finished a document, she would bark out that it was done and then hand it to the person who had rapidly arisen and approached her desk. Then, barely glancing at the room, she growled, "Next." The bearded man appeared once in the doorway—barely turning her head, fingers still moving across the keyboard, she snapped at him, "Did you take the money?" He assured her that he had and withdrew. It gradually became clear to me that this was the woman's own business, and that she was a serious, seasoned professional. On the wall behind her hung a framed diploma that certified that she had completed a seminar in insurance training given by an Islamic holding company. She probably rented the space from the shop owner, who, judging from the lack of custom in his part of the shop, was most likely grateful for the rent and, thus, eager to assist her. When my turn came, I passed her my forms and the answers I had written out on a separate piece of paper. When I began to explain that some of the answers were in English, she waved me off. Businesslike, she tapped the edges of the stack of papers and carbons, rolled the sheets into the typewriter, and reproduced the information flawlessly.

Tesettür, unlike other forms of veiling, has a cachet of politically correct respectability. A man molesting a woman in *tesettür* would be more than a scoundrel; he would be a traitor to a national movement whose intellectuals argue that an Islamic lifestyle is not only

Young women in fashionable tesettür.

respectable and reputable, but morally superior to a Western lifestyle. The honor of the nation is at stake, not only the honor of an individual woman. Women in *tesettür* reported being able to move freely through the city without fear of harassment, unlike women in Western dress, who often complained of being mauled in buses and harassed by men on streets outside their neighborhoods. Secularist women also have complained about the visibly better treatment of women in *tesettür,* like letting them go to the head of the line to get on a bus. I once moved through the city myself in *tesettür* because I was going to see some friends off on their pilgrimage to Mecca: among hundreds of people at the send-off site, I did not want to attract attention as the only woman with head uncovered. Male taxi and *dolmuş* drivers avoided looking at me and kept interaction to a minimum. An old woman placed herself between me and the *dolmuş* driver and insisted on speaking to him for me and handing him my fare money, clearly so that I would not be tainted by even the slightest interaction. Implicit in *tesettür* style is participation in a national social movement that lends the wearer a heightened sense of status, both moral (vis-à-vis secularists) and social (vis-à-vis women who merely cover, but do not veil). However, despite its political cachet, behind the social force of *tesettür* one can discern the familiar principle of *himaye,* guidance and protection by (and from) men.

Neither political cachet nor norms of respectability explain the newer, more assertive styles of *tesettür* veiling. How does one reconcile the revelation of the female shape in a form-fitting dress or suit with the act of hiding one's hair under a *tesettür* scarf? Two answers come to mind.

First, veiling is a form of seduction, simply by virtue of the fact that it emphasizes what is hidden. This is no secret to observers of women in other Islamic countries, where the discreet but effective twitch of a veil speaks as loudly as any Victorian ankle. Having come to inspect her new home on the floor above her soon-to-be in-laws, Mahmure had paused on the landing below and, looking coquettishly at her fiancé, asked whether the workmen had gone. She couldn't go up there to look at her furniture or decide where it was to be placed if strange men were there, she emphasized. Veiled young women sometimes engage in a self-conscious checking for strange males, a kind of preening, demonstrating publicly their virginity and moral standing. It is a kind of flirtation, with overtones of sexual danger in looking.

Second, Islamist veiling in Turkey has taken on a life of its own as commercialized fashion. In 1986, preparing for a visit to Turkey, I shopped for gifts at Filene's in downtown Boston. I spotted a selection of scarves in an attractive leopard print framed in loops of Hermès-style gold chains. I bought several of these for my educated secularist friends in Ankara, thinking that the fashionably "modern" pattern would override any religious overtones that might adhere to a gift of scarves. These clearly were meant to be worn modishly around the neck. For my friends in Ümraniye I purchased larger scarves in flowered patterns, thinking that these could be incorporated into *tesettür*. I had seen similar scarves in Ümraniye the year before. Upon arrival in Turkey, I visited Ümraniye first and presented my gifts. Much to my chagrin, I realized that flowered patterns were sadly out of date, and to my horror, I realized that the new rage in *tesettür* veils was—yes—a leopard-print design, framed in loops of Hermès-style gold chains. Variations of this pattern were everywhere to be seen. With great trepidation, I approached my secularist friends and handed over my gifts, now tainted by association with the "Other" Istanbul. One of these friends, a professional woman, was particularly sensitive about veiling and would react badly to any intimation that veiling was a fashion or was attractive in any way. Of course, I didn't mention that the scarf she was unwrapping was all the rage among Islamists. In fact, neither she nor any of my other friends knew about or noticed this connection (although they'll eventually read about it here). It is likely that they had no occasion for contact with veiled women aside from passing them on the street. It was to my advantage that there was a fashion time lag between cosmopolitan Istanbul and bureaucratic Ankara.

Ideally, to be fashionable, women should purchase new *tesettür* head scarves regularly to keep up with the patterns and colors of the moment. They should have several scarves, each matching a particular coat. There are also suits and dresses to be worn under the coats, again with matching head scarves. The best scarves and coats are made of silk and even the poorest women try to acquire one silk head scarf for special occasions. Many married women in Ümraniye were unable to keep up with the fashion and washed and ironed their one or two good scarves until they were threadbare. Young women, like adolescents everywhere conscious of their standing among their peers, were more likely to be sporting the latest fashion.

Elite Islamist women attended *tesettür* fashion shows. Navaro-Yashin (2002) describes an Istanbul fashion show at which expensive Islamic fashion styles inspired by "the Ottoman Palace" were demonstrated by runway models who matched the Turkish mainstream fashion industry's ideal of tall, thin, and blue-eyed. When the show ended, the professional models removed their veils, donned miniskirts, and, blond hair swinging, made their way through the veiled and bearded audience to the door. Navaro-Yashin tells of a well-off Islamist woman at the fashion show who complained that when she began to veil at age thirty-nine, the sales help at the shops she had frequented didn't recognize her and, because of her veil, began to treat her as someone who wouldn't be able to afford to buy anything in the store. The woman was happy that a more fashionable and recognizably elite *tesettür* style was emerging which allowed her to retain a middle-class identity while following the dictates of her faith.

In other words, while *tesettür* reflects a politicocultural philosophy and is associated with Islamist ideology, it is also deeply conditioned by socioeconomic forces. Indeed, as fashion, the style can be worn without the wearer evincing any overt interest in politics or in political Islam. As a populist uniform and symbol of aspirations for upward mobility, *tesettür* unites people despite differences in social class or political motivation; as fashion, it divides those who can afford to keep up with the latest styles and buy the best-quality materials from those who cannot. The danger of commodification and co-optation by the market was recognized by three young Islamist intellectuals, two of them women, in a discussion published in the Islamist magazine *İzlenim*[2] in 1995. The participants noted that after 1980 the Muslim elite began to attend fancy circumcision and engagement parties at five-star hotels and began to want to make an impression through their dress. Until the founding of the Republic, they argued, women had had a clothing language but it had been taken from them by the Kemalists. Now, Muslims were trying to regain the dignity of pre-Republican fashion, as worn by the style-setting Ottoman upper class. But modern elite, urban Muslims faced a dilemma. On the one hand, they sought an attractive image of their own, a style within which there was room for personal expression. On the other hand, this desire for a unique, personally expressive style opened the movement to the power of the market to foster interpersonal competition and to impose meaning on fashion devoid of ethical content. This would undermine their attempt to create an ethically coherent and unifying style and threaten to fracture the group culture that was one of the movement's main goals.

The panelists' concerns about the danger the market posed to the unity of the movement were prescient. However, the association of Islamist style with elite Ottoman fashion, rather than with popular

styles, contains within it another, though unacknowledged, danger—
that of elitism.

Islamist Elitism

The symbolic content of *tesettür* veiling is highly contradictory. On
the one hand, it incorporates ideas about an "Islamic modernity" in
which women are educated and professionally and politically active.
On the other hand, it refers to values like patriarchal hierarchy, gender segregation, and women's primary role as mothers and their place
in the home. At other times, it is simply a fashion that implies the
wearer is urban, "with it," and upwardly mobile, in intent if not in
fact. This multiple symbolic load put women like computer-literate
Nefise and ambitious Makbule in an awkward situation, when first
one, then another, set of meanings was invoked. In other words,
while the distinctive style of Islamist self-presentation is a key symbol of the Islamist movement, these styles also have a deep cultural
resonance in everyday life.

Gender segregation and veiling, as practiced in the everyday lives
of working-class people, carry multiple meanings, reflecting gender
and class as much as religious or political identity. For these people,
daily hardships deriving from unemployment, poverty, and lack of
adequate infrastructure and educational and health care facilities create fundamental conditions within which family-oriented practices
may be the only viable portals to survival. For women in particular,
obedience to family, submissiveness, and gender-appropriate behavior like veiling and segregation are important for claiming the social
and economic safety net of community membership and family support. These sets of practices can be referenced to a nonelite Muslim
(*varoş*) identity, as well as to an elite Islamist identity. Islamists point
to motivation as the crucial marker of difference.

Islamists have approached the difficulty of distinguishing an
"Islamist" practice by differentiating the commonplace cultural and
religious "tradition" of veiling from veiling that is done as a deliber-
ate act of pious reflection and political activism. Islamist activists
attempt to distance their own cultural actions from those of the surrounding population by claiming that their own veiling is more conscious, more thought out (*şuurlu*). The head of the Virtue Party
Women's Branch in Ümraniye: "My mother is covered [*kapalı*], in traditional covering. Now, our covering is, of course, different from our

mothers' covering. Ours is more purposeful, more researched, more conscious [*şuurlu*] than that in our neighborhood."[3] Another Islamist woman put it this way: "I veil of my own free will . . . not in order to cover my intellect, but because I want to communicate with this [form of clothing] to people, 'Don't see in me the beautiful attributes of woman, but rather the rational, thinking personality, the human being that thinks and has an opinion'" (cited in Seufert, 1997, 425–26, author's translation).

Islamist intellectual discourse (and academic discourse on that discourse) further supports a distinction between "conscious" veiling representative of "cultural politics" and an everyday veiling tainted by everyday motivations. Veiling because it is required by "tradition" or by patriarchal authority is not the same as "conscious" Islamist practice. The Islamist project aims "to introduce the 'real Islam' to social groups with lower levels of education and culture who otherwise experience 'folk Islam'" (Göle, 1996, 113). This top-down approach, reminiscent of Kemalist social engineering, relies, as did Kemalism, on the leadership of educated elites and their modeling of elite styles and lifestyles. In her study of Islamist women, Göle tellingly insists that the contemporary actors of Islamism are "not marginal, uneducated, frustrated groups," but rather university students, future intellectuals and professionals, new elites that she says have moved Islam from the periphery to the center (92, 96). As the young Islamist intellectuals at the *İzlenim* meeting pointed out, *tesettür* style is rooted in the fashions of the Ottoman elite, not the customs of covering practiced by the masses.

Islamists strategically (and consciously) wield cultural symbols like veiling in an attempt to gain social distinction for an Islamic lifestyle. Veiling also hides social distinctions among believers, although this clearly yields a contradiction, to be discussed below. Islamists have attempted to associate such social behaviors as veiling and gender segregation with the meaning complex of urban/modern/educated, challenging social hierarchies that had associated these behaviors in the past with rural/backwards/uneducated/*varoş*. Ideally, this would give veiling the cachet of an elite marker, distinct from mass behavior, and provide a unifying cultural marker for the party and the movement.

Many Islamist women want to use Islam to liberate themselves from conventional patterns of life and patriarchal constraints. While supporting women's centrality in the Muslim family, they believe that

"Take a good look, girl. These are high society." Cartoon by Turhan Selçuk. Used with permission of the artist.

Islamic doctrine also supports women's becoming educated, working, and being politically active. Islamic feminists, as some call them, actively disseminate their ideas in publications and the media. They vary, however, in their prescriptions for the ideal Islamic life. Some emphasize appearance and clothing and a woman's role as wife and mother in a bourgeois household, and agitate for change within those parameters. The magazine *Kadın ve Aile (Woman and Family)*, for instance, contains suggestions for the improvement of women's lives within an Islamic framework. Compare the message of a rural woman Islamist preacher that a woman is "a beautiful jewel that needs to be protected and covered all the time, and only looked at by its owner [i.e., her husband] in complete privacy" (Bellér-Hann, 1996, 41) to the statement of the Islamist woman cited above: "Don't see in me the beautiful attributes of woman, but rather the rational, thinking personality." These views of women are not incompatible, but, rather, differ in degree of emphasis. Indeed, it is not unusual to encounter Islamist activist women who hold both views simultaneously, promoting the centrality of woman in the family while attending university, engaging in professional work outside the home, editing a magazine, or canvassing for votes. As we shall see below, non-elite Islamist women may subscribe to these ideas as well, but are not as free to voice them or to act on them, nor are these ideas necessarily shared by non-elite Islamist men.

Despite efforts by the Islamists to distinguish *tesettür* and its associated lifestyle from their "traditionally lived" context and make of them markers of a different, "consciously" lived Islam, *tesettür* remains associated not just with the Islamist movement, but also with everyday urban life. *Tesettür* is worn by a great variety of women, from middle-class matrons like those attending the fashion show to poor migrants in the urban slums who wish to convey modesty, religious devotion, urban cachet, and the image (if not always the practice) of upward mobility. Some modern, middle-class secularists, although not veiled, lead consciously Islamic lives generally associated with veiling. They may pray and practice a modified yet still gender-segregated use of space. This further complicates any association of clothing and lifestyle with a fixed sociopolitical meaning.

In some respects, the term *Islamist elite* itself is a misnomer, since what is most often referred to is educational status, not necessarily economic status. Two major studies of Islamist women (Ilyasoğlu, 1994; Göle, 1996) took as their subjects educated women who were politically or professionally active, but whose families were migrants and lived in neighborhoods like Ümraniye. Although these women wore *tesettür* and gained status from their education, they were unlikely to be economic elites. Few from a migrant, poor, or working-class background have the means to actually move upwards economically. The families of Islamist businessmen and Islamist Yuppies enjoy a very different lifestyle from the educated, politically active "elites" of Ümraniye. Education, however, is available to the masses, both men and women, thanks to early Republican reforms and to some financial assistance by the true economic elites of the Islamist movement, either through direct assistance or funneled through foundations and the party.

Since cultural differences are associated with class distinctions in Turkey, the differentiation between common, everyday Muslim practice and elite Islamist practice inevitably implies attempts at de-proletarianization. For instance, popular Islamist novels and magazines aimed at an audience of working-class, lower-middle-class, and migrant women often focused on Islamic interpretations of modesty, veiling, gender segregation, and traditional female roles as wife, mother, and homemaker (Acar, 1995, 50). This earned the disapproval of Islamist intellectuals who disparaged such "discourses of 'cheap radicalism and populism'" as an "amalgamation of 'Islamicization and proletarianization'" and "the birth of an 'Islamic arabesque'" (Göle, 1996, 113)—connecting the popular, working-class *arabesk* musical style held in contempt by secularist elites to the implied working-class character of "traditional" Muslim practice.

The most viable avenue for distancing oneself from one's working-class background is education. Groups of *tesettürlü* students form mutually validating nuclei of young people able to wield their clothing and lifestyle in a "conscious" manner in a public field (university, plazas and roads during demonstrations, the media) which is swept clean of other meanings that could adhere from their working-class environment. Mass meetings of Islamist activists are another platform on which symbols can be displayed as having pristine meanings. An image of a unifying, "conscious" Islam can be maintained only in a neutral public space uncontaminated by the socioeconomic background, cultural practices, and contradictory motivations and aspirations of the masses. The economic and intellectual elites who financed and developed an ideological framework for the movement, on the other hand, did not need to fear cultural contamination, since their elite status was unassailable; in any case, like my educated secularist friends, they tended to socialize among themselves. It was Islamists like Nefise and Makbule in Ümraniye that were caught between their "conscious" Islamist political practice and the requirements of their working-class cultural environment.

There is a fundamental contradiction in the Islamist assumption that a "new" politicized, egalitarian Muslim value system can be impressed upon an unenlightened, class-bound, patriarchal Muslim lifestyle and raise it to a higher level. These fields of value and practice already intersect; one is embedded within the other; politics and culture are merged in practice. The attempt to establish one as separate from the other, "elite" Islamist practice as different from—and superior to—the everyday Islamic practice of the masses, leads to a form of Islamist elitism that holds out to nonelite women implicit promises of socioeconomic mobility and professional opportunity, and then betrays that promise. Even though Nefise's world was populated by Islamist activists, and *tesettür* and Islamist activism opened new routes of mobility and action for her, in the end, her world was bounded by the requirements of economic survival and cultural respectability that cling to veiling like the smell of smoke that cannot be washed out.

Educated young women, in particular, have a difficult time putting their skills into practice and forging a permanent professional career. While they can find jobs as secretaries and other office staff, they remain handicapped by a lack of collateral and, thus, access to credit to open their own businesses. Makbule, the young woman working in the Ümraniye municipal offices, was a good example of this. When I visited her in her office, she was wearing *tesettür*, a dove-gray coat and matching navy-blue-and-gray patterned head scarf drawn under her chin and across her bosom. She sat behind a wide L-shaped desk laden with up-to-date technology: two computers with graphics capability, two telephones bristling with buttons, two color printers, and a scanner.

Makbule was a university graduate and had studied accounting at a university on the Black Sea coast and computer science at a major university in Istanbul. Her dream was to open her own accounting business. To do that she needed credit but couldn't get a bank loan without collateral. I asked her if one of the Islamic foundations could lend her money. She answered, "They don't lend money for things like that. If they did, they would do it based on informal relations that already existed between people, so they would lend each other money even if they weren't in the foundation." To open a business, she also needed four years of internship experience. She already had two under her belt, since she had worked as an assistant bookkeeper for a big firm. But she was called in at all hours and on weekends, making it impossible for her to continue there. "Probably because I'm a woman," she offered as an explanation for the extra burden. Her present position at the municipality didn't count as an internship, so she was thinking of changing jobs again.

The ideological polarization of Turkish society also limited her options. One day, I came to her office to find her incensed. She told me she had inquired over the telephone about a job opening at a large company. They had been excited about her qualifications and were eager to interview her. Just in case, so that she wouldn't be wasting her time, she had called back the woman she had spoken with at the company and said, "I just wanted to make sure you know that I wear *tesettür*, in case that makes a difference." The woman told her that in that case, she shouldn't even bother to come in for the interview. Makbule looked at me, quietly seething. "Respect. That's all I want.

232 · Islamist Elitism and Women's Choices

Some respect for my choice to dress the way I think our religion requires us to. I'm not demanding that anyone else dress like this." She waved her hand at the unveiled young woman in a red dress walking by the office door. "There are women who work here who are not veiled. Does anybody tell them they can't work here because they're not veiled?"

Makbule in many ways was typical of the new Muslim woman—educated, ambitious, politically engaged—but her lack of independent access to necessary resources caused her to lose ground in her professional life. She attributed this to being Islamist and being female. Another day, while I sat chatting with Makbule over tea in her office, a man from an office down the hall bustled in and asked her if she used the color printer, obviously desiring it for himself. She got to her feet and defended her printer, insisting that she needed it for the color reports she put out. She asked what he needed it for, and listened while he explained that they were putting out a booklet. Then she told him firmly that he didn't need a color printer for that work and that they could make do with a black and white printer; anyway, the size of paper they wanted to use wouldn't work in this printer. Finally, she offered to do his color work for him, but categorically refused to give up the printer. I left them there, both on their feet, facing each other across the printer, heels dug in.

Some weeks later, I came by the municipal building to have tea with Halil. Halil had lost none of his alert intensity, but was more relaxed and greeted me pleasantly. I sat in a low, black vinyl, padded chair in front of his desk, drinking tea and exchanging news and pleasantries with Halil and other municipal staff members who came by to sit and chat. I congratulated Halil on the recent birth of his son, his first child. He looked very pleased. I asked after Makbule, and Halil told me she had gotten married. I was surprised, since neither she nor our common acquaintances had mentioned that she was engaged. He went to the door of her office to tell her I was here, but found the door locked. He came back and explained that she must be doing her prayers. After about fifteen minutes he tried again. Finding the door unlocked, he stuck his head in to announce me and then beckoned me over. I went in and closed the door behind me. Makbule greeted me effusively from across the broad wooden surface of her desk, noticeably emptier of equipment than last time. The scanner was gone, as was the color printer. I commented that it seemed as though she had lost that battle. Makbule responded that she had resisted as long as possible, but finally an order had come from higher up and she'd had to relinquish the printer. "It wasn't a battle," she assured me. "They needed it more in the other department." In any case, she pointed out wryly, the less equipment she had, the less work she had. She used to handle all the incoming and outgoing faxes of the municipality, but since her fax machine was gone too, she didn't have to worry about that anymore.

I congratulated her on her marriage. She thanked me, but looked rather more thoughtful than the picture of a blushing young bride. I asked if she had met her husband at the municipality, like Nefise. She shook her head no, paused, and then, as if herself musing on the improbability of the events, said that he was a relative of friends of her family. She explained that her brother had come back from the army and was about to leave to work in Germany, so it would be at least a year before she would see him again. "So we decided I would get married so he could attend the wedding," she finished lamely. I noted that she was still working even though she was married, although Nefise had stopped working at her husband's request. Makbule nodded and said that she had discussed it with her husband and that, even though he had said it would be better if she stopped working, they both agreed in the end that it would be alright for her to continue. "But when there is a child. . . ." Her voice tapered off and she looked confused.

Women in the Party

The attempt to establish a separate, "conscious" Islamist culture simply defines away the kinds of dilemmas that Islamist women like Makbule face. In this, as in other ways, it contradicts the populist Islamist political project. The Islamist movement is very much a political project rooted in issues of social justice (if not social class). But the Islamist project is premised upon three contradictory impulses: a populist nonrecognition of class, status, and, in some respects, gender cleavages; the desire to situate itself as the champion of the poor and disadvantaged; and the attempt to reclassify Islamic symbols as separate cultural markers of a superior lifestyle. Describing all movement activists as "Islamist elites" hides distinctions between the economic elite and those with limited opportunities. It adds to the mystique of egalitarianism fostered by the movement and the political party it inspires by extending the label "elite" socially downwards to make it accessible to anyone wearing Islamic dress and engaged in political activism or attending university, regardless of their economic status. It also allows activists to put some social distance between themselves and their nonelite background.

To maintain the fiction of equal status, party activists avoid references to identities, like social class, defined on the basis of economic position. Another means of hiding class differences and other contradictions among party supporters is through particularism, referring identity to the level of the individual. Mr. Akkaya, the managing director of the Ümraniye Service Foundation and an educated, relatively successful businessman, explained that there were no differences among people, in part because they were all Muslims, but also because "everyone is judged as an individual. . . . In the foundation, my rank is different, but in other contexts my level [seviye] is the same as that of other people. The actual level is that of the person; that is the level within which one finds equal conditions."

One manifestation of the implicit contradiction between conscious activist intentions and the varied cultural expectations hidden under the canopy of populism is the difference in construction of women's rights, privileges and motivations by activist women and their male colleagues within the Welfare Party. While many activist women I interviewed in Ümraniye were engaged in the Islamist project in order to carve out new areas of autonomy within the traditional expectations of their community, male activists in the next office were motivated in part by a desire to reinforce traditional female roles and to enhance their own autonomy vis-à-vis women—for instance, by supporting polygyny, which is illegal in secular Turkey. The women were very much interested in using party activism to advance the position of women, particularly through education and work outside of the home. As the head of Ümraniye's Welfare Party Women's Branch put it, "I, too, used to be just like other women in this neighborhood. I sat around and ate and talked, ate and talked. But now I've found myself. I've become active and productive." She firmly believed that women should work outside the home, get an education, and enter the professions. In her study of Islamist activists, Arat also found that women felt empowered by political work. Some saw it as a path "to prove ourselves to ourselves." Others felt that through their activism they had gained back the status, autonomy, and authority they had lost when they decided to veil and found themselves under patriarchal "house arrest." If they were unable to attend university, then party activism was a form of education, a legitimate vocation, an identity, and a way to expand one's networks (Arat, 1999, 36–39).

Female Welfare Party supporters were extraordinarily successful at popular mobilization and it is widely acknowledged that they were in large part responsible for the Welfare Party's success in working-class neighborhoods like Ümraniye. Women made up a third of party membership in Istanbul in 1997 (Arat, 1999, 23). Female activists were responsible for getting out a large part of the vote for the Welfare Party in the 1994 and 1995 elections. In the month before the 1995 elections, in Istanbul alone, the Welfare Party's women's commission worked with 18,000 women and met face to face with two hundred thousand women (Arat, 1997, 67). They worked person to person, building cells of local women attached to the Women's Branch, which, in turn, was guided by the party and took its direction (and much of its financial support) from it.

However, at the time, there were almost no women in the party administration and the women's branches and commissions had no formal status within the party. This latter fact clearly irked some of the women activists, but they assured me that this would change in the near future. Although the lack of formal connection between the Welfare Party and its Women's Branch could be attributed to state laws forbidding political parties from forming special interest branches, it did not explain the lack of women in formal party administration.

Male party activists generally deflected questions about the lack of women in the party's administration by redirecting the question to the issue of banning head scarves in university and the lack of democracy in the system. This disguised internal divisiveness with the artful unity of political symbolism. A government that refuses education to women on the grounds of their wearing a head scarf, they argued, is undemocratic. However, when pressed about the importance of education for women, these same male activists stated simply that women's main role was to be mothers and homemakers, and that women should be educated because that would make them better mothers.

Within the party, there were contradictory views about whether women should work outside the home and whether they should receive training to do so. In an interview with me,[4] Istanbul Mayor Recep Tayyip Erdoğan underscored his belief that women should be fully involved in social and political life, but with several reservations.

> Some work is not suitable for women. It goes against their delicacy, like the work women did behind the Iron Curtain—working in construction, laying roads, and so on. It's natural for them to do other work. They could even be managers of managers. . . . Women's right includes political work. But I support struggle [*mücadele*], not a quota system. . . . A quota means you are helping people; it's an insult to women.

On the other hand, the mayor also believed that "working at home is safer for women. They often get no insurance when they work outside the home. If they are young, they may be molested in workshops and other workplaces. This way they aren't oppressed by the employer."

I asked him whether this meant he believed that, ideally, all women should work at home. He shook his head emphatically and explained:

> Those women who have the talent and the education, those who are engineers and so on, anyway find work. If women have graduated from high school, they should be able to work. But for the others, staying at home at least gives them the possibility of making their own trousseaus [with money earned from the sale of handicrafts]. But it's a stopgap solution. You can't solve the unemployment problem that way.

Both the mayor and male activists, in other words, differentiated between women who were educated and might work at a profession and women who were not educated and would be better off at home than in a job where they could be oppressed and molested.

However, local male activists in Ümraniye, in their discussions and in practice, added the requisite that even educated women's first priorities were husband, home, and children, and that they should stop working at marriage or after the birth of a child. Veiling and the segregation of women within the home meant that women reserved their beauty, their attention, and their labor for their husbands and families. The men categorically resisted the idea that women could or should work outside the home after marriage. This corresponded to the reality of life in much of Ümraniye, where women were under the protection of their family and under the authority of family males. They worked for their family and did not travel far afield from their homes. I know of several cases in Ümraniye where educated professional women and activists like Nefise were required by their new husbands or husbands' families to remain at home after marriage or after having their first child. In some cases this resulted in greatly constrained mobility, including being required to ask permission to leave home to visit nearby family and friends or to shop at the grocery. A common theme in popular Islamist fiction is the quandary faced by Islamist women when they marry and lose the "voice" they had as activists, students, and professionals. Non-Islamist women's popular fiction also takes up this theme; Kemalism, like Islamism, is shot through with contradictions in its expectations of women.

Although activist women in Ümraniye agreed with the idea that women's first responsibility was to make a home for husband and children, they also had very firm ideas about the need for education and work, and not only to make a woman "a better mother." The head of Ümraniye's Welfare Women's Branch asked, if a girl's family didn't send her to school, "what will that girl do at home? . . . She'll either go to a textile workshop or wait at home for her fate [*kısmet*]. That a man should come, see her, like her, and start a family. Why should it be like that?" She would sit at home and "be a consumer, not a producer. But if that girl finishes high school, finishes university, maybe she will work somewhere in some area, and find herself contributing to the country's economy by working."

In Ümraniye, the Welfare-administered municipal offices were staffed by veiled secretaries, intelligent, computer-literate women like Makbule and Nefise. They designed and published the municipality's reports and booklets. The municipality handed out slick presentations (also put together by the veiled secretaries), magazines, newspapers, and brochures giving party and municipal news. Male activists distributed these to cafes, barbershops, and local stores, places frequented by men. When I asked the male activists how the information got to the women, they answered that the men could bring it home if they wanted to. There were segregated computer classes for female students, but no courses were offered to teach married women or housewives skills that would allow them extra income, even income from work at home. There were only traditional handicraft courses and occasional small fairs where they could sell what they made.

This was in contrast to the policy of the previous Ümraniye administration, led by the Republican People's Party, which offered courses in typing, sewing, literacy, and other skills with the express purpose of making women financially more independent. When it took over the municipality, Welfare had, in fact, closed down many of the programs (which had offered such services as skills classes, kindergartens, and, in another neighborhood, a refuge for battered women) that secularist and feminist women's groups had set up on municipal property. In the case of privately owned premises, other tactics were employed—for instance, sending in squadrons of veiled women to pray in the meeting rooms and hallways, discouraging women who might have used the services.

I asked Mr. Akkaya and Mr. Dikmen of the Islamist charity foundation why, given the widespread poverty in the neighborhood, the foundation or municipality didn't offer courses that would teach women skills they could use to earn money for their families. They explained that they tried to take care of the women's money problems through the men. Mr. Dikmen stated, "Women's duty is to take care of the home and children. There is no need for women to work to earn money, and therefore no need for courses like that." When I pointed out that the men were often unable to pay even for schooling for all their children, but that if mothers could earn money they would be able to send their children to school, he answered with a Turkish saying, "Extend your feet to the length of your comforter." That is, people just have to live within their means. I felt that to be a rather hardhearted position, given the much-trumpeted Islamist concern with social and economic justice. Later, Mayor Recep Tayyip Erdoğan, Mr. Akkaya, and Mr. Dikmen separately explained to me that the municipalities and the foundations can do only so much, because of the widespread nature of poverty and unemployment, and that they believed this to be a system-wide problem that could not be solved by training women to work.

In this, the Islamist movement is only the latest in a century of movements of whatever ideological persuasion that have maintained that solving society's problems will ipso facto solve women's problems, and that to think otherwise would be to put selfish individualism before the welfare of the group, movement, community, or nation. Feminists would disagree, arguing that women and their issues have tended to remain on the back burner even after a movement has come to power and that it is only by seizing the initiative as women and as individuals that women can improve their lives. Interestingly, both secularist and Islamist feminists would agree with the need for "consciousness raising," if not about what would constitute improvement. In this, as in some of their other expectations, Islamist feminists and women activists were out of step with the Welfare Party and, in some ways, constituted their own stream of the Islamist movement.

Activists in the Women's Branch did not have the power to affect the party's practices by voting on party policies or even by setting up job training courses for women. Yet they still believed that the party would give women the opportunities they sought. After all, as the head of the Women's Branch had pointed out, women themselves, through their party activities, had became independent and competent, left their houses, "found" themselves. At one level, this is an elevation of women and an expression of the party's avowed principle of not making distinctions (between men and women, veiled and unveiled women, social classes, ethnicities, and so on). On another level, while women were given status in the party, they were not given access to administrative or financial decision-making, except within their own tightly organized but autonomous hierarchies. The party projected an ambivalent message. For instance, while Mayor Erdoğan supported women working, women were only loosely incorporated into the party structure and there were no women in the highest positions.

Nevertheless, as activists, women were partners with men, even if they moved through different circuits. The women, in many ways, were more visible in their distinctive clothing than male activists at rallies and in the streets. In June 1998, hundreds of women in *tesettür* demonstrated in front of universities and marched on Ankara to demand the right to wear head scarves at university. In other words, while activist women were elevated over other women, they were not placed in an equal position to (or elevated over) men, even though they played an equivalent role as grassroots activists. Several hierarchies were in play simultaneously, that both supported and obscured the gender hierarchies in everyday life from which activist women have tried to distance themselves.

Despite their isolation from the center of power and policy-making, female Welfare Party supporters were extraordinarily successful in popular mobilization. They worked person to person building social cells attached informally to the Women's Branch. The Women's Branch, in turn, was guided by and informally connected to the party and municipality. These were the women who sat behind the bookcases during the Peace of Mind Conversations, listening to the municipality's speakers translate party ideology into local cultural and religious codes. These same women used the Quran to explain and justify what were, in some respects, universalist, modernist, even feminist ideas about women's roles that challenged local norms.

Veiling as perceived by women (whether elite or working-class) differed appreciably from veiling as understood by men in the Islamist movement. Activist women in the Welfare Party consciously wielded veiling and gender segregation as central political symbols to try to forge new social identities and concrete possibilities for women within and outside of the movement. The interpretation of these cultural forms by male Welfare Party/Virtue Party activists, however, was influenced by the everyday context of veiling and segregation, in which male control over women's sexuality and movement through space has primacy over women's autonomy and control over their bodies. Dissonance within the party was controlled by populist rhetoric, the judicious use of unifying symbols in neutral contexts, and avoidance of language that would acknowledge cleavages. Party leaders deflected public statements on divisive issues, allowing differences in the lower ranks between men and women activists to be attributed to personal points of view.

Tesettür was a political symbol that unified members of the Islamist movement and the Welfare Party. It also hid class differences among members of the party and itself became a symbol of upward mobility and urban lifestyle, even if the reality contradicted the symbol. Women activists desired mobility—social, physical, and professional. Yet *tesettür* also signified the opposite of mobility: that the proper place of women was in the home. As a fashion, *tesettür* revealed the yawning gap between those who could afford an elite lifestyle, including couture veiling, and those for whom veiling—and associated behaviors like segregation and obedience within a patriarchal hierarchy—were crucial for respectability and security. While the gap between rich and poor, educated and uneducated, was obscured by Islamist populism, the desire to make an Islamist lifestyle an elite lifestyle led Islamists to distance themselves from the masses. This opened the door to a form of Islamist elitism that celebrated economic and status differences, while simultaneously denying them.

The prevalence of these crosscutting currents of meaning also meant that, rather than fitting neatly into categories of Islamist or secularist, "conscious" activist or "traditional" resident, people, in fact, exhibited a continuum of characteristics, beliefs, and behaviors. All were in flux and subject to modification, both by the introduction of new ideas as the Welfare Party closed and the Virtue Party changed under new leadership, and by individuals themselves, as they selected from the smorgasbord of cultural styles that came to be justified under the banner of "Islamism."

One chill evening, Halil and I emerged from the Ümraniye Municipality Peace of Mind Conversations. It was dark, but the sidewalks were smeared with light from shop fronts and a streetlight. Ordinarily, Halil would have been adamant about my staying over and not taking public transport at night, but my aunt was visiting and she was ill, so I had to take the bus back across the Bosphorus. He insisted on waiting with me under the red bus-stop awning until the bus came. The bus took a long time to come that late at night. We chatted a bit about my aunt. After a pause, Halil turned to look out at the cars speeding by and asked me whether I thought it bad that he didn't let Nefise go out to visit and to the shops. Touched that he had sought my opinion on this sensitive subject, I thought it over and, his mother's words in my mind, responded, "She's a very intelligent and talented woman. She might get bored at home and that would cause problems in the long run." I suggested that she could take women-only computer classes, or give computer lessons to women at home. I knew that she was concerned about losing her cutting-edge knowledge. When I had offered to buy her some recent computer manuals, she had responded that they would be out of date as fast as she could read them. He seemed to mull this over, then said, softly, "It's a very hard thing to buy a computer." Shortly after this conversation, Nefise discovered she was pregnant with her first child.

The question presents itself, whether the secularist Ümraniye Women's Center, by contast, would have been able to assist any of these women, either in obtaining or keeping their skills, finding work, starting a business, or keeping their options open in other ways despite being married and raising children. In the following chapter, I will examine the attitudes and practices of secularist activists in Ümraniye.

8

SECULARIST ACTIVISM
IN ÜMRANIYE

Secularist activists in Ümraniye used strategies of organization similar
to those of the Islamists to mobilize residents around an ideologically focused program. But while they were able to carry out educational and charity activities like the Islamists, the secularist activists were
unable to mobilize residents on a sustained basis. They were unwilling
to situate their message within local cultural norms that they associated with the "Other" Istanbul, despite living in Ümraniye themselves.
Their elitism eventually brought about a lack of rapport with the
neighborhood women they were trying to mobilize. The alienation of
the secularist activists from neighborhood networks was exacerbated
when they moved from informally organized cells of local women to
a more inaccessible, formally incorporated Women's Center.

Although the Ümraniye women associated themselves with
Kemalist elites, their relationship with middle-class Kemalist, feminist women outside Ümraniye was complex. On the one hand, they
identified with them and sought their guidance and assistance in their
projects. On the other hand, the Ümraniye women resented middle-
class feminists, whom they accused of being fickle in their support,
looking down on them, and using local women to subcontract
research work without supporting the local women's own projects.
The Ümraniye women's struggle to mobilize other local women

around a Kemalist, secularist, feminist ideology foundered on these status ambiguities—much as Islamist populism might conceivably be undercut by a developing Islamist elitism. In both cases, activists attempted to distance themselves from a *varoş* (and working-class) identity by locating themselves in a different, ostensibly superior, culturally defined category. For both Islamist and secularist "elite" women in Ümraniye, the exigencies of a working-class context (lack of economic resources, limited opportunities, no outside contacts or knowledge of foreign languages) undermined their ability to maintain a high level of political activism and to act out alternative lifestyles.

In 1989, with municipal funding and volunteer labor, a group of local women opened several informal People's Schools in Ümraniye, teaching young women such marketable skills as typing, bookkeeping, and sewing, as well as literacy, child care, art, and music. The core activists were women with some education and means: teachers, pharmacists, housewives whose husbands had steady professional work or owned some property. The women built on their personal ties with others in the community and brought together women in different parts of the neighborhood. At informal meetings in their homes, women were encouraged to get involved in the People's Schools, either by taking classes, volunteering to teach them, or spreading the word among their neighbors and friends. The classes were held in rooms provided by the Republican People's Party–run municipality, such as school rooms on weekends.

Because the association was based primarily on interpersonal relations among neighbors and friends, both conservative and secularist women participated, including women whose families might not have allowed them to join an activity run by strangers. The activists also enlisted women's programs on local television and radio stations, as well as women's periodicals, to popularize and legitimize the schools. The schools were quite successful and "graduated" hundreds of women over their five years of operation. They were closed in 1994 when the Welfare Party won the municipal election and withdrew municipal resources. The following year, a group of women who had been associated with the schools pooled their resources and opened a formally registered Ümraniye Women's Center, with more explicitly political (anti–Welfare Party, secularist) goals. This chapter examines the transformation from the populist, highly personalized People's Schools to formal status as a civic organization, and the consequences of that change.

Young woman learning to sew at the Ümraniye Women's Center.

Despite the ideological contrast between the Islamists and the staunchly Kemalist, secularist People's School activists, I noticed some striking similarities in the way they engaged local people and mobilized them for their cause. Both placed great value on face-to-face interaction and organized people on the basis of cells of neighbors who already knew one another. Both presented their projects as being local and informally organized, while working closely with a political party. Their programs were ideologically inspired, and women played a major role in implementing them. Yet the Islamists seemed much more capable of inspiring sustained participation, even under such conditions of duress as when the Welfare Party was banned. The Kemalist activists, on the other hand, were able to organize women around their projects, but did not seem able to inspire loyalty and interest beyond the projects themselves. When the projects ended, the participants went home.

Suna Onat,[1] a Republican People's Party activist, was the power-house behind the development of the People's Schools. Suna was an alert, earnest, middle-aged woman whose broad smile and energetic manner projected a youthful and infectious enthusiasm. Her hair hung to the base of her neck in a thick, brown braid. She tended to dress informally: skirt or slacks, T-shirt, black sneakers. For formal political events, she put her hair up in a bun and donned a simple, dun-colored suit. She lived with her husband, a schoolteacher, in a settlement of small, whitewashed duplexes on the outskirts of Ümraniye.

On a warm autumn evening, a fellow People's School organizer, Feride, dropped by after dinner and sat with us in the Onats' small yard to have a drink of *rakı,* the popular anise-flavored alcohol. Feride was a trim, animated, coppery blonde with a strong-featured face and a big smile. She grew up in a provincial city on the Black Sea coast. As a child, Feride spent summers in Istanbul visiting her mother's relatives, and moved there after her own marriage. She trained as a pharmacist and, together with her husband, ran a pharmacy in Istanbul. All four of her siblings went to college and lived in different parts of Turkey. She had three children, two sons and a daughter, who had just broken a leg in a car accident. After talking about the accident and her daughter's medical care, she launched eagerly into a discussion of her organizational work.

Suna and Feride explained that they had set up the People's Schools in order to teach women skills that would empower them and give them a source of income, skills like literacy, sewing, typing, cloth painting. They were outspoken about their support for Kemalist secularism; their goal, they said, was the social enlightenment of Ümraniye's conservative women. For Suna and many of the other activists, this meant, ultimately, mobilization of support for the left-of-center Republican People's Party, which they viewed as best representing and guaranteeing these principles. Each activist organized cells of women from her immediate community, resulting in a dozen "schools" spread throughout Ümraniye.

In 1993, at a point several years into the successful running of the schools, the cells were brought together in an overtly political meeting held in a local theater, where the women discussed issues ranging from the environment to spousal abuse. This was made possible in part by the use of the telephone, which enormously amplified the numbers of cells that could be simultaneously mobilized around any given cause. Suna had contacted national women's groups and invited them to send representatives; several did attend, along with other public figures, from politicians to a film star. Suna also contacted established women's centers at universities and asked them to support the schools and the conference. These centers responded with logistical support, lent their expertise in the form of classes in organizing, law, and other subjects for the activists, and made available some connections to the media. Suna tenaciously pursued these media outlets over the telephone, then followed up by bringing brochures about the group's activities to the stations. She complained that, while the media were enticed by the novelty of an event organized by *gecekondu* (squatter-area) women, this interest did not last. Nevertheless, she made the best of the media appearances she was able to drum up. For instance, instead of sending one of the trousered, blond activists to represent the schools on a local early-morning television women's show, she selected an unlettered, veiled woman whom she judged to be particularly well-spoken. Suna's rationale was that the appearance on television of a woman just like the woman next door would legitimate their project and encourage more conservative women to participate and their husbands to allow it. After all, she reasoned, if "Ayşe" next door was on television talking about it, people would think it must be all right. The conference brought together several hundred women. Photos of the event showed women of all ages, in dress ranging from *tesettür* to jeans, seated in the audience or at discussion tables. The schools continued holding classes, the mayor handing women diplomas at "graduation" ceremonies under an array of Republican People's Party flags.

When the Welfare Party won local elections in Ümraniye in 1994, the People's Schools were closed down. The activists complained that the Welfare Party quite literally had locked the doors on the municipal rooms they had been allowed to use under the previous administration. This meant that they lost all their equipment: typewriters, sewing machines, books, cloth and paints, and a knitting machine that someone had donated. They relocated to a small, reasonably priced apartment near the center of town, paying the rent out of their own pockets. Soon, however, they were being harassed by people they associated with the Welfare Party—bearded men and veiled women. The men clogged the halls, their presence, the activists said, intimidating women who wanted to attend the much-curtailed People's School classes. Only two courses were offered, handicrafts and cloth painting, neither of which required much equipment. In these classes, women learned to make accessories, "useful things" like decorated pillowcases, embroidered or painted satin prayer mats, decorative cloths for home religious ceremonies, bed and tablecloths, and children's clothes. Many of these were articles necessary for girls' trousseaus. The group had hoped to add carpet weaving, with two looms promised by the Ministry of Industry and Trade through their contacts in the Republican People's Party, but this never materialized. Suna complained that they were unable to receive state funds because "Ümraniye is a squatter area, a neighborhood left at the margins."

After six months, a dormitory for male religious students was opened on the floor below, making it impossible for the group to continue in that building. The women moved their operations several *dolmuş* stops away, into one room of a relative's office. No classes were held until permanent quarters could be found. Meanwhile, the group prepared the paperwork needed to become an official association.

The Ümraniye Women's Center

The twenty-eight founding members of the Women's Center belonged to several different political parties, some left-of-center, others right-of-center. They were drawn from Ümraniye's lower middle class. Only two were born in Istanbul. Their ages ranged from twenty-three to forty-seven, but most were in their late thirties. Most had a grade school education; a few had finished university. Fifteen were middle-rank (*orta düzey*) housewives who had "a house and car." Their husbands were salaried workers. One woman was a nurse, another a statistician; they included a retired teacher and several pharmacists. All had met through mutual friends.

In order to "prepare [themselves] to found the association," the women reactivated their connection to women's research centers at two Istanbul universities. Through these institutions, over a space of two months, twenty-five activists were given courses two days a week on topics ranging from Turkish economy, politics, and history to human rights, women's rights, and "social progress," as well as on laicism and Islamic law. Suna explained that the group was planning not to teach skills to the neighborhood women, "but to raise their level of knowledge, so that they learn right thinking [*doğru düşünce*]. Our [university] courses were about. . . how we can influence these kinds of people; for instance, show them that things can be different."

A core group of seven women filled out the forms required to petition to become a formal association. A lawyer donated her services. The group used their connections with women's centers, the press, and celebrities from People's Schools conference days to spread word about the new Center's activities. The Center's opening event, an afternoon tea, was held in a rented wedding hall and attracted several hundred women who drank tea, nibbled pastries, and danced to cassette pop and folk music. Dinner events drew a smaller crowd, usually to hear a featured speaker.

As Feride described it, press coverage of the Center's activity when it first opened occasioned many telephone calls from interested women from all over Istanbul. Some calls were simply from working women who wanted events to be scheduled on weekends. Others reflected a typical problem in a society where fewer than one in three women is formally employed (TESEV, 1997, 32). As Feride recounted, "A woman with two grown daughters called. Their economic situation is good [because of the husband's job], but the woman has no economic power and is beaten by her husband. She has wanted to divorce him for some time, but she is afraid her relations with her daughters will be damaged, and, although she can knit, she has no connection to the outside to sell her work." Because of the Center's centralization of its activities, it was unable to help this woman—and others like her who could not travel to the Center's location.

By its second year, the Center had acquired a hundred and fifty members. Each gave a monthly donation ranging from thirty cents to three dollars, bringing together just enough to pay the rent and buy supplies for the courses. The Center's income was supplemented by occasional craft fairs, as well as teas and dinners for which tickets were sold. There was no charge for the courses, but the students were expected to work one day making things for themselves and the next day making things for the Center, which would be sold at fairs to raise money to replace materials. Television, radio, and newspapers were harnessed whenever possible to advertise the events. Women's shows on radio and television were especially receptive to discussing Center events on the air. Center activists passed out handbills, hung up banners, and networked. Feride recalled, "If there were fifty women, they each tried to reach all the women they knew." They represented themselves to the media as "Ümraniye's association" and as "Ümraniye's women's association."

Although the group's activities had become formalized, the activists tried to keep up face-to-face connections within their cells. They continued to visit women when they gave birth, had a celebration, or were ill. "Everyone carries their circle of friends," Feride explained. "That way, you have people who come with a bridge of trust; then they become long-term participants." But the effort to be both a formal, centralized, civic organization and to retain the personal ties of the social cells became more difficult as membership swelled. In the Center's second year, there were about fifty students in the courses; almost all became members. This made it difficult to keep relations personal. Suna worried about this transformation. "You can't keep track of everyone. It takes time and effort to keep up a personal relationship. If you can't turn it into an associational relationship [derneksel ilişki], you lose touch and it can break off."

What had changed since the group became an official association? Suna observed, "It's now a place where women can meet. It has a sign. People knock on the door and ask. They come with problems, especially problems with their husbands, economic problems, help with [finding] jobs, finding brides [for their sons]. Every two weeks or so there is a walk-in. We wouldn't reach these women otherwise. Now they seek us. But they're a different type of woman." According to Feride, "There are different groups. Some never change, some are very uneducated. . . . The covered women come less than before. There are fewer veiled women in the Center. They are more normal, not veiled. Most are like us. We don't want entrenched people [kökten]. We want women who may be veiled, but haven't made up their minds, women who can think."

Emboldened by the experience of the 1993 conference, the group had become more focused on ideology and less on providing service to the community at large. Being a card-carrying member of national "civil society" meant a more politically engaged activism and a winnowing of participants to those best able to assist in this cause—those with time, money and communications skills. Suna explained that their most important goal was a bigger and more participatory association.

> It's not enough to sit and meet for tea occasionally. That doesn't solve problems. We want to turn our attention to people who try to find solutions to problems, who would like to take ownership of their own country and nation. We want people to really take an active leadership role, put in their time and money. Eventually, we want to be effective on every street; we want to have lots of members, eloquent ones. For instance, Welfare closed three libraries. We want to be able to use broad public opinion to pressure them to reopen the

Women learning cloth painting at the Ümraniye Women's Center.

libraries. It was a political decision, so it's hard to influence. [They closed the libraries because] they had a lot of books by modern Turkish and foreign authors. We weren't able to keep control of our libraries, our People's Schools, our kindergartens. If we had been able to organize the people here, we could have challenged them, "How dare you take the people's library," but we weren't able to hold them accountable. If we had a real civil society, we would have been able to. Without that, we become more passive and silent as these things happen. We have no strength. Women are wounded by [the closing of] schools, kindergartens, children's libraries. It tears apart women's lives.

But Feride's account of their relations with local residents was not promising. "The thing is, these women take advantage of what we have to offer, but we can't take advantage of them. When the subject turns to politics, they don't support us. During the period of the People's Schools, we visited them in their homes before the 1994 local elections. They wouldn't give us the time of day. They wouldn't support the Republican People's Party, the party that gave them services. If you didn't have some kind of tie with the husband, then she did whatever her husband wanted."

There also was animosity toward the Center on the part of conservative residents and Welfare Party supporters in the community. It is customary on the annual religious Sacrificial Holiday to dress children in new clothing, but many families find that financially impossible. The Center obtained permission from a primary school in one of Ümraniye's poorest areas to hold a fair on its property selling inexpensive used clothing just before the holiday. The Center activists chose that neighborhood in particular because it was a very conservative area with many veiled women. They collected used clothing from friends and passed out fliers to the schoolchildren to take home. They also hung up a big cloth banner announcing the fair and giving the Center's address. The banner was repeatedly cut down. Before the fair, someone phoned residents of the area, the caller reportedly claiming to be from the Ümraniye Municipality and warning that the clothes to be sold at the fair were dead people's clothes. They alleged that the Center activists were loose women and leftists. After the fair, which netted $182, Feride exulted that, although many of the customers had been veiled, "The first items to go were tight, short, open clothes and jeans."

Two years later, the Center had moved into an apartment in the center of Ümraniye's shopping district. Suna bargained the rent down to $150, but it was still a struggle for the Center women to pay it. They raised between $60 and $90 from each fair, but there was a limit to the number of fairs they could put on, so the money did not go far. In Turkey's centralized political system, parties in power reward their supporters with material support. Once they lose power, these resources dry up. In other words, with the loss of municipal funds, the activists were on their own. They were unable to apply for funding from foreign NGOs, as did many middle-class women's groups, because none of the activists spoke a foreign language, had outside contacts, or experience writing grant proposals. This put the Women's Center in a situation of dependence on middle-class organizations that would subcontract project work to them, whether organizing courses or doing surveys, door-to-door information gathering, or information dissemination. The Center had the advantage of having the connections and local knowledge necessary for completing these projects, but did not have the skills to obtain its own outside funding. The money brought in by these subcontracted projects helped keep the Center afloat, but did nothing to provide a sustained income. Yet, despite the activists' complaints about abandonment and misuse by the "middle class," they allied themselves with Kemalist elites through their ideology, clothing, hairstyles, and, to some extent, lifestyle, which they tried to "teach" to the women who came to the Center. In other words, they reproduced the very class superiority and top-down social engineering that they felt victimized by.

Kemalist Elitism

Feride, her blond hair in a ponytail, bangs obscuring her forehead, held court in her pharmacy. She took phone calls regarding Center business, extolled the Center to her customers, and the other Center women visited her there to sit and chat or discuss business. Among the activists gathered in Feride's pharmacy on a dry, hot September day were Semra, Nazmiye, and Zehra. All were in their late thirties or forties. We sat in a circle of folding chairs in the shop aisle, sipping glasses of tea. Feride wore tight slacks and a form-fitting orange sweater. The women invariably wore slacks whenever they came together, whether at the Center or at the pharmacy.

Semra, a big woman with long, blond hair tied at the nape, was a high school graduate who had studied crafts and taught for a time in the People's Schools. She was also active in the Republican People's Party's Women's Branch. A hearty, easygoing grandmother, she was a housewife and lived in a relatively new apartment complex in Ümraniye. Her husband, she readily volunteered, had a white-collar job. Nazmiye, a dark, tired-looking woman in her fifties, was a retired teacher and, although an activist, had developed an interest in the crafts the Center was teaching and was herself taking the course on cloth painting. Zehra was a short, tidy woman with a tough voice and firm gestures, her brown hair worn incongruously in a soft flip. Her husband ran an appliance repair shop and they lived in the same newly minted section of Ümraniye as Hasan and Sevgi. Zehra told me that they owned the three-story building they lived in. She and her family occupied one of the apartments; the others were rented out. Her husband's shop was on the ground floor in the back of the building; in the front, Zehra had opened a tearoom and simple restaurant (it served only *mantı*, a yeast-based ravioli).

At the pharmacy, Feride's husband fielded calls and saw to customers while the women talked. A teenage male assistant kept the tea brewing and our glasses topped up. Feride was unable to spend much time away from the pharmacy because a female pharmacist needed to be on duty at all times to deal with female customers who might not wish to explain their problems and needs to a man. On the occasions when she could get away, on late afternoons and weekends, the women would meet at the Center, three small rooms overlooking Ümraniye's main street. Two of the rooms were used as classrooms and for storage. The windowless center room was furnished with a donated desk, comfortable chairs, and a coffee table. A cheap but colorful woven kilim decorated one wall. Tea brewed continually on a potbellied stove that also served to heat the rooms in the winter. More rarely, the women visited each other in their homes.

Some days, the Center activists gathered at Zehra's restaurant. It had an outdoor terrace and a large indoor room. The walls of the room were decorated with craft items Zehra had made herself. On one such day, a group of Center women sat around a table. In addition to those who had met in Feride's pharmacy, several other women from the neighborhood joined us. All had been active in some way in the Center. One young woman, dressed in a feminine suit, introduced herself as a pharmacist. She spoke little but smiled gently and inclined her head delicately in the direction of whoever was speaking. Zehra rushed around, seeing to our tea and serving plates of *manti* nestled in spicy yoghurt sauce. The food was prepared in the kitchen by a woman in village dress, a threadbare cotton head scarf framing her sweating face. A woman from the neighborhood, dressed in slacks and long-sleeved sweater, her hair in a ponytail, sat drinking tea with her young daughter at another of the round tables covered with frilly cloths. Occasionally, Zehra sat and chatted with us, telling the story of her son who had been badly beaten in a fight. On the street, he had met a girl he hadn't seen in a long time and had impulsively kissed her on the cheek, offending the man who accompanied her. Although the activists placed great emphasis on the ways in which their lives differed from those of Ümraniye residents like Hasan and Sevgi, the lives of Zehra and her family shared certain basic patterns of gender relations and even gender segregation. As Zehra talked, several young men came into the room, but, seeing only women, left again. Zehra called out to them that they should stay, saying, "It's fine." They returned an hour later, as we were leaving.

The women complained about the Center's lack of money and seemed bitter about the lack of support by what they called "middle-class women's groups." This was a big change from the early days of the Center two years before. They claimed that middle-class organizations wouldn't help them now that the Center was no longer in the news, and that, while these organizations subcontracted project labor to them, they didn't share the financial benefits. "There is a class difference," Feride explained. She had gone to a meeting of an umbrella women's organization that incorporated several women's groups. "I listened to them talk about what needed to be done—women's rights and so on. But none of them ever *did* anything. Most of them have never been in a neighborhood like Ümraniye, never crossed the border. They have money, but it's all empty talk." The Center had been given a project to carry out by one of the middle-class organizations, a legal-rights group: going door to door advising women of their rights under the law. The Center women found the work rewarding, but chafed at the fact that the organization had refused to help pay for Center expenses like rent. They felt they were being used as pieceworkers by middle-class groups that had the money, but not the access to the neighborhood.

Feride pointed out that the important difference between the Center and other groups was that the women at the Center worked door to door, "eye to eye." "There's no other group [in Ümraniye] like us." I asked whether they only visited people they knew. Feride answered, "No, strangers too." But another woman disagreed. "Not really. These are people that, say, 'Ayşe' knows." In other words, they visited people who knew people that they knew. Their aim, they explained, was to develop trust. "Other groups and political parties don't bother. They're in and out. They come from outside, and they don't come all the time. The element of reciprocity is important in developing this trust." Nazmiye chimed in, "Take a rose, give a rose." They discussed among themselves how important it was to give something back to the people they visited. "What if you meet them on the street after that [and you haven't given them anything]?" It was important to keep up relations, they agreed. This was particularly difficult when they had carried out a survey for the State Planning Organization with minimal funding. They knocked on more than three hundred doors, this time the doors of strangers, to ask women questions on a long questionnaire, sometimes personal questions about income and other private matters. The process took at least one-and-a-half hours per questionnaire. "We had nothing to give the people when we were done." The State Planning Organization survey work also had been onerous because of the lack of personal connection. They had had to talk their way into some of the homes. Often husbands or mothers-in-law forbade women to answer. One husband accused the interviewer of being a thief and wanted to throw her out when she began to ask about income. The Welfare

Party, they agreed, also operated with "eye to eye reciprocity." But, they noted, it had more money than they did and thus could give things to people.

There was also a spirited critique of another association that had recently begun operating in Ümraniye. The women claimed they had taught the women of this association everything, sharing the training they themselves had received from middle-class organizations and university women's centers when they had first opened. But now this group had money, whereas their own Center did not. "This other group has rented offices on the main street, with a secretary who sits there and processes anyone who comes in, with or without a head scarf. They come in, the secretary takes their name, stamps their paper and sends them on through to the class. Inside is a bookkeeping teacher who doesn't make any personal connection, just says to herself, 'I'm a hired bookkeeper.'" What made the Center women so irate was that the other group just taught the women skills, without reaching out to them or making a personal connection so that they could change their way of thinking. "They don't ask, 'Do you need anything? What can I do for you?'" The Center women found it unconscionable to pass up the chance to expose veiled women to a different ideology, the implication being that the message would only get through if there was a personal connection. One was not helping women by just teaching them skills.

This ideological approach was evident in their behavior at the Center when neighborhood women arrived for courses, taught either by a volunteer or a government-appointed teacher. All the activist women wore slacks, in stark contrast to the neighborhood women who generally wore conservative, baggy clothing, voluminous coats, and head scarves. If the students wore head scarves, the Center women suggested they take them off. "We're all women here. There's no need to keep that on your head." Occasionally, derogatory comments were made about women who insisted on keeping their head scarves on—comments not directed at the women present, but impugning in general the backwards traditions that kept women covered in an otherwise modern society. The students did not react to these comments, but kept working, heads bowed in concentration, an oversized black plaster bust of Ataturk looming over them from a corner of the room.

While this type of interaction may be understood simply as reflecting anti-Islamist sentiment or a lack of respect for *varoş* life on the part of Kemalists, it also demonstrates a fundamental flaw in political strategy. The local Kemalist activists were not economic elites, but, in effect, aligned themselves with the Kemalist elites, who had since the early days of the Republic monopolized the definition of middle-class "modernity" (and thus the parameters and symbols of upward social mobility) in Turkish society. The activists attempted to raise their own local status by raising themselves above other locals on a civilizational yardstick. (This is a process that bedevils the Islamist movement as well, as discussed in the preceding chapter.) This alignment with the elite was as evident in the women's choice of clothing, and derogatory comments about the clothing and lifestyles of other locals, as in their self-defined mission to convert them to a "modern" lifestyle.

They planned to do this, in part, by requiring that women come to the Center in the central part of Ümraniye, rather than situating the classes nearer to their homes or providing services in the homes. The activists believed it was necessary for the women to learn to move about in public space and important for them to have a life outside of their homes. They acknowledged that this was an imposition on women coming to the Center, given the amount of work and responsibility for child care they had at home, and the fact that some had difficulty coming up with the money for bus fare. But they perceived the solution to be subsidizing the women's travel (for which the Center did not have the money), rather than a change in organizational method. One activist made the connection between Kemalism and social class more explicit when she bragged to the Center activists, to me, and reportedly to women in the classes that her husband had gotten a white-collar job and that she herself had begun attending university classes, to which, she added pointedly, she took a taxi. She explicitly connected her ability to go back to school at the age of forty to "the advanced, modern state of the Turkish nation, where women have the right, and indeed the duty, to advance themselves."

Elements of Successful Mobilization

Two elements of successful mobilization in Ümraniye were informality and the face-to-face nature of interaction, particularly for conservative women who would not have been allowed by their families or husbands to join formal associations and to participate in public demonstrations or campaign activities where they could come into contact with strangers. Like the ambiguous nature of Islamist activities, the informal status of the Kemalist women's activities was less than clear. Even when they were not officially registered as an association, the volunteers who ran the People's Schools had received financial and in-kind support from the Republican People's Party and the municipality. The women's political meeting in the theater, for instance, had been organized and sponsored by the Republican People's Party and had been designed to increase support for the party and to impart the Kemalist, secularist ideology it represented. Party flags, portraits of the mayor, and other political symbols were often in evidence at People's School events.

The face-to-face, personal aspect of the activists' activities was an important but also insufficient explanation of their mobilization successes. Suna suggested that the idea to organize in social cells came from leftist groups in the 1970s that had organized street by street and cell by cell. Yet, by itself, organization on the basis of face-to-face cells was not sufficient to inspire loyalty. In the 1970s, leftist activists went to the squatter neighborhoods, lived among their inhabitants, painted their houses, helped harvest crops in their home villages, but did not manage to win their loyalty. After the 1980 coup, the military cracked down on the left, and many of these activists were turned in to the police by the very people they had lived among and helped. Suna argued that the development of social cells lay behind the Welfare Party's success in Ümraniye. "[The left] had refined it. But it has been nourished by the Welfare Party." Yet the People's Schools, too, had been organized in this way. As with the 1970s leftists, face-to-face, informal relations aided interaction with the neighborhood and allowed cells of women to join together for particular activities in the public realm, but did not inspire loyalty or create a foundation for sustained activism. The women's group, once it was formally incorporated as a women's center, lost the loyalty of neighborhood residents, who would come for classes, but not engage in Center activities beyond that.

If informality and personalization defined both secularist and Islamist strategies, their different outcomes illustrate that these are insufficient to explain successful mobilizing. Where, then, should one look for an explanation? Three things distinguished Islamist activists from secularist activists: the fact that they popularized their ideological message; the means by which it was delivered (including the cultural language of transmission); and the resulting mystification of class and status differences. Although the secularist group was composed of local people with roots in the community, although they operated on a face-to-face basis, organizing as cells, and although they offered local women services and skills, they did not popularize their message, nor did they translate their ideas about the characteristics of a modern Kemalist lifestyle into a form that fit with local normative values. Indeed, the women assumed that they stood in opposition to local values and that it was their responsibility to "enlighten" the local women and encourage them to emulate their own enlightened lives. This attitude was shared by some Republican People's Party activists as well—and by the 1970s leftist activists, often students from middle-class homes who entered the squatter areas in order to enlighten and assist the local population. When activism becomes the handmaiden of ideology, it disconnects from local culture and reveals hierarchies of status and class. Service acquires an ulterior motive, rather than being seen as an expression of populist concern on the part of people "just like us."

By 1998, the number of women participating in Center activities had declined. The Center had become, like thousands of others on the books, a civic organization with shallow membership. It no longer attracted women from conservative households, who probably felt unwelcome and suspicious of the motives of a "feminist" organization.

One afternoon, I was waiting for Suna in Republican People's Party headquarters in central Istanbul. Since she was in a meeting, I was thrown into conversation with some men in the office, also waiting for the meeting to end. I described to them the face-to-face, "neighbor-next-door" populism of the Welfare Party's approach to mobilizing the working-class population and asked them, "Why don't you do something like that?" A man in his mid-thirties, wearing a suit, immediately snapped back, "We don't have time for that sort of thing. We're a modern party." Another man across the room looked thoughtful and asked, "Didn't we used to do something like that? Sit in coffeehouses in the neighborhoods and talk to people?" A third man barked, "Who has time for that kind of thing nowadays?"

Since the Republican People's Party was unable to muster enough votes in the 1999 election to gain representation in parliament, clearly its activists were doing something wrong. Perhaps, like the Women's Center activists, they believed that a modern political party and a modern civic association can be ideologically engaged without having to fit the round pegs of "modern" ideas into what seem to be the square holes of "traditional" relations. A secularist/Kemalist ideological focus by itself should not be an impediment to successful mobilization. Despite the classification of a *varoş* lifestyle as patriarchal, Islamic, and backward, the secularist nationalist ideals of Ataturk in some form pervade working-class, as well as elite and middle-class, populations—much as, in practice, religiosity, veiling, gender segregation, and patriarchal family relations can be found in middle-class and elite families, too. Given the ideological complexity and diversity of social life at all levels of society, it might be expected that successful mobilization would be possible regardless of the ideological impetus. Yet one finds that secularist, Kemalist, and feminist (these are often conjoined as associational foci) associational activities and party platforms do not inspire sustained followings and loyalty in neighborhoods like Ümraniye, even if the activists are local, not outsiders, and even if their modus operandum—face-to-face informality based on relations of trust and reciprocity—was similar in some respects to that of the Islamists, who tended to be more successful in this regard.

The difference between successful, sustainable mobilization in Ümraniye and short-term, more utilitarian support is not just a consequence of ideology—the message—nor of the face-to-face quality of rapport and the resulting personalization of the message, although these are important. The message must also be popularized, so that it can be acquired by the local population, made its own, hitched to the various needs and motivations that inspire local activists, voters, and participants. Popularization—embedding ideas within local norms and values—and personalization—transmitting the message in the context of social relations based on familiarity, trust, and reciprocity—hide class differences, at least initially. This allows working-class people to feel that they share a common cause with middle-class professionals and merchants and with educated elites. This seeming paradox of embedding the "modern" in the "traditional" stymies groups trying to mobilize working-class people on the basis of secularist/Kemalist ideology. But this confusion is due in large part to the inability (or unwillingness) to recognize that what are denigrated as "traditions" characteristic of the *varoş* may, in fact, be a powerful basis for thoroughly "modern" phenomena, like political mobilization, civil society, and women's empowerment. Informality and personalization of an ideological message mobilize social movements only if they are populist, not elitist, and respect local cultural norms instead of trying to "subcontract" the norms of an elite class, as the Women's Center activists did.

Kemalist/feminist women's projects provided women with skills that, under ideal circumstances, might have enabled them to earn an income, thereby expanding their range of options, perhaps making it possible to leave an abusive husband or open a business. The Islamist movement, despite its lack of support for women's income production, opened the gate for women's political activism. The popularization and personalization of its ideological message expanded the meaning of religious symbolism, whether of clothing or behavior, and legitimated women's expanded political roles. *Tesettür* became a badge of ideological equality between men and women and between social groups (like workers and business owners) that otherwise represented competing interests.

Of course, the Islamist and Kemalist/feminist movements contained within them contradictions and people with competing ideological and pragmatic goals. This led to drawbacks on both sides. While Islamic foundations embedded women within the family and did not allow them an independent economic role, secularist associations seemed to regard women (and their problems) as separate from their families, making it difficult for women to attend activities and to incorporate what they learned into their daily, family-based routines. Many feminist or Kemalist projects focused only on women's needs, either because they assumed that women's earning income would automatically improve family welfare, or because they did not wish to reinforce women's traditional homemaking roles. Such programs typically ignored women's home duties and cultural prohibitions about venturing far from home, requiring them to travel to project centers "so that they leave the house," but providing neither bus fare nor child care. Not surprisingly, women's participation in such projects tended to be patchy and short-term and the projects not self-sustaining. Most importantly, the personalization of the ideological message and informality of organization must be combined with popularization—the embedding of structure, means, and message within a local cultural idiom. For this reason, the Islamists in Ümraniye were better able to hide potentially divisive contradictions than a movement that adamantly claimed the "modern" high ground and refused to engage in a vernacular politics.

CONCLUSION

Vernacular politics is an autonomous, grassroots political process, incorporating a variety of actors and views, in which local networks work in tandem with political parties and civic organizations in a sustained social and political movement. It is generally associated with an ideological platform, but, on closer examination, the outward appearance of homogeneity and unity under an ideological banner breaks down when differences of background, motivation, and gender are taken into account. These differences filter and distort both ideological message and political practice. Potentially divisive differences within the movement are kept at bay through (1) shared populist rhetoric, issues, and symbols; (2) the personalization of political relations; and (3) situating the ideological message within a local context of shared communal values and interests. A local politics thus becomes national, while carrying within it the coalitions and contradictions that reflect local and national diversity.

Why use a new term? The term *vernacular politics* gets us beyond such circuitous discussions as whether civil society is formally or informally organized, autonomous or controlled (it can be both simultaneously), or whether political mobilization based on religion has a place in modern democracy. A new term shakes loose our expectations and preconceptions of political and social boundaries and leads us to ask crucial questions about the connections between people and processes. In its simplest sense, the term *vernacular* means domestic or indigenous. However, its recent trajectory of meaning in the fields of language, geography, and architecture reflects the same preoccupation with distinguishing a kind of atavistic, communal cultural existence from "modern" political and historical consciousness that has afflicted discussions of civil society and political mobilization.

The term is used in these fields to mean indigenous or local styles of speech, space, or form. Implicit in many of these applications are assumptions that nature is set apart from history, relationships from power, custom from structure, informal from formal, the traditional from the modern, and the ephemeral from the permanent. Communities characterized by vernacular architecture, for instance, have been described as being "without political status, without plan, ruled by informal local custom, often ingenious adaptations to an unlikely site and makeshift materials" (Jackson, 1984, 327). Such communities do not have monuments to remind residents of "long-range, collective purpose, of goals and objectives and principles" (323). Vernacular landscapes are populated by communities ruled by tradition and custom, where identity derives from family membership and goals are functional and short-term. It is a landscape entirely remote from institutionalized politics, law, and capital markets.

These sorts of distinctions parallel those made by European social philosophers in defining civil society as distinct from family and community and devoid of the rhetoric of kinship and love, duty and welfare. In the modern era, it is argued, such rhetoric was appropriated instead by the nation-state and became the language of nationalism. Partha Chatterjee, in his rereading of discussions of civil society by Locke, Montesquieu, and Hegel, argues that these authors have suppressed the "narrative of community" that he sees flowing through liberal, capitalist society, a narrative that "those who celebrate the absolute and natural sovereignty of the individual . . . refuse to recognize" (1990, 124). Vernacular politics, by contrast, is the process by which community narratives may intersect with political formations that self-consciously foster the construction of a national identity.

Civil society, as a concept, evolved in tandem with Western philosophical thought about the superiority of reason, rationality, and exchange as a basis for social order and morality, over bonds of God, king, and family. In this classic formulation, civil society is associated with contractual models of individual relations and with liberalism in a free marketplace of ideas and interests. As de Tocqueville observed about nineteenth-century America, "Feelings and opinions are recruited, the heart is enlarged, and the human mind is developed, only by the reciprocal influence of men upon each other. . . . [T]hese influences are almost null in democratic countries; they must therefore be artificially created, and this can only be accomplished by associations" (1984 [1835], 200).

Are associations the last resort of societies no longer "united amongst themselves by firm and lasting ties, [where] it is impossible to obtain the co-operation [sic] of any great number of them, unless you can persuade every man whose help you require that his private interest obliges him voluntarily to unite his exertions to the exertions of all the others" (202)? Or can associational and, by extension, political life be grounded in "firm and lasting ties" in a democratic society? What public roles can kinship, religion, and cultural norms of cooperation play in a democracy?

Robert Putnam, in his masterful analysis of civic traditions and democracy in Italy, suggests that networks of civic engagement based on norms of reciprocity and mutual trust do strengthen democratic government. Areas with strong civic traditions of voluntary cooperation, he writes, embodied historically in guilds, communes, and traditions of mutual assistance, are characterized by better government and a more developed economy than those areas dominated by "force and family" (1993, 178). Kinship and religion play ambiguous roles in this analysis. "Familism" can be hierarchical and authoritarian. Kinship, Putnam suggests, can impose hierarchies between and within families that make civic solidarity less likely. But he points out that kin also form horizontal, cooperative networks composed of people of equivalent status committed to mutual aid. With regard to religious groups, Putnam suggests they are characterized by both equality and hierarchy, with some denominations evincing more horizontal networks and others more vertical linkages (173). This was quite clearly borne out in the Turkish example, where the Islamist movement was grounded both in horizontal *imece*-based networks and in the paternalistic *himaye* of patron-client relations.

Nevertheless, Putnam believes that "strong" interpersonal ties based on kinship are less important for democracy than the "weak" ties of acquaintanceship and shared membership in civic associations. This is because the latter support wider cooperation between unrelated groups (175). The civic actor in this view is presented as a rational actor looking for value among available forms of association, whether of kinship or community. Mutual trust, Putnam writes, is a kind of collateral, and customs of mutual assistance are founded on a sense of mutual value to the participants. Both community solidarity and individual benefit are desirable values (167–69). Putnam's insight was that civil society need not always consist of associations of individuals alienated from one another and brought together by shared interests, but rather that civil society might also be informally organized around ties of trust, personal history, and mutual obligation (if not kinship). While this challenges the classical understanding of civil society, it continues to view associational life through the lens of "rational" choice.

Other scholars have examined the interaction of kinship, religious affiliation, and other "informal" relations with civil society and political institutions, but without breaking out of the basic terms of debate that situate actors within (or outside of) "rational" categories of association: institutional civil society, private interest, or a politics based on shared interests. Two particularly richly painted analyses of grassroots political life are those of Singerman and Bayat. Diane Singerman's (1995) detailed account of the political context and consequences of daily life among Cairo's lower classes focuses on informal networks, but deals only indirectly with civic organizations and the Egyptian political system, apart from its treatment of patronage ties with local politicians. Asef Bayat (1997) analyzes "street politics" in squatter neighborhoods of Tehran before, during, and after the Iranian Revolution. These collective efforts took the form of organizations, syndicates, and informal, grassroots, cooperative activities, but remained a "politics of the poor." Informality, Bayat suggests, facilitated autonomy from state control, with many advantages for the poor. More hybrid movements, such as cross-class popular support for the Iranian Revolution, have been explained as the result of recruitment of the poor by outside groups and organizations (Kazemi, 1980, 118–19), common interests (Nowshirvani and Clawson, 1994, 229), and the mobilizing power of Islam (Weiner and Banuazizi, 1994, 1).

My own use of the term *vernacular* to apply to political process does not make assumptions about "natural," informal collectivities versus permanent, autonomous structures of political and legal decision-making. Rather, I assume that vernacular politics is predicated upon and inseparable from an underlying formal structure.

Vernacular politics expresses (and is expressed through) local cultural norms and idioms, but also takes advantage of available structural vehicles that might include political parties, religious or ethnic institutions, and civic organizations. Like all political processes, it also must accommodate itself to such structural limitations as type of government, regulatory laws, and degree of press and organizational freedom. Sheila Carapico, in her study of Yemeni civil society, makes the point that civic activism could be based on formal, autonomous organizations or on religious and tribal mechanisms, depending on the economic state of the nation and the degree of political liberalism. The civic realm, in other words, straddled the government's public sphere, the business sector, and "the private affectionate space of families," developing a variety of formal and informal routes to civic activism (1998, 11).

In Ümraniye, vernacular politics was a populist, neighborhood-based politics grounded in norms of reciprocity and mutual obligation expressed as neighborliness and legitimated by reference to Islam. It was expressed as grassroots activism coordinated within the Welfare Party, the municipal government, and an Islamic foundation. It shaped itself to and was shaped by the requirements of the national political system and economy. In other words, it was characterized by multiple links between social networks and local political and civic structures, all of which were embedded in culturally distinct and historically specific forms of community and nation.

Populism and Hybridity

Populism is both a cultural and a political project. It relies on a direct appeal to the people unmediated by associations or party politics. Rather, charismatic leaders and people "just like us" personally guide each individual into the movement. At the same time, populism is a strategy by which political parties mobilize people to support party interests while seeming to pursue their own. At its best, the hand on the elbow is so light that its direction is unnoticed. Civic organizations ply the middle ground, being both an expression of the needs and interests of local people and a conduit for popular mobilization by the party. Neither set of interests necessarily guarantees a liberal or a democratic agenda, nor do they necessarily coincide. This is not classic ward politics, although it resembles it in some respects. That is, it is not only a mobilization to vote for a particular party, but rather the awakening of a social movement that is simultaneously a product of local values and ties and broader social and political goals. The movement may provide support for a particular political party, but is, in the end, independent of it.

Under its populist mantle, vernacular politics accommodates a hybrid constituency and a variety of interests and motivations, some conflicting. Differences within society (whether they be of gender, social class, ethnicity, or sect) mean that the fit among symbols, organizations, and interests is bound to be imperfect. In Ümraniye, democracy was commonly espoused at Islamist rallies, yet interpreted in many different ways by local activists, some equating it with Islamic law. The meaning given to Islamic law itself varied from a legal system that permitted polygyny to a vehicle of self-fulfillment or simply a metaphor for a just society. Many female activists perceived one of the goals of the Islamist movement to be the education of women to work outside the home, while male activists in Ümraniye tended to believe the reverse. Organizational cohesion also is not a given; despite its successes, the Welfare Party was far from the only institution claiming to represent the Turkish "Muslim."

These differences vanish from view under the powerful beam of a projected unity of symbols, ideological rhetoric, and mass public action. The public expression of shared cultural values is an important factor in the success of contemporary Muslim popular movements because it represses community factional and class divisions. A common cause, underscored by public protests, crystallizes the sense of a city- and nationwide Muslim identity and community consciousness. As the ideological message of a movement is translated into shared local cultural norms and practices, internal disagreement on issues and goals becomes personalized and its potentially divisive effect is scattered. Vernacular politics brings a hybrid population together around a political and ideological agenda, but this agenda is personalized and popularized by situating it within a context of shared norms, idioms, and interpersonal trust.

This hybrid aspect differentiates vernacular politics from a grassroots politics of the poor. Nor is it a politics of the like-minded, since beneath a symbolic coherence and shared concern about social and political issues, interpretations of basic issues vary, as do the activists' motivations and goals. It is true that the Welfare Party provided the most successful public structure within which complex and fragmented Muslim communities could express class issues within an idiom of social solidarity and cooperation, rather than class antagonism. But the party did not represent only the disadvantaged. A "politics of the poor" does not explain the Welfare Party's support from an extremely varied constituency that included industrialists and professionals. Nor, indeed, can it explain the participation of the poor, since in a patently poor neighborhood like Ümraniye, the activities of the Welfare Party municipality and its partner Islamist foundation barely dented the poverty and extensive need.

Nor is vernacular politics solely a politics of identity. In the aftermath of the eclipse of communism, there has been a rush to declare the end of class-based politics and the nascence of identity politics. The premise of identity politics is that non-Western subaltern populations attempt to rival the social status of generally Westernized, secularized elites by setting up an alternative elite lifestyle grounded in local identities. This lifestyle may be grounded in ethnicity or religion and often is legitimated by reference to a religious or ethnic movement.

One example of this is the use of *tesettür*, a highly specific form of veiling, in Turkey's Islamist movement. Legitimated by reference to national political ideologies and transnationally circulated Islamist ideas, *tesettür* was part of an attempt to establish an alternate elite in a country where the definition of status for at least two generations had been monopolized by a Westernized, secular, urban, educated professional class. While veiling was not new in Turkey, its commodification (Islamic fashion shows) and politicization (mass demonstrations to protest banning of veils at university) were part of a larger bid by a new cadre of intellectual and economic elites to establish their lifestyles, clothing, history, means of doing business, and political ideals as an alternative, native form of "modernity." While the masses may have engaged in this form of veiling and supported the protest movement, elite Islamist veiling also was a marker of difference from the masses. In the end, the bid for credibility of an alternative Islamic elite lifestyle is not the same as a bid for populist acceptance of the lifestyle of the subaltern masses.

The Broader View

Clearly, this is a process that cannot be unique to Turkey or even to Muslim societies. Religion provides a rich symbolic, behavioral, and ideological field that both resonates with the local everyday and can unify a diverse national movement. Scholars of Latin American social movements have long recognized the role of local networks based on trust and the mobilizing potential of new religious forms like liberation theology and the political uses of religious and other local institutions. However, the new hybridity of urban (or suburban) life also is an important factor in vernacular politics, as are the resulting coalitions of political actors with very different goals. Religion can play an important role in this new politics, not simply as a mobilizing ideology, but in obscuring, at least temporarily, competing interests.

The new, unaffiliated, Christian megachurches in the United States, the fastest growing congregations in that country, could profitably be examined in this light. Like the Islamist movement, their seeming ideological coherence masks a diverse following, and, despite an elaborate institutional infrastructure, their message is delivered face to face and embedded in local norms. Their potential for political mobilization is immense, given the blurring of boundaries between religious, state, and civic institutions that has emerged in the late 1990s. The administration of President George W. Bush, for instance, has suggested a program of funneling state assistance through "faith-based organizations." Democratic Senator Bill Bradley has said that religious organizations are crucial to building a "civil society" (Tumulty, 1999, 58).

The mostly Protestant megachurches[1] are notable not only for their size (with thousands in attendance), but also for drawing in a variety of Americans of different denominations and lifestyles, as well as people with little history of churchgoing. The churches have been remarkably successful at building not simply sacred congregations, but also secular communities. Part of their success is due to a flexible and broad-based structure that offers a wide variety of opportunities for participation, from seminars on parenting, meetings for seniors and "women in the workplace," men's retreats, and grief support, to baseball leagues, music, drama, and dance.

Despite their size, the churches personalize relations among members by organizing people in small groups of no more than ten members. (Some churches call them "cells.") Groupmates ideally become "neighbors" and "family" who comfort members if a parent dies, help them move to a new apartment, take them to a doctor's appointment, or step in if their children need to be picked up after school. Some groups are for singles, others for married couples, while others are selected according to age and sex or by location. Groups meet for Bible study or religious discussion, but also to organize the volunteer work members do for the church. The Willow Creek Community Church in South Barrington, Illinois, for instance, has 1,400 small groups. Each has a group leader, responsible to a team leader, and so on, up the line to the pastoral staff (Trueheart, 1996, 54).

The churches strive to become "culturally indigenous" to the populations they are trying to reach (43). That means, in American suburbia, contemporary music, personal testimonials, and dramatic presentations—multimedia pastoral messages, rather than sermons. They also cater to the everyday concerns of their members by offering needed services, from babysitting to dating advice. They stress these services in sophisticated advertisements that are not immediately recognizable as church-based. The larger national culture and economy also have played a part in the success of these churches, as people feel that their workplaces are no longer secure and their communities are declining, and they are dissatisfied with their government. The climate in Washington, as discussed above, has opened the door to links with political parties and government institutions.

Like the Islamist movement, the Christian megachurches, in their wide sweep of members, bring potentially divisive contradictions into the flock—divisions over abortion and homosexuality, for instance, as well as segregation by race and ethnicity. Some of the churches attempt to overcome these divisions by stressing spiritual renewal over issues, or by counseling compassion; others compartmentalize differences by supporting minority-specific churches.

The parallels to the Turkish Islamist movement are startling, from the personalization of the movement through the use of "cells," the translation of its ideological message into local cultural norms, the emphasis on neighborliness and fictional kinship, mutual assistance, and volunteerism, to the focus on people's everyday concerns, downplaying religion. The Islamists, like the megachurches, have managed to mobilize a disaffected but varied part of the populace in a manner that blends religion with culture and everyday life, community with civic organization, and opens the door to political action through poorly defined links with political parties and state institutions.

In its hybridity and ability to obscure it, Welfare/Virtue Party populism also bears some resemblance to the nature of prerevolutionary popular movements in Iran.[2] These drew together coalitions of religious leaders, liberal nationalists, and bazaar merchants in common cause against an entrenched power-holding class associated with the West. The Khomeinist clerics mobilized the urban working class, many of them migrants living in shanty towns, who had not been successfully organized by the Iranian left, much as Welfare/Virtue took over the rhetoric and goals of the Turkish left after it had been crushed in the aftermath of the 1980 coup. The clerics built on already existing grassroots cooperative activities, neighborhood associations, and other organizations that incorporated local migrant networks based on kinship and neighborliness. The poor organized not for any ideological (religious) purpose but to secure such basic needs as housing and jobs. Indeed, increased religious rhetoric and activity in the years preceding the Iranian revolution did not connote an increased devotion to religion. Rather, religion served as a national rallying point and organizational framework to achieve the national goals of a populist social movement based on nonideological local community networks.

Although Khomeinism attacked the establishment, the movement was careful not to undermine private property and the interests of the petty bourgeoisie. After attaining victory over the old order, Khomeinists focused on changing cultural and educational institutions, rather than on changing the economic order. This reflected the ambiguity and contradiction inherent in a movement that wanted to protect the middle-class private property of its elite leaders, yet strengthen the state's control over society as a whole and provide social benefits to the lower classes that had supported the movement.

As in Turkey, contradictions between the interests of an Islamic elite and those of the masses were obscured by Islamic symbolism, imagery, and rhetoric representing the unity of all Muslims and a classless Islamic society characterized by social justice. Once in power, however, social and political fault lines came into relief, and Khomeini's followers monopolized the leadership and vision of the new state by eliminating those with different goals from the political scene. This is the challenge facing the Islamist movement in Turkey as well. As soon as political decisions had to be made, positions of power allocated, and resources distributed, pressure began to mount to accommodate the differing aspirations and goals of its hybrid coalition of followers.

Contemporary Iran provides another illustration of the adaptive, cultural nature of Islamist politics. Adelkah (2000) writes that contemporary Iranian society and politics are shaped by a cultural tradition, the ideal lifestyle and ethic of the *javânmard*, or "man of integrity," which has been redefined by the modernization of Iranian society. In a kind of "permanent improvisation," the *javân* ethic has adapted to such changes in Iranian society as the development of private enterprise and urban culture, a stress on individual autonomy, respect for the rule of law, and social activism among women (1, 4). The *javânmard* is selfless and courageous, and develops trust and networks of contacts through the generous giving of gifts. Adelkah's point is that, along with the transformation of Iranian society in the 1990s, the *javân* ethic, always a part of everyday life, has become institutionalized in charitable organizations and financial networks and has opened up a new political public space. The social qualities of the *javânmard*, Adelkah argues, can be turned into political qualities on the basis of which politicians present themselves to the public and by which the public evaluates them. Politics and public space are defined not only by rational action (or religious ideology), but also by the strategic skills of giving and receiving, by "the economics of beneficence," and by public generosity, in what Adelkah calls "open-handedness as a political movement" (53, 67).

What is important here is that this is not simply an expression of an Islamic idea or of political Islam, but rather it is "the way in which Iranians are fashioning their daily life, and thus inventing their modern life (or a form of modernity that is their own)" (8). Equally important, for purposes of comparison with the Turkish case, is Adelkah's observation that the institutionalization of *javân*-based networks as charitable institutions means that these become partners in dialogue with the state (73). Like *javân*, the Turkish *imece* ethic was transformed by forces at work in society, particularly urbanization, commercialization, and globalization, to form the foundation of new institutional and political forms that did not neatly fit such categories as traditional or modern, formal or informal, cultural or political.

"Islamist mobilization," then, whether in Turkey or Iran, may not really be about religion, despite the high-decibel Islamic rhetoric. Instead, Islamist mobilization may be part of a process of indigenous modernization that reshapes culturally distinct lifestyles and ideals, institutionalizing and commercializing them and linking their everyday practice to new forms of public life and political practice. Rather than a homogenous religious movement, Islamist mobilization can be a political process that brings together new coalitions of people with varied and often highly practical goals. It is sometimes difficult to see hybridity and difference, as well as local networks and the practical concerns of everyday people, behind the seeming single-mindedness of religious identification, rhetoric, and justification. Religion is a wide parasol that throws these differences into shadow and casts a unifying, but ultimately illusory, penumbra.

POSTSCRIPT

The bulk of the research for this book was carried out between 1995 and 1998, and writing was completed in 2000. Since then, several interesting developments have occurred that speak directly to the thesis of this book.

The Virtue Party was banned in June 2001, with the conservative faction, under Necmettin Erbakan, and the reformist faction, under Recep Tayyip Erdoğan, going their separate ways, each faction founding a new party. Under the figurehead leadership of Recai Kutan, the conservatives founded the Felicity (*Saadet*) Party. This party continued the heritage of strong, centralized leadership and religious rhetoric that had characterized previous Islamist parties. In August 2001, Recep Tayyip Erdoğan founded the Justice and Development Party, whose acronym in Turkish is AK ("white, unblemished"). Its symbol is a lightbulb, a radical departure from the animal and plant symbolism of most previous parties, and one that occasioned some ridicule in the press.

The Party, as it came to be called, diverges significantly from previous Islamist parties and, in some ways, from other political parties. The seventy-one party founders, none of whom are politicians, are relatively well educated, represent a range of ages, and include twelve women. They are active in business, law, education, medicine, and civil society organizations. The party has developed an organizational form that relies on internal balloting and membership votes rather than on appointments and decisions made by the leadership, and it has instituted term limits. In other words, the horizontal and more egalitarian characteristics of the grassroots organization described in this book have penetrated the structure of the party itself. Given the reliance of the party on a power base of relatively independent civic networks, it is not surprising that the influence of these networks should have filtered upward. This book has argued that the success of the Islamist parties in the 1990s rested less on their religious message than on their unique organizational ability to incorporate a wide variety of local voices and desires into the national political process on a continual basis. The reformists have taken this one step farther and developed a new style of party.

The platform decidedly avoids reference to Islam and expresses support for laicism as a fundamental requirement of democracy and, notably, freedom. The essence of laicism is spelled out in the Party Principles: laicism is "the state's impartiality toward every form of religious belief and philosophical conviction," meaning that "the state, rather than the individual, is restricted and limited by this." On a much publicized visit to Ataturk's tomb, the symbolic center of Kemalist secularism, Erdoğan closed his inscription in the visitors' book with the words "What you have entrusted [to us] is in safe hands." This movement away from an Islamic message should not be surprising, since the Virtue Party platform has long rested on other issues.

Shortly after the party was founded, the state prosecutor warned the party that it was in violation of the law on two counts: founding members of a political party may not wear head scarves, but half the female founding members did; and Erdoğan's previous conviction on charges of violating Article 312 of the Turkish Constitution made him ineligible to found or lead a political party. (Article 312 refers to the crime of "inciting people to hatred and enmity on the basis of ethnic, religious, regional, and sectarian differences"; Erdoğan's crime, discussed in chapter 4, had been to read a poem at a rally.) As of this writing, the issues surrounding the Justice and Development Party are unresolved. There has been discussion that the six veiled founding women might resign and that Recep Tayyip Erdoğan might be replaced as party leader by Abdullah Gül. Whether this will satisfy the Constitutional Court and prevent the party from being closed down is uncertain.

It is also worth mentioning that in August 2001 the European Court of Human Rights ruled, in a 4 to 3 decision, that banning the Welfare Party did not violate human rights laws, because Turkey had legitimate concerns about the party's threatening its democratic society. The three dissenting judges issued a separate statement in which they wrote that nothing in the statutes or program of the Welfare Party was hostile to democracy, and that they contested the decision to ban a party solely on the basis of declarations by some of its leaders.[1] The issue of the relationship between democracy and rights clearly has not been settled, and the case of the Islamists in Turkey brings together all the contradictions inherent in this fundamental philosophical question.

After the September 11 terrorist attacks on the United States, the Islamists in Turkey reacted in a predictably varied manner. The more radical and confrontational newspapers and politicians, including some from the Felicity Party, claimed that there was insufficient proof to implicate Osama bin Laden. They repeated conspiracy theories positing Israeli involvement in the attacks and expressed sympathy for the Afghan Taliban.

Moderate Islamist politicians in the Justice and Development Party spoke out against terrorism in general and the Taliban and bin Laden's Al-Qa'eda terror network in particular, and they tried to delink the incidents of September 11 from Islam. Before the terror incidents, most Turkish Islamists had disowned Taliban practices as being unrepresentative of Islam, so the fact that conspiracy theories and pro-Taliban statements abounded after September 11 should not be construed as active support and sympathy for bin Laden's organization, at least by the majority of mainstream Islamists. Discussions of conspiracies and government cover-ups are everyday fare on the Turkish street, so it is not surprising that these suspicions should attach to the September 11 attacks as well.

The Islamist press also expressed concern about the spread of the United States' war against terrorism to other countries, especially Turkey's neighbor Iraq. Once American bombing in Afghanistan began to produce civilian casualties, there was a great deal of concern for the humanitarian dimensions. This concern was shared to a large extent by the liberal establishment, both in Turkey and abroad. For a segment of the Turkish population, the intensive coverage of civilian casualties stoked Islamic sentiment; for leftists, it stoked anti-American sentiment. But these are broad generalizations for a variety of reactions that changed as individual circumstances changed. In particular, the larger Turkish economic and political context influenced public reaction.

At the time, Turkey was living through one of the most severe economic crises in its history, so public opposition to sending Turkish troops to fight in Afghanistan had less to do with a reluctance to fight against fellow Muslims than with the questions of who would pay for such an expedition and whether Turkey would be compensated (having already experienced enormous financial losses after assisting the United States' efforts in the Gulf War against Iraq) and with the concern that Turkish soldiers' lives not be traded for an economic bailout by the West. The distrust of mainstream political parties, perceived to be corrupt and unresponsive to national needs, also fed suspicion of government intentions, whether Turkish or American. For the most part, however, people were focused on economic survival. Turkish reaction to the attacks of September 11 is better understood as reflecting national preoccupations rather than Islamist participation in or sympathy for international terror groups.

To argue that Islamism is an intensely national phenomenon does not rule out transnational connections and influences. Saudi Arabia and other Islamic countries have long financed mosques, Islamic publications, and other activities in Turkey. Turkish Islamic associations are active in Central Asia and in Europe. But while the term "vernacular politics"—a style of mobilization based on personal networks loosely allied with organizations (which need not be nationally based) and national political forces—might be used equally to describe the activities of Turkish Islamists and a movement like Al-Qa'eda, this does not in any sense imply a connection between them.

There is no question that the post–September 11 atmosphere encouraged the more illiberal elements of society, whether radical Kemalist, leftist, or Islamist, confirming them within their ideologically entrenched positions. However, their peculiar understanding of liberalism—that is, the belief that progress, however defined, is attainable through ideologically inspired social engineering or a kind of benign repression—precedes September 11 and is shared by more moderate groups in Turkish society. More often than not, this involves the control of social expression in public spaces, whether that means banning veiling or banning alcohol. Nevertheless, the desire to join the European Union, and the kinds of internal transformation discussed in this book, are steps on the road to a more liberal democracy.

NOTES

Introduction

1. I am grateful to Ariel Salzmann for suggesting the term *vernacular politics*. Salzmann (1999) uses the term in a somewhat different sense in her work on late Ottoman society.
2. At the party, the hands of the bride and female friends and family are dyed red with henna to celebrate her impending marriage.
3. See, for instance, Duben (1982), Güneş-Ayata (1996), and Kağıtçıbaşı (1996).
4. These processes are described in detail in Eickelman and Piscatori's (1996) insightful and exhaustive account of the sociopolitical context and symbolic politics of Muslim political practice in a variety of locations around the world.

1 | The Political Economy of Culture

1. A leader of the Islam-oriented Virtue Party approved the national celebration of Valentine's Day for the first time in February 2000.
2. The political party founded by Ataturk. The Republican People's Party was in power until Turkey's first multiparty elections in 1950.
3. Official unemployment figures remained at this level until the mid-1990s when they began to decline somewhat.
4. Navaro-Yashin (2002) notes that *tesettür* coats and scarves were described by shopkeepers who sold them as being rooted in Ottoman times, a part of Turkish history, and "authentically Turkish," yet were

advertised as being foreign made *(yabancı mal)* to imply better quality, and, indeed, were often made of imported cloth. Çınar (1997, 32) also has pointed out that the image projected by Turkish Islamists is based on an orientalist image of Ottomanism and Islam that originated in and is aimed, in part, at consumption by the West. In other words, although the Islamist-secularist dialogue is constructed as a national dialogue, based on competing versions of local "authenticity," both are embedded in a global marketplace of ideas and images. Navaro-Yashin (1999) also argues that Islamist "authenticity" is reactive, a response to secularist fears.

5. It was unclear whether these were birth names or chosen names. On at least one occasion, an activist introduced herself to me by saying, "They call me . . . ," an unusual locution.

2 | Religion and Politics in the Everyday

1. For information on Ümraniye, see the entry in *Istanbul Ansiklopedisi* (1994, 341), and the sociological survey by Erder (1996). Güvenç and Işık (1998) link type of industry, employment, region of origin, neighborhood of residence, and housing status in Istanbul, creating combined ethnic/occupational/residential maps of the city.

2. The evening before the wedding, the women of both families get together in a henna party at which they generally sit and chat over nuts and cake. The younger women often dance. In a series of rituals, the bride's close friends symbolically escort her out of her unmarried life and family home into a life with her husband and mother-in-law. The palms of the bride and guests are painted red with henna paste, thus the name.

3 | The Institutional Expression of Islam

1. The headman *(muhtar)* is the elected representative of a *mahalle* neighborhood.

2. For a general discussion of Turkish Islam, with particular attention to the Alevi, see Shankland, 1999. On the Alevi, also see Çamuroğlu, 1997, and Yavuz, 1999c. Mélikoff, 1992, discusses Sufism.

3. The government has denied supporting Hizbullah. For a detailed account of Hizbullah and other radical Islamic groups, see Narlı, 1996, 48–52.

4. For an in-depth discussion of the order, see Mardin, 1994, and Özdalga, 1999.

5. For more on the Fethullacılar, see Aras, 1998; Narlı, 1996, 42–45; Özyürek, 1997; and Yavuz, 1999a, 1999b. Fethullah Gülen's life story is told in Can, 1996.

6. For an analysis of the writings of Said Nursi and the Nurcu movement, see Mardin, 1989.
7. The tradition of the Prophet Muhammed's example.
8. Interview with Hashim Bayram, CEO of Kombassan Holding, Boston, January 27, 1999.
9. Buğra describes an interesting contrast in positions on these issues between the Islamic business community as represented by MÜSIAD (The Association of Independent Industrialists and Businessmen) and the conservative labor union confederation Hak-İş (1999, 40–53).
10. A pseudonym.

4 | Generation X and the Virtue Party

1. As the internal battle heated up, news reports in spring 2000 began to refer to the split within the Virtue Party as one of the renewers *(yenilikçi)* versus traditionalists *(gelenekçi)*.
2. Interviews with Mayor Erdoğan, Izmit, June 27, and Istanbul, June 29, 1998.
3. The Alevi are an Islamic minority noted for their heterodox interpretation and liberal practice of Islam. See Shankland (1999, 132–68) for a comprehensive description.
4. These writings and the political ideologies based on these ideas construct Turkic identity as racial, rather than ethnic. I use the term race as it is used by these ideologists, although ethnic chauvinism might be more accurate.

5 | Populism: Democracy is Peace of Mind

1. The term used, *sevgi,* also means love and compassion.
2. White (1994, 96–97) discusses the use of the term in common Turkish rituals of exchange and as a marker of social indebtedness.
3. Some conservative women in Ümraniye did not wish to have their photos taken if there was an unrelated man in the same frame, even a bystander in the background.
4. Founder of the Mevlevi religious order.
5. *Turkish Daily News,* Turkish Probe, June 14, 1998, p. 18.
6. Ibid.

6 | Civil Society: In Whose Service?

1. Some hospitals held patients hostage until their bill was paid.
2. A pseudonym.
3. Berik (1995), Çinar (1989), and White (1994) describe piecework and subcontracting in Turkey during this period.

7 | Islamist Elitism and Women's Choices

1. A rotating savings club meets at regular intervals, alternating among the homes of its members. At every meeting, each woman gives a set amount of money to the hostess. In this way, each member, in turn, receives a large lump sum of money that she might not have been able to save on her own. The system works on trust and guaranteed attendance, so savings clubs only include women who know each other well.
2. "Giyim kültürümüz üzerine bir tartışma," *Izlenim,* Nos. 23–24 (July–August, 1995), 26–37. Participating in the discussion were Peyami Gürel, Fatma Karabıyık Barbarosoğlu, Ayşe Böhürler, and Ilhan Kutluer.
3. Activist women preachers in the countryside also differentiated between themselves as "knowledgeable" and ordinary women as "ignorant," using distinctive Islamic clothing and neo-Ottoman references to mark this distance (Bellér-Hann, 1995, 39, 41–42).
4. Istanbul, June 29, 1998.

8 | Secular Activism in Ümraniye

1. Like the names of other Ümraniye activists, this is a pseudonym.

Conclusion

1. They are also called full-service churches, pastoral churches, apostolic churches, "new tribe" churches, new paradigm churches, seeker-sensitive churches, or shopping-mall churches. This discussion is based on Truehart (1996).
2. This account of prerevolutionary Iran was taken from Abrahamian (1993), Bayat (1997), Hegland (1987), Kazemi (1980, 1991, 1995), and Weiner and Banuazizi (1994). In a broader context, Lapidus (1988) discusses the unifying potential of Islam in the wake of economic change, urban migration, the development of new social forms, and increasing economic stratification.

Postscript

1. "Europe Rights Court Backs Turkish Ban on Islamist Party," *International Herald Tribune,* Aug. 1, 2001, p. 3.

BIBLIOGRAPHY

Abrahamian, Ervand. 1993. *Khomeinism: Essays on the Islamic Republic.* Berkeley: University of California Press.

Acar, Erhan, and M. Güvenç. 1992. A study on the housing conditions of industrial labor. In Ilhan Tekeli, Tansı Şenyapılı, Ali Türel, Murat Güvenç, and Erhan Acar, *Development of Istanbul metropolitan area and low cost housing,* 210–35. Istanbul: Turkish Social Science Association et al.

Acar, Feride. 1995. Women and Islam in Turkey. In *Women in modern Turkish society: A reader,* ed. Şirin Tekeli, 46–65. London: Zed Books.

Adelkah, Fariba. 2000. *Being modern in Iran.* New York: Columbia University Press.

Ahmad, Feroz. 1993. *The making of modern Turkey.* London: Routledge.

Akinci, Ugur. 1999. The Welfare Party's municipal track record: Evaluating Islamist municipal activism in Turkey. *Middle East Journal* 53, no. 1 (winter): 775–94.

Aras, Bülent. 1998. Turkish Islam's moderate face. *Middle East Quarterly* 5, no. 3 (September): 23–29.

Arat, Yeşim. 1997. Islamist women challenge the boundaries of citizenship. In *Human development report: Turkey,* 67. Ankara: The United Nations Development Programme.

————. 1999. *Political Islam in Turkey and women's organizations.* Istanbul: The Turkish Economic and Social Studies Foundation.

Bayat, Asef. 1997. *Street politics: Poor people's movements in Iran.* New York: Columbia University Press.

Bellér-Hann, Ildikó. 1995. Women and fundamentalism in northeast Turkey. *Women: A Cultural Review* 6, no. 1: 34–45.

Berik, Günseli. 1995. Towards an understanding of gender hierarchy in Turkey: A comparative analysis of carpet-weaving villages. In *Women in modern Turkish society: A reader,* ed. Şirin Tekeli, 112–27. London: Zed Books.

Buğra, Ayşe. 1998. The immoral economy of housing in Turkey. *International Journals of Urban and Regional Research* 22, no. 2: 303–17.

————. 1999. *Islam in economic organizations.* Istanbul: The Turkish Economic and Social Studies Foundation.

Çamuroğlu, R. 1997. Some notes on the contemporary process of restructuring Alevilik in Turkey. In *Syncretistic religious communities in the Near East,* eds. K. Kehl-Bodrogi, Kellner-Heinkele, and Otter-Beaujean, 25–34. Leiden: Brill.

Can, Eyüp. 1996. *Ufuk turu: Fethullah Gülen Hocaefendi ile. . .* Istanbul: AD Yayıncılık.

Carapico, Sheila. 1998. *Civil society in Yemen: The political economy of activism in modern Arabia.* Cambridge: Cambridge University Press.

Çarkoğlu, Ali, and B. Toprak. 2000. *Türkiye'de din, toplum ve siyaset.* Istanbul: The Turkish Economic and Social Studies Foundation.

Ceyhun, Fikret. 1988. The politics of industrialization in Turkey. *Journal of Contemporary Asia* 18, no. 3: 333–57.

Chatterjee, Partha. 1990. A response to Taylor's "Modes of civil society." *Public Culture* 3, no. 1 (fall): 119–32.

Çınar, Alev Inan. 1997. Refah Party and the city administration of Istanbul: Liberal Islam, localism and hybridity. *New Perspectives on Turkey* 16 (spring): 23–40.

Çinar, E. Mine. 1989. Taking work at home: Disguised female employment in urban Turkey. Working Paper 8810. Chicago: Loyola University of Chicago School of Business Administration.

Cohen, J. L., and A. Arato. 1994. *Civil society and political theory.* Cambridge: MIT Press.

DPT (Turkish State Planning Organization). 1983. *Vakıf.* DPT publication no. 1899. Ankara.

Darnton, Robert. 1984. *The great cat massacre.* New York: Basic Books.

Delaney, Carol. 1991. *The seed and the soil: Gender and cosmology in Turkish village society.* Berkeley: University of California Press.

———. 1993. Traditional modes of authority and co-operation. In *Culture and economy: Changes in Turkish villages.* ed. P. Stirling, 140–55. Hemingford: Eothen Press.

de Tocqueville, Alexis. [1835] 1984. *Democracy in America.* Edited by Richard D. Heffner. New York: Penguin Books.

Dilipak, Abdurrahman. 1994. Interview. *Express* 1, no. 2 (February–November): 12.

Duben, Alan. 1982. The significance of family and kinship in urban Turkey. In *Sex roles, family and community in Turkey,* ed. Ç. Kağıtçıbaşı, 73–99. Bloomington: Indiana University Turkish Studies.

Eickelman, Dale F., and J. Piscatori. 1996. *Muslim politics.* Princeton: Princeton University Press.

Erder, Sema. 1996. *Istanbul'a bir kent kondu: Ümraniye.* Istanbul: İletişim Press.

GDF (General Directorate of Foundations). 1997. Internal document, 11/12/97.

Gökçe, Birsen, F. Acar, A. Ayata, A. Kasapoğlu, I. Özer, and H. Uygun. 1993. *Gecekondularda ailelerarası geleneksel dayanışmanın çağ daş organizasyonlara dönüşümü.* Ankara: Turkish Prime Ministry, Women and Social Services Administration.

Göle, Nilüfer. 1996. *The forbidden modern: Civilization and veiling.* Ann Arbor: University of Michigan Press.

Gönel, Aydın. 1998. *Araştırma raporu: Önde gelen STK'lar.* Istanbul: Turkish Economic and Social History Foundation.

Gülalp, Haldun. 1997. Globalizing postmodernism: Islamist and Western social theory. *Economy and Society* 26, no. 3 (August): 419–33.

———. 1999a. Political Islam in Turkey: The rise and fall of the Refah Party. *The Muslim World* 89, no. 1 (January): 22–41.

———. 1999b. The poverty of democracy in Turkey: The Refah party episode. *New Perspectives on Turkey* 21 (fall): 35–59.

Güneş-Ayata, Ayşe. 1996. Solidarity in urban Turkish family. In *Turkish families in transition,* ed. G. Rasuly-Paleczek, 98–113. Frankfurt-am-Main: Peter Lang.

Gürsoy, Akile. 1994. Mosque or health centre? A dispute in a *gecekondu.* In *Islam in modern Turkey: Religion, politics and literature in a secular state,* ed. Richard Tapper, 84–101. London: I. B. Tauris.

Güvenç, Murat, and O. Işık. 1998. *1990 sayımında Istanbul: Açımlayıcı araştırma için yöntem önerisi ve üç örnek çalışma.* Ankara: Middle East Technical University Faculty of Architecture, Department of City and Regional Planning.

Hefner, Robert W. 1990. *The political economy of mountain Java.* Berkeley: University of California Press.

Hegland, Mary Elaine. 1987. Islamic revival or political and cultural revolution? An Iranian case study. In *Religious resurgence: Contemporary cases in Islam, Christianity and Judaism,* eds. R. T. Antoun and M. E. Hegland, 194–219. Syracuse, N.Y.: Syracuse University Press.

Hıncal, Sinan. 1994. Benim oyum refah'a. . .! *Express* 1, no. 6 (March-December): 6–7.

Ilyasoğlu, Aynur. 1994. *Örtülü kimlik: Islamcı kadın kimliğinin oluşum öğeleri.* Istanbul: Metis Yayınları.

Istanbul ansiklopedisi. 1994. Ümraniye Ilçesi. In vol. 7, 340–41. Istanbul: Turkish Ministry of Culture and Turkish History Foundation.

Jackson, John B. 1984. *Discovering the vernacular landscape.* New Haven: Yale University Press.

Kağıtçıbaşı, Çiğdem. 1996. *Family and human development across cultures: A view from the other side.* Mahwah, N.J.: Lawrence Erlbaum Associates.

Kandiyoti, Deniz. 1988. Bargaining with patriarchy. *Gender and Society* 2, no. 3: 274–290.

Karpat, Kemal. 1975. The politics of transition: Political attitudes and party affiliation in Turkish shantytowns. In *Political participation in Turkey: Historical background and present problems,* eds. E. D. Akarlı and G. Ben-Dor, 89–119. Istanbul: Boğaziçi University Publications.

Kasaba, Reşat. 1997. Kemalist certainties and modern ambiguities. In *Rethinking modernity and national identity in Turkey,* eds. Sibel Bozdoğan and R. Kasaba, 15–36. Seattle: University of Washington Press.

Kazemi, Farhad. 1980. *Poverty and revolution in Iran: The migrant poor, urban marginality and politics.* New York: New York University Press.

———. 1991. Peasant uprisings in twentieth-century Iran, Iraq, and Turkey. In *Peasants and politics in the Middle East,* eds. Farhad Kazemi and J. Waterbury, 101–24. Miami: Florida International University Press.

————. 1995. Models of Iranian politics, the road to the Islamic revolution, and the challenge to civil society. *World Politics* 47, no. 4 (July): 555–74.

Kearney, Michael. 1996. *Reconceptualizing the peasantry: Anthropology in global perspective.* Boulder, Colo.: Westview Press.

Kentel, Ferhat. 1995. L'Islam, carrefour des identités sociales et culturelles en Turquie: Les cas de Parti de la Prospérité." *Cahiers d'études sur la Méditéranée orientale et le monde turco-iranien (CEMOTI),* no. 19 (January-June): 211–27.

Keyder, Çağlar. 1997. Whither the project of modernity? Turkey in the 1990s. In *Rethinking modernity and national identity in Turkey,* eds. Sibel Bozdoğan and R. Kasaba, 37–51. Seattle: University of Washington Press.

Kiray, Mübeccel. 1999. Modernleşmenin temel süreçleri. In *International conference on "History of the Turkish Republic: A reassessment,"* vol. 2, 161–68. Istanbul: Economic and Social History Foundation.

Kramer, Gudrun. 1993. Islamist notions of democracy. *MERIP* 183 (July-August): 2–8.

Lapidus, Ira M. 1988. Islamic political movements: Patterns of historical change. In *Islam, politics and social movements,* eds. Edmund Burke III and I. Lapidus, 3–16. Berkeley: University of California Press.

Mardin, Şerif. 1989. *Religion and social change in modern Turkey: The case of Bediuzzaman Said Nursi.* Albany: State University of New York.

————. 1994. The Nakşibendi order in Turkish history. In *Islam in modern Turkey: Religion, politics and literature in a secular state,* ed. Richard Tapper, 121–42. London: I. B. Tauris.

Meeker, Michael. 1994. The new Muslim intellectuals in the Republic of Turkey. In *Islam in modern Turkey: Religion, politics and literature in a secular state,* ed. Richard Tapper, 189–19. London: I. B. Tauris.

Mélikoff, I. 1992. *Sur les traces du Soufisme Turc: Recherches sur l'Islam populaire en Anatolie.* Istanbul: Isis.

Mercan, H. Murat, and I. Belge. 1997. Analysis of the chief prosecutor's reply to the Welfare Party's defense. *Turkish Daily News,* October 27, p. A6.

Nalbantoğlu, Gülsüm Baydar. 1997. Silent interruptions: Urban encounters with rural Turkey. In *Rethinking modernity and national identity in Turkey,* eds. Sibel Bozdoğan and R. Kasaba, 192–210. Seattle: University of Washington Press.

Narlı, Nilüfer. 1996. Moderate against radical Islamicism in Turkey. *Zeitschrift für Türkeistudien* 9, no. 1: 35–59.

———. 1999. The rise of the Islamist movement in Turkey. *Middle East Review of International Affairs,* no. 9 (September): np.

Navaro-Yashin, Yael. 1998. Uses and abuses of "state and civil society" in contemporary Turkey. *New Perspectives on Turkey* 18: 1–22.

———. 2002. The market for identities: Secularism, Islamism, commodities. In *Fragments of culture: The everyday of modern Turkey,* ed. Deniz Kandiyoti. London: I. B. Tauris.

Navaro-Yasin, Yael. 1999. The historical construction of local culture: Gender and identity in the politics of secularism versus Islam. In *Istanbul: Between the global and the local,* ed. Caglar Keyder, 59–75. Oxford: Rowman and Littlefield.

Norton, Augustus Richard, ed. 1995, 1996. *Civil society in the Middle East,* vols. 1 and 2. Leiden: Brill.

Nowshirvani, Vahid F., and P. Clawson. 1994. The state and social equity in postrevolutionary Iran. In *The politics of social transformation in Afghanistan, Iran and Pakistan,* eds. M. Weiner and A. Banuazizi, 228–69. Syracuse, N.Y.: Syracuse University Press.

Öncü, Ayşe. 1995. Packaging Islam: Cultural politics on the landscape of Turkish commercial television. *Public Culture* 8, no. 1 (fall): 51–71.

Özdalga, Elisabeth, ed. 1999. *The Naqshbandis in western and central Asia.* London: Curzon Press.

Özyürek, Esra G. 1997. "Feeling tells better than language": Emotional expression and gender hierarchy in the sermons of Fethullah Gülen Hocaefendi. *New Perspectives on Turkey* 16 (spring): 41–51.

Putnam, Robert D. 1993. *Making democracy work: Civic traditions in modern Italy.* Princeton: Princeton University Press.

Sağlam, Erol. 1994. Kara ekonomi 100 trillion. *Hürriyet,* November 1, p. 9.

Salzmann, Ariel. 1999. Citizens in search of a state: The limits of political participation in the late Ottoman empire. In *Extending citizenship, reconfiguring states,* eds. M. Hanagan and C. Tilly, 37–66. New York: Rowman and Littlefield.

Savaş, Vural. 1997. *Refah partisi iddianamesi ve mütalaası.* Istanbul: Fast Yayıncılık.

Şenyapılı, Tansı. 1992. A new stage of gecekondu housing in Istanbul. In *Development of Istanbul metropolitan area and low cost housing,* Ilhan Tekeli, Tansı Şenyapılı, Ali Türel, Murat Güvenç, and Erhan Acar, 182–209. Istanbul: Turkish Social Science Association et al.

Seufert, Günter. 1997. *Politischer Islam in der Türkei: Islamismus als symbolische Repräsentation einer sich modernisierenden muslimischen Gesellschaft.* Stuttgart: Franz Steiner Verlag.

SFYDP. 1995. *Seventh Five Year Development Plan (1996–2000).* Ankara: Turkish State Planning Organization.

Shankland, David. 1999. *Islam and society in Turkey.* Huntingdon: The Eothen Press.

Singerman, Diane. 1995. *Avenues of participation: Family, politics, and networks in urban quarters of Cairo.* Princeton: Princeton University Press.

Sönmez, Mustafa. 1997. Bu gelir dağılımıyla AB kapısından girilmez. *Hürriyet,* April 20, p. 16.

Tekeli, Ilhan. 1992. Development of urban administration and planning in the formation of Istanbul metropolitan area. In Ilhan Tekeli, Tansı Şenyapılı, Ali Türel, Murat Güvenç, and Erhan Acar, *Development of Istanbul metropolitan area and low cost housing,* 3–111. Istanbul: Turkish Social Science Association et al.

TESEV (Turkish Economic and Social Studies Foundation). 1997. *Human development report: Turkey.* Ankara: United Nations Development Programme.

Toksöz, Fikret. 1996. Dernekler. In *Cumhuriyet dönemi Türkiye ansiklopedisi,* vol. 2, 366–378. Istanbul: Iletişim Press.

Toprak, Binnaz. 1996. Civil society in Turkey. In *Civil society in the Middle East,* ed. Augustus R. Norton, vol. 2, 87–118. Leiden: E. J. Brill.

Trueheart, Charles. 1996. Welcome to the next church. *The Atlantic Monthly,* 278, no. 2 (August): 37–58.

Tumulty, Karen. 1999. Taking a leap of faith. *Time,* June 7, p. 58.

Türkeli, Nalan. 1996. *Varoşta kadın olmak: Günlük.* Istanbul: Gökkuşağı Press.

Weiner, Myron, and A. Banuazizi. 1994. Introduction to *The politics of social transformation in Afghanistan, Iran and Pakistan,* eds. M. Weiner and A. Banuazizi, 1–31. Syracuse, N.Y.: Syracuse University Press.

White, Jenny B. 1994. *Money makes us relatives: Women's labor in urban Turkey.* Austin: University of Texas Press.

Yalçın, Soner. 1994. *Hangi Erbakan.* Ankara: Öteki Yayınevi.

Yavuz, M. Hakan. 1993. Nationalism and Islam: Yusuf Akçura and Üç Tarz-i Siyaset. *Journal of Islamic Studies* 4, no. 2 (July): 175–207.

———. 1997. Political Islam and the Welfare (*Refah*) Party in Turkey. *Comparative Politics* 30, no. 1 (October): 63–82.

———. 1999a. Towards an Islamic liberalism: The Nurcu movement and Fethullah Gülen. *The Middle East Journal* 53, no. 4 (fall): 584–605.

———. 1999b. Societal search for a new social contract in Turkey: Fethullah Gülen, the Virtue Party and the Kurds. *SAIS Review* 29, no. 1 (Winter): 114–43.

———. 1999c. Media identities for Kurds and Alevis in Turkey. In *New media in the Muslim world: The emerging public sphere,* eds. Dale Eickelman and J. Anderson. Bloomington: Indiana University Press.

Zevkliler, Aydın. 1996. Türkiye'de vakıflar. In *Cumhuriyet dönemi Türkiye ansiklopedisi,* vol. 15, 1347–1440. Istanbul: Iletişim Press,

Zürcher, Erik J. 1997. *Turkey: A modern history.* London: I. B. Tauris.

INDEX